WELSH WINTER CLIMBS

by

Malcolm Campbell
and
Andy Newton

CICERONE PRESS,
MILNTHORPE, CUMBRIA

WELSH
WINTER CLIMBS

by

Malcolm Campbell

and

Andy Newton

CICERONE PRESS
MILNTHORPE, CUMBRIA

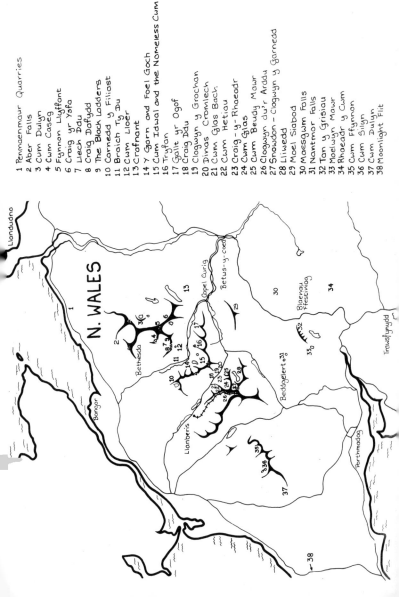

N. WALES

1 Penmaenmawr Quarries
2 Aber Falls
3 Cwm Dulyn
4 Cwm Caseg
5 Fynnon Llyffant
6 Craig yr Ysfa
7 Llech Ddu
8 Craig Dafydd
9 The Black Ladders
10 Carnedd y Filiast
11 Braich Ty Du
12 Cwm Lloer
13 Crafnant
14 Y Garn and Foel Goch
15 Cwm Idwal and the Nameless Cwm
16 Tryfan
17 Gallt yr Ogof
18 Craig Ddu
19 Clogwyn y Grochan
20 Dinas Cromlech
21 Cwm Glas Bach
22 Cwm Hetiau
23 Craig - y - Rhaeadr
24 Cwm Glas
25 Cwm Beudy Mawr
26 Clogwyn du'r Arddu
27 Snowdon - Clogwyn y Garnedd
28 Lliwedd
29 Moel Siabod
30 Maesgwm Falls
31 Nantmor Falls
32 Tan y Grisiau
33 Moelwyn Maur
34 Rhaeadr y Cwm
35 Cwm Ffynnon
36 Cwm Silyn
37 Cwm Dulyn
38 Moonlight Flit

First published as Winter Climbs in North Wales
by Richard Newcombe, 1974.
Reprinted 1977, 1979. Second Edition 1980.

This edition published 1988, reprinted 1996, 1988 & 2005.

ISBN 1 85284 001 3

For
Dave and Ian; Ian and Steve
Always pushing, always vital

We shall not find the seventh grade
beyond the sixth, but in ourselves

Ivan Ghirardini

Front Cover:
John Barry on the 'easy' pitch of Cloggy's classic
BLACK CLEFT (V/VI). Photo: Dave Alcock.

Rear Cover:
'Standing Room Only' - ABER FALLS 1986.
Photo: Malcolm Campbell

ACKNOWLEDGEMENTS

All guidebooks are based to a certain extent on previous works, and the authors would like to thank Rick Newcombe, for his two previous editions, and for his help and advice during the production of this guide.

The contributions from John Sumner and Martin Crook were invaluable, and Mick Fowler was able to shed some light on many, often unrepeated routes. Nigel Nix's help with some of the outlying areas has added significantly to the scope of the guide.

Thanks also to the following, in no particular order, for descriptions, comments, photos and advice: Wil Hurford, Ian Carr, J.Neville Sanderson, Paul Trower, Paul Williams, Paul Airey, Andy Beverridge, Graham McMahon, Frank Corner, Chris Ayres, Steve Ashton, Mike Woolridge, Rosie Walmesley-White, Stu Cathcart, Dave Alcock, John Barry, Terry Storry, Howard Jeffs, Dave Woolridge, Ian Fox and Dave King.

Thanks also to; Amstrad for the word power, the publishers for their patience, and all the climbers at Pete's Eats, Plas y Brenin and Arvon's for their comments, even if we seemed to ignore most of them!

And last, but certainly not least, Denise Long for her late nights at Plas y Brenin and the beautiful drawings which resulted.

Malcolm Campbell
Andy Newton

CONTENTS

INTRODUCTION

Although this latest edition has been substantially revised to accommodate new climbs and new crags it still embodies and draws inspiration from Rick Newcombe's detailed and wide-ranging accounts in the two earlier editions.

Winter climbing has seen an unprecedented boom in popularity over the six or seven years since publication of the last edition and with a number of really excellent winters in this period there has, not unnaturally, been a surge of exploration and a consequent plethora of new routes on a whole range of new crags. *If it ices up, climb it!* seems to have been the attitude and this has led to new climbs being established in such diverse places as Cwm Silyn and Aber Falls, Craig Ddu and Cadair Idris.

Alongside this boom a new outlook has emerged; involving perhaps a totally new 'clientèle', more akin to the rock climbing fraternity than to the mountaineers, within whose domain winter climbing was once firmly entrenched. Technical difficulty is now pursued for its own sake by climbers who are not mountaineers; frozen 'smears' in quarries are sought in preference to Lliwedd's icy ribs and grooves; new climbs are recorded even before frozen beards have softened; accurate blow-by-blow descriptions are demanded ... for 'the Times They Are A'Changin'! Whilst we, the authors of this guide, regret the passing of the romantic Golden Age of British Winter Climbing (violins and sighs!), we are not ostrichs on the way to becoming dodos! It's your sport (and ours!) - do with it what you will: we are only observers and we are trying to provide the service that *most* of you want.

Consequently, this guide differs in some ways from its predecessors. It contains descriptions of many more short 'outcrop' climbs: it offers fuller descriptions where they are available and appropriate: it attempts to tackle the grading dilemma. It also offers advice on mountaineering issues for climbers who are seduced onto the tops by the promise of glistening ice only to find deep fresh snow, storm force winds and zero visibility. Of course this information is available elsewhere in a number of excellent instructional manuals, but the odd pearl of wisdom contained herein is aimed at the climber of action, whose reading is confined to guidebooks.

'Activists', and those with a need for 'extreme adventure' will doubtless be critical of any attempt to make the sport more 'accessible'. But this guide is not aimed at them. For most of these people, winter climbing is a game of exploration and adventure. Certainly, experienced winter mountaineers will need no guidebook or grading system to promote their climbing and the authors offer anyone in this category the opportunity to close the book at this early stage - and to refuse all the 'clues' it contains (so long as they've actually *bought* the book!). Happy Adventuring! But for other lesser mortals, the information is here should you want it. But take only what you need and leave the rest to discovery and chance. And afterwards, when your adventure is over, there will be many a fine yarn to spin over pints of ale, toasting around a blazing fire.

One of the problems of writing a winter guide where there are so many routes spread over such a wide area and where the majority of climbs (400 of them!) are out of condition for 360 days a year, is that it is practically impossible to have climbed and checked everything. So we haven't! This means that **descriptions and grades of some of the less popular climbs should be treated with caution**. In these cases, although we may have relied to some extent on rumour, hearsay and common sense, the basic information is all there: you should be able to find the climb with reference only to this book and an OS map; its grade will approximate to that given (as far as they ever do!); and you should be able to get down safely (assuming you can get up!) - what more could you ask? Oh, yes - and there's the odd bit of humour, just to discourage anyone who may be taking things too seriously.

Have fun!

THE CLIMBING AREA

Previous editions have covered a massive area of land and this revision further extends the boundaries of the climbing area. From Aber Falls to mid-Wales, and from Llangollen to the Llyn Peninsula ice forms with astonishing regularity in cold winters. In fact, the tourist guide to the waterfalls of Wales, as a companion volume to this book, has done much to push the boundaries outwards from the traditional heartland of Snowdon and its satellites! And the further you get from Snowdon the more scope for exploration and imagination there seems to be, based on a careful study of the OS map. Almost any steep stream or wet crag is a potential winter playground given the right weather conditions.

The area has been sub-divided into twelve smaller sections (see

CONTENTS), and although at the current stage in development some of these areas can only boast a handful of routes the intention is to set up some sort of framework into which future new routes can be slotted. Inevitably, the bulk of the climbing is in the Snowdon/ Glyders area, but other areas are becoming increasingly developed. The extent and pace of this development can easily be gauged by a comparison with the previous edition. It should be remembered, though, that search and rescue services may well be less effective in some of the more esoteric outlying areas, thus enhancing the feeling of isolation in these wilder places. Access, too, may be a problem in areas outside the traditional stamping grounds of the Snowdonia National Park and here, climbers should keep a low profile and avoid antagon- ising other land users at all costs. This is particularly true of areas around Nantlle in the west and the Arans to the south where access has traditionally been a controversial issue. Read the notes on 'Approach' and keep up to date with current access agreements through the columns of the mountaineering press.

WINTER CLIMBING CONDITIONS

The close proximity of the Welsh mountains to the sea and the frequent arrival of Atlantic depressions pushing very warm, moist air over the area, even in the depths of 'winter', conspire to produce generally unpredictable and unreliable conditions for winter climbing. Conditions are often similar to those experienced on the lower lying crags of Glencoe. Suitable conditions **can** exist at any time between the start of November and the end of April, but they can come and go overnight. If you're planning to grab some snow and ice in Wales, it's usually a good idea to throw in a pair of rock boots and a good book, such is the fickle nature of our winter!

Two main weather patterns usually produce good, but quite differ- ent winter climbing conditions:-

1. High pressure to the north or north-east of Scotland will bring settled, generally dry, and very cold weather to Wales. This will, after a few days of temperature below or close to zero, produce water-ice conditions on the popular lower-lying crags of Llanberis and Idwal, as well as on the less popular crags scattered around the fringes of the main area.

    Unfortunately, it is impossible to say how many days of frost are needed to bring certain climbs into condition as this will depend on how wet things were before the freeze and the severity of the frost. In ideal conditions even the big ice-falls can form surprisingly quickly. However, pure water-ice which forms rapidly under these conditions will be very brittle. Generally, the inclusion of snow in water-ice will produce a more secure medium (opaque, white ice) for the ice-climber.

In these cold spells there may or may not be much snow on the hills. Higher level routes may **look** to be 'in nick' (ie. snow covered), but unless this snow has already consolidated during less cold weather before the freeze-up, this weather pattern is unlikely to produce good climbing high up on the mountains. There may be little ice (with a few notable exceptions) and the snow will be loose and powdery. However, to compensate for this lack of good climbing high up many low-level watercourses which drain the hillsides may be frozen solid and under these conditions provide excellent sport, often giving a long succession of short ice-pitches to be savoured or spurned according to taste!

2. A succession of well-spaced depressions tracking eastwards over the far north of Scotland and slowing down in the process, can give warmer, stormy westerly conditions alternating with cold NW showery airstreams. This will generally provide the 'snow-melt-freeze' cycle which is essential to produce good snow conditions high up on Snowdon, Crib y Ddysgl, the Glyders and the Black Ladders. During this sort of weather pattern low-level ice routes will rarely be in condition and the snow may not lie below 600m.

The most reliable and long-lasting snow conditions can usually be found on the Clogwyn y Garnedd face of Snowdon, the Cwm Glas face of Crib y Ddysgl and in Cwm Cneifion on Glyder Fawr. Although the upper sections of the deep gullies of the Black Ladders do hold snow well, their lower sections tend to rely more on water-ice. Many of the larger Grade I gullies can be in excellent condition during fine weather late in the season when their ribbons of old snow freeze to hard névé overnight. At a higher grade, the ice-falls of the Devil's Kitchen cliffs are often the first to come into condition in a freeze.

To summarize then - most winter climbs in Wales are in condition at some time each year, but will only succumb to an opportunist approach. Ice waits for no man - or woman! Study the weather patterns, retain a local sage with a telephone, keep a full tank of petrol in the car: and make sure your boss knows about the elderly relative in Bangor with the 'dicky' heart!

STYLE OF ASCENT

Until fairly recently, the strict code of ethics which applies to summer rock climbing seems not to have had any obvious parallel in winter climbing, where safety considerations have always been felt to override any altruistic wish to play by the rules. However, as with modern rock climbing, winter climbing too seems to be developing as a separate sport in which the pursuit of technical difficulty is of increasing importance. And the more technical the sport becomes, the more complex is the set of rules required to maintain the challenge of the activity.

The very use of axes and crampons adds a technical artificiality which does not exist in rock climbing (cf. sticky boots?) and which creates some problems as regards the emergence of a natural code of ethics. In particular, the debate centres on what constitutes acceptable aid in an activity which is only possible by using the aid which is fundamental to the design of modern hand and foot tools. It is obvious that the challenge of ascending steep, thick ice might be better described as a grading of A1, given that it is a simple matter to aid it on tools, placing ice-screws and resting at regular intervals. Of course, it is an arbitrary and fine line which distinguishes hanging from a tool via a wrist-loop in one case and via a sit harness in the other, but it is probably important to recognise the difference in **style** and to try to aspire towards cleaner ascents in one's own climbing.

The grades in this guide reflect this philosophy and are offered on the arbitrary and quite illogical assumption than hanging fröm the wrists is acceptable for whatever reason, whereas clipping in and hanging from the harness either to place gear or for a rest, reduces the effective grade of the climbing, if that is something that concerns the climber. At the same time, it should be recognised that clipping in is usually preferable to falling off...! The heroism of summer has no place for the armoured warrior of winter!

The discussion above relates to what has been described as the 'Competitive Ethic' and breaches of this are mere matters of individual conscience and consequently of little real importance to other climbers.

A matter of greater concern, however, is a breach of the 'Environmental Ethic', which is always a potential threat when winter climbers carry and indiscriminately use rock pegs. Because of the difficulty of obtaining secure anchors in heavily iced cracks, even with modern nuts, it has traditionally been recognised that carrying and using pegs in winter is both sensible and acceptable, even after it became unfashionable to do so when repeating established routes in summer.

It is only recently that winter climbers have strayed on to popular summer rock climbs, but it is a growing and irreversible trend, and the use of pegs on such routes will inevitably cause conflict, with hours of endless debate in the pubs, cafés and magazine columns. The peg which appeared at the top of the first pitch of *Charity* on the Idwal Slabs during the winter of 1986 and has remained there ever since, is a salutary example of what can happen when the ethics of the elite becomes the mores of the masses. Crampon scratches too will offend many but there seems to be little that can be done about this.

This guide takes the view that whilst it is sensible to carry a few pegs their use should in all cases be restricted to situations where no other adequate protection can be arranged, and in the case of winter ascents of summer rock climbs special efforts should be made to avoid unnecessary damage to the rock through the use of pegs, axes or crampons.

Whilst peg scars and crampon scratches may be unsightly and offend other climbers, the stripping of vegetation from many mountain crags is much more an offence against Nature herself. Vegetation is usually present for the same reason as ice - an abundant water supply - so winter climbers often find themselves on cliffs with a well developed and possibly rare, flora: cliffs, indeed, which are rejected by rock climbers for exactly this reason. These steep faces are in many cases the last safe haven from widespread grazing for some of the rarer Arctic/Alpine plants. Safe, that is, until recently. For now (Ice-)Man rushes in where sheep fear to tread!

No one is suggesting that climbers should steer clear of all vegetated cliffs: all that is needed is a little awareness of the mountain environment; a sensitivity to other living things; a gentleness, perhaps. So try to avoid clearing turfy ledges in the search for runners and belays, and tread carefully in your porcupine Koflachs! Remember just how many years it has taken for plant life to establish its toe-hold in these wild, inhospitable places before you consign it carelessly to the scree slope below. Fight the mountain, but don't de-flower its maidens!

DESCRIPTION OF CLIMBS

In general, detailed route descriptions such as appear in current rock climbing guides are inappropriate for winter climbs in view of the varying effect of snow and ice build-up on the topography of the crags. This is particularly true of major snow gully lines where stances are normally taken when anchors present themselves, or when the rope has been stretched to breaking point!

However, for some of the more technical (difficult?) climbs described in this guide and where it is customary to tackle particular pitches in a particular way, then some description of this has been given. This being the case, users should bear in mind that an 'icy groove' as described may well refer to the rocky corner or uniform snow slope which confronts them - or it may not!

Easy ground may be assumed to be Grade I.

LEFT AND RIGHT

The terms left and right are relative to the direction in which the climber is facing when the text is relevant, ie. facing the cliff when ascending, and facing outwards in descent. When there is any likelihood of confusion, approximate cardinal directions (N,S,E,W) have been added.

However, in the section on descents in the introductory notes to each crag, left and right assume that the climber is **facing** the crag, rather than actually descending.

GRADING SYSTEM

At best, the grading of a winter climb should only be thought of as a rough guide to 'normal' difficulty when in 'average' climbable condition. Extremes of snow and ice (or lack of it) can make a nonsense of many of the grades in this book. For example, the waterfall at the back of the Devil's Kitchen can range from impossible (or 'futuristic', for those who cannot accept impossibility!) right through to Grade I when banked out, as it was in 1979.

Not only can conditions alter the *technical* grade of the climbing, but they will also affect the seriousness of the lead. For example, thin ice may be no more difficult to climb than thick ice, but it will probably not afford secure ice-screw protection: buttresses which are heavily iced may make the location of rock belays and runners much more difficult. It would be easy to make out a good case for having no grades at all!

The ubiquitous Scottish I to V system was originally devised to describe winter climbs in Scotland, which were often major routes on remote and serious mountain faces and the grade V was intended to be used only for such climbs, where frequent grade IV pitches (the hardest **technical** grade of snow and ice climbing) were encountered. Also it is clear that the application of this system to Wales is not wholly appropriate as much of the climbing is pursued for technical rather

13

than mountaineering satisfaction, owing to the lack of big, remote faces. However, for historical reasons Welsh winter climbing has adopted this system of classification and many present grades are somewhat meaningless. Sadly, I have heard Point Five quoted as 'a good Idwall III' and whilst there may be **technical** comparability, the author of such remarks does seem to have missed the point (unintentional pun!).

The introduction of Grade VI has further complicated the issue. Although it is obvious that there exist nowadays longer and steeper ice-pitches to which one might ascribe a grade V irrespective of the nature and length of the route as a whole, it is arguable whether their ascent with all the paraphernalia of modern ice-climbing technology is any more difficult than, say, the first ascent of Zero or Smith's Route on the Ben, climbed before the introduction of hooking tools.

And the most recent developments in Scotland, which are only just appearing in Wales, involve climbing steep rock in winter conditions, either by brushing off the snow and using hand-holds, or by torqueing axes in cracks or using them to skyhook face holds. On summer HVS ground that is clearly harder than an ascent of, say, Cascade in good condition. So does it qualify for grade VI ... or VII? Or, as I suspect, have we outgrown the grading system with the diversity of modern winter climbing? Or is it winter climbing at all, and might it not be better described by rock climbing grades?

So, in an attempt to grasp the nettle, this guide uses a modified grading system in an attempt to assist the user in the selection of a climb to suit their style and ability.

A numerical technical pitch grade is introduced from 1 to ? roughly equating with the current Roman numerical grades and being open ended to allow for difficult mixed pitches but taking no account of other aspects of the route such as length, seriousness, remoteness, protection, belays etc. For routes which are thought merely to be outcrop problems, the technical grade of their crux pitch has been adopted as an overall grade and the overall seriousness/sustainedness can be assessed from reading the description. The definition of what constitutes an outcrop and what a mountain crag, is obviously subjective and open to argument, but the number of pitches, its isolation and the ease of escape are obviously important factors.

It is expected that continuous thick ice would never warrant a grade higher than 6 and that 7 and above be reserved for modern routes with a predominance of difficult mixed climbing on steep ground. It is clear that such pitches exist, but have generally had so few ascents that it would be arrogant to scatter such grades around. However, it is to be hoped that climbers making repeats clutching these new ideas will offer their opinions of the difficulty based on this principle. The process of providing full pitch grade information cannot obviously be completed in one fell swoop, so only those routes where it is known or can be guessed have been thus amended in the hope that once the seed has been sown later editions will be able to complete the task. The concept of pitch grades is not a new one and we can claim no originality here: it was the late Al Rouse who originally published the idea, although he himself may have got it second-hand.

Ascents of difficult rock climbs in winter conditions have largely been omitted except for a passing reference: rock climbing guidebooks (and grades too, possibly) are more useful and appropriate here.

For routes which are more in the traditional winter climbing mould, ie. those involving snow, ice and mixed ground on the bigger, more remote mountain crags, the old Roman numerical system is retained but some crucial pitch grades are given where they are both known and thought to be relevant. Currently, Grade VI is offered as the upper limit but VII's and VIII's may well exist ... I await your advice! As a general guide, the overall grade does not normally differ by more than one or two from the technical grade of the hardest pitch and the relationship between these two grades should be interpreted in a similar fashion to 'E' grades and technical grades in summer.

For those climbers who are familiar with the wide differences in the style and grading of climbs on Ben Nevis and in the Cairngorms it will probably be useful to know that the grades in this guide will be found to be somewhere between the two - the ice is harder and steeper than on the Ben, whilst the buttresses are easier than in the Gorms! In fact Welsh winter climbing probably combines the best of both areas!

The grading won't be perfect - the variability of conditions will see to that - but it can never be worse than before and may even be a lot better.

PITCH AND ROPE LENGTHS

Despite the valiant rearguard action still being contested by champions of the furlong, fathom and chain, the authors of this guide, whilst lamenting the passing of the good old foot, have reluctantly accepted that the metre is here to stay, and have followed current trends accordingly.

As readers of earlier editions will have realised, most of the pitch lengths quoted were only approximations at best and consequently the metric conversions have been rounded to the nearest 5m, rather than offering mathematically accurate but pointlessly pedantic equivalents. Thus 50ft. becomes 15m rather than 16m, and so on. It is also hoped that those recording new routes will do so along these lines.

On some routes the division into pitches occurs naturally, whilst on others, different climbers may pause at different points as dictated by conditions and their skill at excavating anchors! The pitch length given and thus the position of the stance should be taken therefore only as a rough guide, to be adapted to prevailing conditions by exercise of the climber's judgement.

All climbs in this guide can be tackled with 45m ropes. The current trend towards 50m will increase the likelihood of finding belay anchors - but will certainly not guarantee it. Most climbers will find double 9mm ropes to be most suitable for winter climbing, particularly on routes above Grade II, where it may not always be possible to force an ascent. Retreat with a single rope from high on a major route in winter could be a memorable experience!

Where a pitch is described as being longer than one rope length the suggestion is not that intermediate anchors don't exist, nor that ropes should be tied together, but that the line is obvious and that climbers take stances as they see fit.

TIMES

Previous editions of this guide have followed the traditional Scottish idea of giving a climbing time for each route. This was presumably included to give some indication of how sustained the climb was thought to be as most people would in any case be able to arrive at their own estimate based on overall length and difficulty.

The authors of this edition feel that route descriptions already contain sufficient information (overall grade, some pitch grades, length, text, etc.) for users to make their own projection about how long it will take them to complete any of the climbs. In any case, we don't know how well (or badly!) you climb!

Furthermore, there are few routes in North Wales of a sufficiently long, serious and remote nature, for climbers who having chosen within their ability, bearing in mind prevailing conditions and started at a sensible time, need to worry about how long it's going to take them to get to the top. Only the big routes on Lliwedd and the Black Ladders are liable to lead to time pressure - but don't quote us on that!

However, to satisfy the traditionalists may we offer, somewhat tongue-in-cheek, the following adaptation of the time-honoured Naismith's Rule! To calculate the approximate time for an average party in good conditions, climbing as a roped pair and pitching all the way (not always the case, in practice, of course) try this:-

Allow 48 minutes for every 100m (125m per hour) at Grade I and II, and multiply times for harder climbs by half the grade.

> eg. For a 300m Grade V:
> 3 x 48mins. = 2hrs. 24mins.
> 2hrs. 24mins. x 2.5 (½ the grade) = 6hrs.

No time allowed for photographs, food or changing the batteries in your calculator!

It's not perfect but it's at least as good as the times in other winter guidebooks. Climbers may find times somewhat ungenerous for the longer grade I and II's, particularly if they only run out short rope-lengths, but it should provide some sort of yardstick by which they may make some assessment of their competence. Generally, the more competent the party the faster the time. If anyone finds the above formula to be well out, then perhaps they should examine their own climbing style before writing to tell us!

STAR RATING SYSTEM

The currently fashionable system of rating the quality of climbs by a system of one to three stars has been retained - it would be more than the authors' lives were worth to abandon such a pillar of the establishment! However, the stars have not been scattered like confetti, as all the climbs in the guide are worthwhile in the right conditions, and any climb thought worthy of a star must be exceptional in some way.

To qualify for a star a route must have good climbing and be a natural line, commonly in condition. Climbs which are already popular will inevitably warrant stars, almost by definition. Three stars indicates an outing of tremendous character in a superb position offering winter climbing comparable with the best in Britain. The number of stars awarded to recent climbs which have had few, if any, repeats, have been deliberately kept to a minimum - some first ascentionists have a tendency to rave about their creations whilst others adopt a more modest style of reporting.

But remember that quality goes hand in hand with conditions - so don't blame us if the starred route of your choice turns out to be a pile of choss!

FIRST ASCENTS

Unlike Scotland, Wales has no tradition of recording first ascents in winter and it's only in recent years that such information has become generally available. As a result, some of the routes claimed in recent years may well have been ascended in the past. Joe Brown and Martin Boysen between them probably climbed everything in the 60's, but unfortunately they can't remember exactly what they did! If they didn't do them, then Archer Thomson almost certainly did!

We believe that a first ascents list is an interesting and popular part of any guidebook and we started in this edition to compile one. Unfortunately, with so little information available it has proved to be a fruitless task. Currently we have details of the probable first ascents of about 10% of the climbs but felt that this did not warrant publication at this stage. However, we hope that the production of this guide will generate sufficient interest for climbers to come forward with details of ascents of routes which they may have felt to have been firsts at the time.

If there **is** a route which you think you may have done the first ascent of, or you know who did; or if you know of any climbs not recorded; or you do any new climbs in the future, please write to us via the publisher - Cicerone Press, Police Square, Milnthorpe, Cumbria, LA7 7PY. Don't worry if you're unsure of dates - just tell us what you can remember. Hopefully, in this way we may be able to include something worthwhile in the next edition.

Information on new routes may also be recorded in the book at Pete's Eats in Llanberis, or the one in the Plas y Brenin bar.

BELAYS AND RUNNERS

One of the great attractions of climbing in winter is that although life can be uncomfortable there is often no great technical difficulty. Modern tools and clothing have done much to make life bearable on steep, snowy faces; but because of the inherently shattered nature of many of the classic north facing crags in winter and the variable quality of their frosty mantle, the sport is unlikely to attain the level of security often demanded of rock climbs. No bad thing, some might say!

All belay anchors should automatically be treated with suspicion. Frost shattered rock presents a superficially attractive array of spikes, threads and cracks, but any security offered is only as good as the icy gel coat bonding it all together. Contact threads between boulders are particularly vulnerable to rupture under load as are small wire placements. Friends can be useful in winter and will absorb a certain amount of expansion of cracks but they won't grip in iced-up parallel-sided, or flared cracks.

One advantage of using pitons is that expanding cracks become obvious after a few hammer blows. However, few climbers these days have much experience of pegs - and there's more to it than most people imagine. A few hours spent in the company of Doug Scott's *Big Wall Climbing* - if you can get hold of a copy, followed by a bit of surreptitious practice at the local quarry, is to be recommended before attempting to nail up any icy gullies.

In Wales, it is rare to find a sufficient depth of consolidated snow to accept a deadman and a properly buried horizontal axe will usually provide more security in shallow, firm snow if good rock anchors are unobtainable. A well constructed stance, or seat, together with a safe, dynamic belaying technique will help to reduce loads on belay anchors, as will an early runner.

All winter climbers should practise the waist belay and know when to use it in preference to other belay devices. Either learn to use it **safely** with a modern harness, or just use a belt. Practise holding sliding falls (no crampons!) on steep snow slopes with safe run-outs until it feels comfortable. But beware, for the ubiquitous body belay is probably the single most abused technique in the whole of climbing.

Modern ice screws, if correctly placed, offer reasonable security where the ice is at least six inches thick but never place two screws closer than, say, a metre apart and don't hang from them for too long! The pressure will begin to melt the ice. One solution for belays is to place both tools to take the weight so that the attachment to the screws is *just* slack. Remember also that screws, particularly snargs, have a nasty habit of popping out in the sun.

One might imagine from the general scarcity of anchors in winter that it isn't too important to carry a lot of gear. Well, it's certainly true that you won't need a lot of krabs but at the same time it's generally a sound idea on most routes to take a good selection of nuts and Friends, a few screws and some pegs, particularly blade types. If there are only three anchors in 150m it would be a shame not to be able to use them!

EQUIPMENT

It is assumed that climbers using this guide will be equipped with all the modern tools of the trade: two well-designed, curved or inclined hand tools (normally one with an adze head, and the other with a

19

hammer head) complete with wrist-loops adjusted to length, and a pair of rigid-soled boots fitted with crampons which have ice-climbing front points protruding at least 2cm beyond the toe of the boot. Although most grade I's and II's can be climbed with a single axe, 'bendy boots' and any old crampons, the limitations of this equipment will become apparent on some of the harder routes, and add a notch or two to the effective grade.

Those who have graduated to winter climbing from rock climbing may not have used a helmet for some time. Well, now's the time to dig it out again, because no one in their right mind (well, almost no one!) goes ice-climbing without a helmet. Lumps of ice falling from 50m above, where your partner is clearing a stance tend to be both heavy and fast-moving: students of physics will understand the significance of this!

As far as clothing is concerned, lots of thin layers are better than one thick one. A good system when actually climbing is thermal underwear, thin sweater, polar jacket, and 'shell' clothing - but walk in wearing as little as is comfortable. A couple more tips: never wear cotton clothing next to the skin, sew elastic loops to your mitts, and wear something around your neck - a polo neck without the sweater is ideal.

In addition to the hardware and basic clothing, it is usually sensible in winter to go into the hills carrying a rucksack with a few items of basic survival equipment in it. These include: small first aid kit; head-torch (with battery and bulbs); spare sweater or lightweight duvet jacket; full water/windproof overgarments; polythene emergency bivvy bag; some spare food (chocolate etc.); flask of hot liquid; map and compass; spare gloves; balaclava (to go under helmet).

Of course, experience will teach you when you can leave some of these things behind, but when climbing on the higher mountain crags it is sensible to have most of them most of the time. And don't leave your rucksack with all these bits in it at the bottom of the crag - they won't be much use down there when the going gets tough!

MAPS AND NAVIGATION

Navigation is as much a skill of winter climbing as belaying is. The following lists of skills should be acquired:

Basic map interpretation - reading contours
Lifting a bearing from the map
Walking accurately on a bearing
Measuring distance from the map

Measuring distance (up to about 500m) on the ground by counting paces.

Few climbers acquire these skills by climbing - but in white-out conditions (which are fortunately rare in Wales), they can be life-savers. It's impossible to describe just how frightening it can be in a true white-out where nothing at all on the ground is visible, and there is no horizon. Without a map and compass and the ability to use them, safe progress cannot be made. In such situations staying roped-up is the only sensible course of action. The answer is to practise in controlled situations - and then it's down to experience and judgement.

A good map and compass are the basic tools - a Silva Type 4 is probably as good a compass as any, and although the 1:50,000 Land-ranger series of maps is adequate, detailed navigation is much easier with the new Pathfinder 1:25,000 sheets. But beware when purchasing maps - there are still some old series sheets in the shops, even dressed up in new covers. Look inside for detailed metric (10m) contours with major contour intervals in multiples of 50m. Older maps either have feet or strange contour numbers, eg. 152m.

Apart from the maps quoted for each crag (1:50,000 Landranger 115, 123, 124 & 125), the following 1:25,000 sheets may be found to be useful.

Pathfinder   Sheet 66/76 Bethesda (Gwynedd) - CARNEDDAU
                    Sheet 65/75 Snowdon & Betws y Coed
                    -SNOWDON & GLYDERS

Outdoor Leisure Series
                    Sheet 17 - most of Northern Snowdonia
                    Sheet 18 - Bala area
                    Sheet 19 - Harlech (Rhinogs)
                    Sheet 23 - Cadair Idris

And don't forget to protect the map from the elements - wind and wet can reduce a new map to nothing in a matter of minutes.

COLD INJURIES AND FIRST AID

In winter, mountaineers suffer an increased risk of **hypothermia**, particularly in windy conditions. Prevention is better than cure and good clothing, lots of food and not being over-ambitious usually does the trick. Should it occur, the situation is potentially serious - recognise and treat early signs by food, warm clothing and retreat (or the least energetic option), as later signs (collapse, unconsciousness) may prove untreatable on the climb.

21

Frostbite can and does occur in British condition. Toes and fingers are the traditional areas affected but nose, ears and cheeks are even more common as these are often left uncovered. Check each other for white spots appearing on the face, particularly in very windy weather and carefully re-warm. Frostbite is usually the result of carelessness - as soon as the feeling is lost in an extremity spend some time re-warming it - don't just ignore it. Doing strenuous exercise will usually restore cold hands and feet. Run uphill - or do lots of pull-ups on your ice-axes!

There are a few basic principles of **First Aid** which are worth knowing:

1. Unconscious casualties should not be left lying on their back - roll them into the **Recovery, or ¾ Prone, position,** and check for breathing and pulse. If either is absent use expired air resuscitation and/or external cardiac compression - if you don't they will certainly die, so don't worry if you are not absolutely sure how to do it.

2. Take care when moving if spinal (neck and back) injuries are suspected - particularly avoid **forward** bending at the waist and twisting movements.

3. Most bleeding is stopped by **firm and continuous direct pressure over the site of the injury.**

4. Do not give food, drink (even water) or drugs to seriously injured casualties.

5. When trying to keep a casualty warm remember to insulate underneath.

6. Keep a timed record of the level of consciousness - this is invaluable later.

7. When dealing with an accident to someone else, **look after yourself** too.

AVALANCHES

With the dramatic increase in the numbers of those participating in winter mountaineering of one sort or another there has been an inevitable rise in the number of accidents, a significant proportion of which are caused by avalanches. Unfortunately, many climbers venturing into the hills in winter have either very little or perhaps worse, misleading information about the nature of the problem. There are two widely held and potentially dangerous misconceptions which can lead to complacency and false reassurance in conditons of real avalanche risk:

1. ***Avalanches are only a serious problem in Alpine-type mountains.***

    NOT TRUE - Whilst it is evident that avalanches of truly devastating proportions generally only occur in the larger mountain ranges, smaller snow slides are a common feature in any hilly area which receives snowfall and it doesn't require much to dislodge a climber on front-points in a gully. Furthermore, there are frequent reports of avalanches in Britain a kilometre wide and involving snow layers in excess of one metre thick. These are significant avalanches by any standards.

2. ***Avalanches only occur in thaw conditions***

    NOT TRUE EITHER - A rise in temperature **can** certainly increase the likelihood of avalanche in some conditions, and will usually bring the risk of cornice collapse, but it is also the case that increases in temperature can equally lead to a more rapid consolidation of the snowpack, and hence, an actual reduction in the risk. By far the greatest threat to winter mountaineers and skiers is posed by **dry, cold snow slab avalanches** on slopes in the lee of recent or prevailing winds - and this risk is usually greatest within 48 hours of significant snowfall or deposition. The influence of *wind* in the British Isles is far more significant in the creation of potential avalanche hazard than *temperature.*

Tragedies in recent years, involving experienced climbers, on the Black Ladders and in Parsley Fern Gully have illustrated the sad lack of real knowledge about snow structure and avalanche prediction among many mountaineers. In an attempt to encourage safer practices in winter, some brief notes are included below, but all users of this guide are urged to consult one of many authoritative works now available on the subject. The following three volumes will be found to cover the topic with clarity and in depth:-

A Chance in a Million? by Barton & Wright pub. SMT

Avalanche Safety for Skiers and Climbers by Daffern pub. Diadem

Mountaincraft and Leadership by Langmuir pub. Scottish SC & MLTB.

This latter volume also contains much useful information on general winter mountaineering techniques.

Main Types of Avalanche

1. **Powder**

   These occur most commonly during or immediately after snowfall in calm conditions (ie. with no wind) and are rare in Wales. They may occur in gullies, over buttresses, or on open slopes, usually starting from a point and fanning out as they collect more snow. They may be quite large on medium angle (less than 45°) slopes, but normally take the form of regular releases (spindrift avalanches) of small quantities of snow on steeper slopes. These are most commonly experienced in gullies with large exit fans leading out onto extensive snow-catching plateaux areas (eg. Trinity Face on Snowdon, and the Black Ladders). Although these spindrift avalanches are unpleasant, they are rarely dangerous unless the climber is taken unawares and off-balance.

2. **Wet Snow**

   These are associated with major thaw conditions, and are most common on south facing slopes in the Alpine ranges in spring. Melt water percolates the snowpack and washes away the bond which one layer has developed with underlying layers, or in some cases, the ground where this has a smooth surface (grass, small scree or rock slab). They frequently emanate from just below buttresses, moving slowly downhill and spreading out as they gather more snow rather like a rolling snowball. Slopes which are prone to this type of avalanche are easy to spot as there is frequently evidence of small wet slides on the surface. Although they are quite common, in Wales they are generally small, fairly predictable and thus easily avoided.

3. **Slab**

   These are the commonest of all British avalanches and represent the most serious threat to climbers. A slab avalanche involves a whole section of the slope or gully breaking away simultaneously with no obvious warning and occurs most commonly on slopes between 30° and 45° (although slopes of little more than 20° have been known to avalanche in this way). Most Grade I gullies involve slopes of this angle, as does the ground leading up to the foot of many crags.

   The most common type of slab consists of wind-damaged crystals deposited on the more sheltered slopes in the lee of the prevailing wind and these can build up rapidly to several feet in depth. Slabs begin to accumulate with local wind speeds of 15 knots or so (soft slab), and their surfaces become increasingly hard as the wind speed in the deposition area increases (hard slab). Wind slab is much denser than new snow, because its crystals have been pulverised by the wind allowing them to pack together and form a strong, welded mass. It has a chalky, unreflective appearance; breaks into compact blocks; may have a rippled surface; is squeeky when walked on; and leaves very well defined footprints. Soft slab is frequently found just beneath cornices and crags, whereas hard slab is more common on exposed slopes and ridges. Changes in wind direction can cause erosion and transport of existing slabs and their re-deposition on slopes with different aspects. This may thus produce fresh avalanche danger, **even when there has been no fresh snowfall.** Many climbers confuse potentially dangerous soft wind slab with powder which poses less of a threat.

Whilst the existence of wind slab on slopes of the appropriate angle should always be noted with concern by climbers, two further factors are necessary for any avalanche to occur: there must be poor bonding between the slab and the next layer down the snowpack; and there must be a trigger. If the layers **are** poorly bonded, or a lubricating layer of small, rounded or fragile crystals is sandwiched in between, then the mere presence of the climber on the slope may be enough to cause fracture. In practice, most mountaineers involved in avalanches are themselves the triggers - avalanches should not be seen as Acts of God which hurtle down upon the poor, innocent climber from above.

Practical Evaluation of Snow Slopes
From the above considerations, it is therefore recommended that climbers physically examine the bonding of the various layers before venturing onto open slopes, or into gullies where the snow is anything other than firm névé. This can best be done by cutting a small snow profile, or snow pit vertically down through the snowpack, preferably to ground level, but for convenience, where the snow is particularly deep, at least as far as the old, stable base layer. When choosing a site for the profile, choose a safe, protected spot which has the appropriate aspect, and which seems to be characteristic of the whole slope. The various layers and their boundaries should then be critically examined. A potentially dangerous condition will exist where two adjacent layers exhibit markedly different snow characteristics in terms of any of the following: **HARDNESS, WETNESS, CRYSTAL SIZE**

A simple check on the adhesion of any suspect layers can be made by cutting around a block just above the pit and encouraging it to slide. Where there is some doubt as to the security of slopes after an examination of this nature, it should be remembered that the steeper the slope upon which these conditions exist, the greater the risk of fracture; and the deeper the unstable upper layer(s), the more serious the consequence of a release.

Further Safety Precautions

1. The stress (ie. tendency to fracture) is greatest on **convex** sections of slope - these should be avoided where possible in favour of **concave** sections.

2. When traversing a slope under a crag, try to stay as close to the rock as possible. Avalanches usually leave a thin strip of snow anchored to the crag.

3. When approaching gullies, do not do so in a direct line, but try and identify from protruding rocks and stones, faint ribs under the snow where the cover is less deep. These islands of safety, combined with a high traverse at the very foot of the crag will offer a safe approach.

4. When in wide snow gullies, stay as close to the sides as possible. Better still, **avoid Grade I snow gullies altogether when they have lots of fresh snow or wind slab in them.** (eg. the Trinities, Parsley Fern, Easy Route in the Nameless Cwm, the Y Garn gullies etc.).

5. Study the weather pattern (direction and strength of wind, snowfall, temperature, etc.) of the previous few days to determine likely snow conditions and which aspect slopes may be dangerous (lee slopes).

If You are Caught in an Avalanche

1. Try to jump clear, or plant your axe and try to hang on to avoid or delay being swept away.

2. Shout to attract attention so that you are seen.

3. Try to discard axe and rucksack.

4. Try to 'swim' to remain on the surface and try to get to one side.

5. Cover your mouth and nose, and try to create a breathing space in front of your face as the snow comes to rest.

6. Try to free your limbs as soon as possible after the slide has stopped - the debris will consolidate very rapidly making further movement impossible.

7. Conserve energy and try to remain calm. Rescuers on the surface

may not be able to hear your shouts.

If You are a Witness to an Avalanche
REMEMBER, *IMMEDIATE* SEARCHING SAVES LIVES

1. Mark the point from which the victim was swept away, and the point at which they were last seen. This will give an indication of where to start searching.

2. A quick search of the whole area below the last seen point should be made, looking for visible signs. Leave any items of equipment you may find where they are - these will offer further clues.

3. Observe silence whilst searching, and **LISTEN.**

4. If this fails to locate the victim, immediately organise a more thorough search and probe systematically with ice-axes. Continue searching in this way until assistance arrives.

5. Sending for help is a **LOW PRIORITY** compared with using all available hands for searching. Remember, victims who are dug out immediately have an 80% chance of survival, whereas those who remain buried for 3 hours only have a 10% chance: and rescue team help will generally be more than 3 hours away.

6. If a victim is uncovered and not breathing, clear the airway and commence E.A.R. before treating other injuries.

RESCUE

In the event of an accident occuring which requires rescue services or medical assistance, phone 999 and ask for 'Police'. Do not make a special effort to reach or contact a Mountain Rescue Post - just go to a phone. Give details of the incident, including the exact location (crag, climb, pitch, etc.), how many injured, nature of injuries, time of incident, etc. If the injuries are particularly serious and you feel that a helicopter might be required, then make this point over the phone. Always wait at the telephone until the Police arrive for further information - do not return to the scene of the accident without informing the Police.

If you have to leave a seriously injured casualty on the hill, make them comfortable, leave them in a sheltered spot and belay them securely if they are still on the crag. Mark the location clearly if there is likely to be any difficulty in re-locating it in bad weather. If you *have* to leave an unconscious casualty, ensure that their airway is clear and their position keeps it that way, and leave a note explaining what you're doing in case they should recover consciousness while you're

away. But always try to attract the attention of others rather than leave
a seriously injured casualty on the hill alone.

1. CARNEDDAU

This massive rolling upland with its remote and hidden cwms, stone-walled by huge and rambling crags has a subtle splendour which is in marked contrast to the instant and rather vulgar grandeur of the peaks which cluster around the heart of Eryri. Here the summits are modest; no thrusting extroversion or naked spires but wild, shy plateaux, embarrassed, it would seem, by their baldness and bare dominance of the main ridge.

But the advent of the winter snows raises these Cambrian Cairngorms to new heights. The uniformity of the terrain gladly accepts this welcome gloss and offers to the adventurous traveller on ski the prospect of effortless gliding, whilst the shortcomings of many of the crags as summer playgrounds now lie deep beneath a glistening mantle of ice and snow. And the stiffening resolve of summer's sagging turf offers a unique opportunity for venturing onto the frozen buttresses of forgotten crags.

Of course, Ysgolion Duon is the showpiece and rightly so. Recent hard winters and modern techniques have brought this rambling Gormenghast of a crag out of the Dark Ages; but by no means have they beaten it into submission. The climbing remains serious and the situations are remote. Fortunately, perhaps, the current popularity of this one major crag has diverted attention away from some of the other fine winter climbing areas in the Carneddau and has allowed explorers and romantics to cherish and enjoy an isolation which is uncommon in these days of easy access and abundant leisure. Craig y Dulyn and the almost Alpine terrain of Cwmglas Bach behind Carnedd Dafydd, still offer much scope for exploration at all levels.

On the less popular crags, only a few of the possible routes are included in this guide: many more have probably seen the passage of earlier pioneers with no wish to record their explorations and maybe many other lines still await the first anguished squeal of metal on rock. Who knows and does anyone really care? The Carneddau remain aloof from the absolutism of modern mountaineering. An icy wind, screaming in the manes of its wild ponies barely pauses for breath as it races down from the ridge into sunless dungeons of grey rock. And the climber is left clinging to a tenuous toe-hold on this Rock of Ages; lost in the magnitude of Nature and insignificant in her shadow.

1.1 CRAIG Y DULYN

Grid Reference: 698668 (OS Sheet 115 Snowdon)
Altitude: 600m - 700m
Aspect: E to SE
Climbing Conditions:
As most of the climbing on this relatively low-lying crag is on steep water-ice and its aspect ensures that it gets quite a lot of sun in the morning, a prolonged period of cold weather is required. Furthermore, it is inadvisable to tackle routes on Weeping Wall on sunny days, even in cold spells, because of the serious danger of massive icicle collapse! Consolidated snow and a long period of frost will produce some interesting possibilities on the steep right-hand section of the crag.
Approach:
The quickest approach is by car from Tal y Bont into Cwm Eigiau via a gated road, parking at 731663. From here a rough farm track leads NW across the bounding ridge of the cwm into the valley of the upper Afon Dulyn. Either continue SW up the track to Melynllyn where a path leads down to the Llyn Dulyn dam, or more directly, leave the track beyond the stile at 720669 and contour into the valley bottom, approaching the N-end of the lake via a marshy plateau area.

This very wet and vegetated crag receives a copious water supply from the eastern slopes of **Garnedd Uchaf** and **Foel Grach**. Steep ground extends for over 1km along the west side of **Llyn Dulyn**, although the wettest and steepest section is that at the northern end where three major (and many minor) watercourses pour over the vegetated crags situated above and to the right of the steep section rising directly from the lake. A straight wall running up from the lake to the crags is a readily identifiable feature of this region. **Fairy Falls** takes the right-hand watercourse, starting to the right of the wall.

Further right, the crag becomes bigger and steeper, and its aspect becomes more southerly. This is **Weeping Wall**, a very wet, steep and vegetated area rising above an easy-angled rake, and tapering from nothing at the left-hand end to 100m on the right. **Quicksilver** takes a line of ice-falls above the bottom of the rake, rising the full height of the crag.

Remarkably, there is no documented evidence of the other obvious lines having been climbed, but this seem difficult to believe...?

Descent:
The easiest descent is down grassy slopes well to the right of Weeping Wall, but a more awkward direct return may be made in good visibility down the rake to the right of Fairy Falls.

FAIRY FALLS   60m   IV/V   **

Exhilarating climbing on steep water-ice in the modern idiom.
Start by scrambling up a shallow snowy gully to the right of the stone wall until discretion requires the use of the rope.
1.   30m   (5)   Start from the right and climb the bed of the gully until it is possible to move up into an alcove on the right via a steep iced slabby ramp. Move out left and climb the steep ice curtain to a belay on screws.
2.   30m   (5)   Weave steeply in and out of the huge chandeliers to reach easier ground.

QUICKSILVER   140m   IV/V   **

The central line on Weeping Wall gives an exciting outing beneath the Damoclean icicles!
Start to the right of the foot of the easy rake, where an icy ramp leads up to the main line of ice-falls.
1.   40m   (5)   Climb the ramp leftwards and move up to below the free-standing pillar. Muscle up this to gain an icy ledge with good rock belays in a corner at the back. Don't look up!
2.   50m   (5)   Step down onto the steep iced wall on the right and climb it rightwards until an overhung groove leads back left to easier ground and poor belays.
3.   50m   (3/4)   Directly to the top of the crag, taking the largely

avoidable bulges in one's stride!

1.2 CWM FFYNNON CASEG

Grid Reference: 678650 (OS Sheet 115 Snowdon)
Altitude: 800m - 900m
Aspect: N
Climbing Conditions:
The climbing is predominantly on snow, and will therefore be most enjoyable when the underfoot conditions are firm and consolidated after periods of alternate freeze and thaw.
Approach:
Tracks leads east from the farm (639660) above the pumping station in Gerlan (parking is a problem here - take care not to block the road, or antagonise the residents), past a number of disused slate tips and sheep pens along the north side of Afon Caseg. The true right bank of the stream is followed, crossing various tributaries, to its source at the tiny lake in the base of the cwm. Allow 1¾ hours from Gerlan.

This tiny cwm has a wild and remote air, and is a stormy place in strong SW winds. It holds snow very well, and was the scene of a most impressive wind slab avalanche in 1963.

Descent:
Either reverse Col Route, or traverse the summit of Yr Elen and descend its ENE ridge, contouring back into the cwm at a convenient level.

The snow slope direct to the summit of **Carnedd Llewelyn** contains two shallow depressions (Grade I) which have some merit for those of carbon-fibre calves and a penchant for the diretissima!
Unfortunately there are few continuously steep lines, but an ascent to the col between **Carnedd Llewelyn** and **Yr Elen** can be made using one of the following approaches:

COL ROUTE 150m I
A pleasant approach to either summit under firm, safe snow conditions which takes the slopes to the left of the steeper, buttressed area at the head of the cwm.

COL GULLY 150m I/II
This is the first gully to the right beyond a slight buttress. It is quite steep to finish.

ELEN GULLY 150m I/II

*Bill Wayman attacking the crucial icicle on the first pitch
of THE DEVIL'S APPENDIX (VI). Photo: Malcolm Campbell.*

The next gully to the right is similar, although not quite so good.

To the right of this route further small rocky buttresses and gullies leading to the SE ridge of **Yr Elen** offer opportunities for the more adventurous to frighten themselves, although nothing substantial has been recorded in this area.

1.3 CRAIG YR YSFA

Grid Reference: 693637 (OS Sheet 115 Snowdon)
Altitude: 600m - 860m
Aspect: E
Climbing Conditions:
The crag is relatively low, receives only moderate drainage and is largely clad in a tall, tenacious heather. Consequently, much of the winter climbing is rather disappointing, bearing in mind the promising gully-buttress-gully structure of much of this rambling crag. However, a substantial covering of well-consolidated snow will provide traditional sport in many of the gullies.
Approach:
Approach from the Conwy Valley as for Craig y Dulyn, but from the parking place at 731663 follow good tracks past the left-hand side of Llyn Eigiau across the river and into the cwm proper. From the old mine workings at 702635, re-cross the river and follow paths along the bed of the cwm before slanting up left to the crag. 1½ hours from car to crag, assuming the road from Tal y Bont (sections of 1 in 3!) is negotiable, which it frequently isn't in winter!
Alternatively, and most commonly, approach via the tarmac road (on foot!) from the A5 east of Ogwen (688602) to Fynnon Llugwy, then cross Bwlch Eryl Farchog and descend a steep, awkward diagonal path into Cwm Eigiau and the south end of the crag. 1¾ hours from the A5.

This large and complex crag is conveniently divided into three sections: the **South Crag, The Amphitheatre** and the **North Crag** which are encountered in that order as one approaches from the Ogwen side over **Bwlch Eryl Farchog. South Crag** is a rambling, vegetated collection of buttresses divided by a number of shallow gullies; **The Amphitheatre** is an atmospheric, broad gully defined on the left by the slender rib of the classic 'Diff', **Amphitheatre Buttress**, and on the right by a magnificent, soaring wall of clean rock where **Mur y Niwl, VS,** wends its summer way through some particularly unfriendly-looking territory; **North Crag** to the right would probably not warrant description were it not for **The Great Gully**, a route whose summer grade, Very Difficult, is a most apt and literal description of its ascent!

But all too often the crag disappoints even the most ardent supporters of obscure wintry esoterica. Its heathery gullies and out of condition rock climbs pay scant regard to the weapons of modern winter warfare. Tricouni and tweed will often gain better purchase here than Grivel or Gore! None of the security of vertical ice can be expected in the dark recesses of an Arch, Bending or Avalanche under a curtain of deep powder snow clinging to vertical heathland!

Amphitheatre Buttress is usually sporting (and difficult!) but hardly a winter route; **Great Gully,** also sporting is usually better described as E4 than Grade IV: but notwithstanding its shortcomings, Craig yr Ysfa is a crag which will always repay a visit. Its traditional winter climbing is part of every climber's apprenticeship, and a day spent in its isolated splendour with rope and axe will later be recalled with affection and good humour in the company of like-minded spirits - probably under the influence of the other kind!

Descent:
The safest way off is to follow the path southwards above the crag to regain Bwlch Eryl Farchog. The awkward summer descent into the left-hand (facing out) side of the Amphitheatre can be even more awkward in winter, and can only be recommended to the experienced, and then only under substantial and well consolidated snow cover.

SOUTH CRAG

The steep heathery slopes of the descent path from the col gradually merge into the left edge of the buttress, and the first climb starts some 20m or so to the right.

PINNACLE GULLY 200m II

Although shallow the gully is well-defined throughout its length, and may be recognised by the rotting, flake pinnacle in the upper section.
1. 200m   The gully is steep at first with numerous short pitches, but eases towards the top.

Beyond the obvious rib right of **Pinnacle Gully,** a scree/snow shoot runs out of a deep recess in the centre of **South Crag.** This recess contains two gully lines separated by a narrow rib. The right-hand groove/gully is **Bending Gully,** which forks about after 100m, whilst **Arch Gully** is the less conspicuous groove to the left. High on the crag is a depression, **The Cirque** into which both **Arch Gully** and the left branch of **Bending Gully** lead.

ARCH GULLY 300m IV/III *

Although undistinguished in its lower section, there are a number of excellent pitches above The Cirque. Bending Gully, and its left branch may well be a better start. The crux chimney can be quite hard.

1.   160m   (2/3)   A continuous groove, either snow, heather or a mixture of both leads eventually to a thin flake belay on a heathery rib just beneath The Cirque. This flake is probably the first rock anchor of any substance.

2.   50m   (2)   Move right to join the left branch of Bending Gully and follow this via a short pitch to The Cirque. The entry to the cleft is obvious - the exit less so, but move hopefully up to belay on a huge block in the centre of the gloomy chasm.

3.   45m   (4)   The Arch Pitch. The eponymous chockstone hovers above, whilst below, an icy chimney bars the way. It looks hard, and is! (Don't bother trying to lasso the chockstone!) Once through The Arch a bulge is taken on the right, and the easier gully leads to some spikes and a tiny cave beneath a smaller chockstone.

4.   45m   (3/4)   The short, smooth overhanging chimney above suggests a lengthy retreat. However, a hidden groove on the left allows height to be gained before swinging across right to the easy upper section of the gully and the top.

BENDING GULLY   260m   II

Not a particularly good line as the main gully peters out into the heather slopes higher up. The hidden centre section is of fair interest. Start 20m right of Arch Gully in the recess below the conspicuous groove/gully.

1.   100m   Follow the obvious gully line taking the right fork at the junction until it bends sharply rightwards.

2.   100m   Follow the V-groove rightwards up a succession of short pitches.

3.   60m   Where the gully line disappears take to the snow slopes on the left to gain the summit.

To the right is an area of heavy vegetation and overlapping slabs extending into the next gully, which is some 40m to the left of the obvious rib of **Amphitheatre Buttress.**

AVALANCHE GULLY   240m   II

A rather uninspired gully, although in icy conditions the first 100m where most of the difficulties are concentrated, can offer enjoyable climbing.

1.   30m   Climb a shallow ice-groove, or traverse in from the right along ledges.

2.   30m   A 10m ice-step followed by easier climbing.

3.   15m   A 5m ice-pitch followed by a move right and up into the

wide, easy central section of the gully.

4. 165m   Straight on to the final steepening, a chimney on the right which provides a fitting climax.

To the right is **Amphitheatre Buttress** which remains a rock climb in all but the most extreme of winters, and although it will always provide a sporting day out for competent parties, a full description here is not thought to be justified.

Right again is the massive atmospheric cleft of

AMPHITHEATRE GULLY   250m   II/III   *
It is entered via a wide, easy-angled snow slope, leading enticingly to the foot of the impressive Right Wall, with its concentration of fine, steep rock climbs. Thus drawn in, the climber suddenly feels trapped and the urge to escape to the wide open spaces below in a whooping glissade of relief must be suppressed. Beyond this point the back of The Amphitheatre steepens as two major rocky ribs intrude from above, dividing the broad gully into a number of smaller, steeper ones, each of which offers the tantalising prospect of escape from this awesome Crucible into the fading daylight some 150m above.

'A' GULLY (II) is in the back left-hand corner, and provides a relatively straightforward exit. To the right is the first rock rib, characterised by a huge pinnacle at half-height. Between the two ribs is 'B' GULLY (III), the most direct exit, containing a number of awkward steps which may (sometimes!) be skirted on the right.

Further right, immediately beyond the second rib lies 'C' GULLY (II/III), while 'D' GULLY (II) is a shallow, poorly defined depression diverging from 'C' Gully after a pitch or so. In fact, the whole area between these two gullies is quite broken and will generally provide the easiest exit of all, particularly if well banked out. However, care should be exercised in deep snow as there may be considerable avalanche danger in this region and it may be safer to use one of the steeper exits.

Right of **Amphitheatre Gully** lies

NORTH CRAG
The large broken buttress whose precipitous south face forms the Amphitheatre Right Wall is split centrally by a gully which vanishes into the hillside after 110m. This is often mistaken for its Greater neighbour!

VANISHING GULLY   350m   III/IV
After a good and quite awkward start 240m of steep broken ground

must be negotiated to reach the summit. However, it is possible, if not exactly easy, to traverse off left and descend into the lower section of Amphitheatre Gully.

1. 20m   Climb past an awkward step to a prominent cave.
2. 35m   Leave the cave and go up to a chimney. Climb this steeply and over chockstones above, to a narrow, steep section.
3. 20m   Climb the narrow icy cleft with difficulty, either within or without.
4. 35m   Vanish!
5. 240m   Trend initially right, then back to the centre of the buttress to finish.

GREAT GULLY 300m IV/V ★★★

Although frequently wet in summer, there is rarely sufficient ice in winter to satisfy the monkeys with their banana picks. A large party, copious quantities of food, a torch, encouraging words and an early start will be found to be of far greater value than leading edge technology within the confines of these dark walls and caves. After hours of struggling up verglassed cracks and chimneys, even Guides have been forced to bivouac with their clients beneath the infamous Great Cave Pitch!

The difficulties diminish considerably in conditions of heavy, consolidated snow, but this is both rare and unsporting.

The start is about 50m higher up, and around to the right from Vanishing Gully, and is less obvious than might be imagined.

1. 45m   (1)   Easily up the gully to the start of the difficulties.
2. 65m   (4/5)   Two bulges lead to the foot of The Door Jamb, a too-wide chimney which may be climbed by an iced wall on the left in good conditions, or by variations to the right, but never directly!
3. 10m   (3)   Continue with interest and more variations on the right to the foot of the depressingly obvious chimney.
4. 30m   (5/6)   The Chimney Pitch. Encouraged by some good runners, wide bridging or a steep crack in the right wall leads to ledges and an awkward icy groove on the right. Or avoid the challenge by a detour to the right from lower down (4).
5. 100m   (4)   Various bulges of powder and rock (which are always harder than they look) interspersed with easy scrambling leads to the cave.
6. 15m   (5)   The Great Cave Pitch. The struggles of the leader may be more readily imagined than seen. Apart from the odd spark from flailing crampons or blunted pick, darkness reigns. Fight to surmount the chockstone at the rear of the cave, traverse the

verglassed left wall to reach the outer chockstone, and crawl through the hole into the upper gully and daylight. Phew! Or bivouac...? Those lacking in moral fibre may avoid this pitch completely by a detour to the right from lower down, but think of the shame!

7.   5m   (4)   An innocuous little rocky bulge taken on the left proves deceptive at the end of the day.

8.   30m   (1)   Easily to the summit.

1.4   FFYNNON LLYFFANT

Grid Reference: 685645 (OS Sheet 115 Snowdon)
Altitude: 950m - 1,060m
Aspect: East
Climbing Conditions:
This high cwm accumulates and holds large quantities of snow, on which the climbing relies. After heavy snowfall and westerly winds there may be cornice and avalanche problems just below the main ridge.
Approach:
There are numerous approaches, all of them lengthy! But perhaps the best is via the SE corner of Melynllyn (approach as for Craig y Dulyn), whence a short climb up a wide, steep basin to the west gains the SE spur of Foel Grach. From here an almost level contour to the SW leads easily into the cwm. (2hrs. from the car.)

This wonderful little cwm nestling high on the NE flanks of mighty Llewelyn is probably the highest in Snowdonia, and although it lacks grandeur, there is a great air of pastoral tranquility. Unfortunately perhaps, man's presence is all around in the form of the scattered remnants of an old aeroplane. A sobering reminder to all who seek to conquer; but with the snows we are spared such sadness.

The climbing is modest, yet for those who seek the solace of untrodden snows, there is great appeal up here, spoilt only by the necessity of arriving on the Great Carneddau Highway close to the summit.

Descent:
The climbs finish on the NE ridge of Carnedd Llewelyn, and to return to the cwm this ridge may be followed down until the crags have been passed, whence a simple descent may be made. But from the summit of Llewelyn the world is your oyster.

The three climbs described are all to the west of the small lake in the bottom of the cwm, and take shallow gullies to join the NE ridge and the main footpath.

SOUTH GULLY 150m I
A straightforward snow climb up the broad depression finishing virtually on the summit.

CENTRAL GULLY 120m I
The shallow snowy gully directly west of the lake some 100m right of South Gully.

NORTH GULLY 100m I
A well-defined, easy-angled gully about 75m to the right again, above the north end of the lake.

Other possibilities exist, particularly on the small buttresses, but these are best left for individual discovery and re-discovery.

CWM LLAFAR
1.5 YSGOLION DUON
THE BLACK LADDERS

Grid Reference: 670630 (OS Sheet 115 Snowdon)
Altitude: 700m - 970m
Aspect: N
Climbing Conditions:
This enormous crag is both wet and vegetated in summer, whilst in winter its northerly aspect and exposure to snow-laden NW winds blowing up Cwm Llafar ensures a good covering of snow. These qualities make it an ideal winter climbing crag. However, as the most difficult sections of all the climbs are to be found on the lower half of the crag, temperatures need to be quite low to produce the good ice and frozen turf which make some of the more difficult climbs possible.
Approach:
The traditional approach is from Gerlan above Bethesda where a narrow track leads to the Welsh Water Authority pumping station (639667). Currently (1988), access to the path through the station is prohibited, so use a gated field to the right to gain a stile. Although this is a right of way, attempts have been made to prevent access through the gates, so climbers should use some discretion as to their choice of access. Parking is also an acute problem, both for climbers and residents.
The gently rising path into Cwm Llafar then crosses the stream a couple of times and passes through several gates. It follows the right (true left) side of the cwm, and leads in about 1-1¼hrs. to the slopes below Llech Ddu. Continue past some huge boulders, and in a further 300m, keep right of the remains of an old moraine. Eastern Gully now lies straight ahead, Western Gully is approached diagonally to the right up the steep slope. A further ½hr. gains the

foot of the climbs.

As already mentioned, there have in recent winters been numerous problems with parked cars causing irritation and inconvenience to local residents in Gerlan, and it is now suggested that in good weather climbers consider the alternative approach from Ogwen, either via Cwm Lloer and then NE to the top of the crag, or via Ffynnon Llugwy and thence NW up the spur of Craig Llugwy to the same place. Descend into Cwm Llafar and the foot of the crag by heading WNW from the narrow section of the main Carneddau ridge, just to the north of where the Craig Llugwy spur joins it and contouring around below Eastern Gully (1¾hrs. to the top of the crag). Although it is a marginally longer approach, it gives a faster and easier descent to the south on completion of the climb - assuming that the climb is completed! - and alleviates the parking and access problems in Gerlan.

This colossal Gothic crag forms the back wall of **Cwmglas Mawr,** and is nearly 300m high throughout its length, offering few real lines of weakness or escape. It extends fully 1,000m from the blunt spur which separates the cwm from **Nant y Graig** to the NE, to the fine narrow ridge **Grib Lem,** which links the top of **Llech Ddu** to the summit of **Carnedd Dafydd.**

The lower third is split by a number of broad terraces. These are quite deeply incised by steep drainage lines and give good, straightforward ice-pitches to the broadest of the terraces, above which is the main rock band occupying the middle third of the crag. The upper third is often more broken and lays back somewhat, providing a welcome relief after the rigours of the previous pitches. However, care must still be exercised here as there may be large accumulations of wind slab below the ridge, particularly after strong southerly winds. There have been two tragic avalanche accidents here in recent years and prudence is clearly indicated in less than perfect snow conditions.

Four major gullies divide the crag. **Eastern Gully** lies on the left edge and runs up from right to left whilst **Pyramid Gully** starts in the same area and runs up to the right and is not readily seen. To the right, the steep triangular **Pyramid Buttress,** with its impressive ice-falls on the lower tier intervenes before **Central Gully** is reached. This is the largest and most obvious snow gully and to its right the sprawling mass of **Central Buttress** culminates in the fine arête of **Flanders,** towering above the deep, classic **Western Gully,** which is almost in the centre of the crag despite its name.

To the right again, the crag continues for a further 400m past icy, vegetated grooves and steep, imposing rock walls. Here the terrain is neither inviting nor readily identifiable and there is a certain sameness about the routes. They are steep, thinly iced and poorly protected!

Almost anything *might* be climbable; it's really just a matter of courage, conditions and imagination!

The location of climbs on The Black Ladders in the mist is never straightforward. It's probably best to become familiar with the deep gullies (Eastern, Central and Western) in good visibility and work from these in the mist, although one often has to climb a pitch or two up the lower ice-falls before locating anything! Such conditions of poor visibility can only be recommended for a first visit to those possessing an unusual drive for exploration and uncertainty!

Descent:
Either reverse one of the two approaches from Ogwen or return to Cwm Llafar from the main Carneddau ridge as described in these approaches. The further one goes along the ridge towards Carnedd Llewelyn before descending leftwards, the easier the descent can be made.

The extreme left-hand end of the crag curves and gradually fades into the hillside, but the lower tier is still quite steep in this region and develops six or seven very good slabby ice-falls, about 50m long. Above the right-most of the ice-falls, **Eastern Gully** slants leftwards into the last of the rock, bounded on its left by:

EASTERN ARÊTE 200m II/III
The vague left-hand bounding arête of Eastern Gully may be followed throughout, starting up the iced slabs and then following the ridge more easily above. Easier options exist to the left.

EASTERN GULLY 200m III *
The centre section is easy, and escape here is possible onto the easier slopes on the left. The direct line of the gully is barred at the bottom by a steep, icy buttress with slabs and overhangs.
1. 45m (3) In good conditions climb the last ice-fall on the slabby buttress directly into the lower basin.
An easier start is possible from 30m to the right under steep walls from whence the highest leftwards traverse line may be taken in two pitches with one awkward step into the lower basin.
2. 65m Follow the central depression to the fork, although escape is possible to the left.
3. 90m The right-hand exit is steeper and probably better.

PLAYSCHOOL 200m III
This route takes a subsidiary gully line in the buttress between the two main gullies starting some way up Eastern Gully.
1. 45m (3) As for Eastern Gully into the lower basin.

2.   45m   (3)   Continue up the gully until it closes in, and then climb a 20m ice-fall on the right wall and follow the flow of ice into a subsidiary gully.

3.   110m   (3)   Follow the shallow gully via three ice-pitches to the top.

PYRAMID GULLY   200m   IV   **

The route slants rightwards from the foot of Eastern Gully to arrive at the crest overlooking Central Gully. Its line is hidden from the usual approach and is best seen from the left-hand side of the crag.

Start just right of the easier start to Eastern Gully, below a short steep ice-fall.

1.   45m   (4/5)   Climb steep snow to the ice-fall. Climb this into the gully proper and belay on the first rocks on the left.

If this initial pitch has not formed, as is often the case, the start to Eastern Gully may be taken, moving right along ledges to rejoin the main line.

2.   35m   (4)   Move back right into the gully and climb the excellent ice-pitch. Exit on the right to poor belays.

3.   120m   (1)   Easily up the gully to a snow crest, then left to the plateau.

JACOB'S LADDER   180m   IV/V   *

About 30m right of Pyramid Gully a steep corner fills with ice in a hard winter and gives the start of this route. The initial pitches are good and hard, but the upper section lacks line and quality although it can be difficult in less than perfect snow conditions.

1.   35m   (5)   Climb the very steep ice, first left then straight up to a snow terrace (peg belays).

2.   35m   (5)   Move right along the terrace to a rounded arête. Go straight up icy grooves and frozen vegetation to easier ground.

3.   110m   (2)   Go diagonally right to the crest overlooking Central Gully which gives the best finish.

PYRAMID FACE DIRECT   185m   V   **

An excellent outing which, after accepting the challenge of the right-hand ice-fall takes a line of right facing grooves in the steep middle section. Directly below the apex of the pyramid a steep 45m curtain of ice springs from the first terrace. Start below this.

1.   45m   (5)   Climb a groove, then the ice-fall to the terrace as directly as strength permits.

2.   80m   (6)   Move 6m left and continue via an iced arête and groove passing an overhang by moves to the right.

3.   60m   (4)   Continue more easily to the top in the same line.

PYRAMID BUTTRESS 185m IV *

Another fine mixed route up the right-hand side of the Pyramid, almost on the blunt arête overlooking Central Gully and avoiding the full-frontal assault of the previous climb on the lower ice-fall.

1. 45m   Take a diagonal line across the main ice-fall from well to the right, turning each of the steeper bulges on the left to gain the terrace.
2. 60m   Move right and zig-zag up ledges and short walls just left of the arête.
3. 80m   Easier ground now leads to the top, either straight up or by moving right to the crest.

CENTRAL GULLY 300m III **

This is the deepest of the gullies and slants from right to left as it rises. The main difficulties centre on the exit from an overhung cave just below half height which may be impossible to achieve without recourse to either technique or variation!

Start well down the hillside below the gully in a frozen stream bed.

1. 75m   (3)   Climb ice in the bed of the lower gully.
2. 20m   (2/3)   Climb a snow groove in the direct line of the gully to poor belays.
3. 25m   (3)   Climb diagonally right across steep ice into the gully.
4. 35m   (1)   Easily up snow to the cave.

Alternatively, in conditions of little ice a somewhat easier (2/3) start may be made via a short chimney behind a flake, 30m to the right of the main line, followed by an easy traverse leftwards along the highest ledge to gain the gully some distance below the cave.

5. 15m   (4/5)   Unless very well banked out, a direct exit from the cave may be found to be too hard. Even exponents of wide bridging may find the tendency to invert irresistible!

However, the cunning will find a way round on the left, starting with a traverse some 20m below the cave; but even this is not straightforward!

5a. 45m (3/4)   *Traverse left along rising ledges to the arête where a 10m awkward wide groove gains access to easier ground and ledges leading back into the gully past an exposed step. With luck, the cave will now lie below!*

6. 130m (1/2)   Straight up the fine narrow gully to the plateau.

GALLIPOLI 250m V *

This route takes a direct line up the left-hand side of the sprawling Central Buttress just to the right of Central Gully. Unfortunately little is known about it except its existence! It appears to start from the easy angled amphitheatre some 80m below the cave of Central Gully. From here ice smears and vegetation lead up on the right to a terrace, whence a leftwards traverse and a short wall gain a terrace below a continuous groove/chimney line (obvious when seen from below the right-hand end of the crag) which is followed to easier ground on the upper buttress.

PASSCHENDAELE 300m IV/V *
A wandering line slightly right of the centre of the buttress finishing on the crest of Flanders above Western Gully. The climb was formerly known as Central Buttress.
Start halfway between Central and Western Gullies.
1. 125m   Climb short, steep snowfields and rock steps to the highest terrace. Traverse left below the steep walls to a short groove leading to a ramp.
2. 75m   Climb the rightward slanting groove for 12m. It then becomes a ramp and finally opens out onto steep snow which is climbed diagonally to the right.
3. 100m   Go straight up grooves, linking small snowfields to the crest and so to the top.

On the right-hand side of the buttress, the left-bounding arête of **Western Gully** is a steep wall in its middle section, but tapers down to a fine, pinnacled ridge soaring above the gully in its upper section. This arête is the substance of the summer route **Flanders HVS,** and although the narrow upper ridge involves classic mixed climbing under heavy snow, the lower pitches lack logic (but **not** difficulty!) in winter and never really accumulate either snow or ice. The climb has, nonetheless, been followed religiously in winter and is a hard and memorable outing. An early start is recommended!

WESTERN GULLY 320m V ***
One of the great Welsh Classics and not to be underestimated. The crux often involves difficult mixed climbing on thinly iced rock, and the whole middle section of the climb is nicely sustained. One of the later climbs to come into condition as it is not dependent on frozen vegetation. In common with all the climbs on the crag, it can be very difficult to located in mist, although a stream bed on the lower slopes is a guide to the line. It is customary to start 15m left of an ice-boss at the foot of the gully, although numerous variations are possible to reach the level of the main terrace.
1. 100m (2)   Climb ledges and snow slopes to reach the gully

proper, or better, ice in the line of the gully.

2.   40m   (3)   Directly up the gully to a large cave.

3.   15m   (4)   Traverse right around an arête and cross to below an obvious groove.

4.   30m   (5)   Enter the groove with difficulty, climb right a little then back left to the gully and up to another large cave.

5.   15m   (5/6)   Crux. Climb the steep slab on the right - some people manage to do it FREE! - to easy snow and up to a belay.

6.   20m   (4)   Negotiate a bulging boulder and enter the easy upper gully.

7.   100m (1)   Easy snow to the top.

Variation: RIGHT-HAND FINISH   120m   IV/V   **

For those with daylight and strength to spare, further difficulties may be sought on the right wall of the gully just above the crux slab of the gully.

6a. 25m   (4)   *Climb the ice-fall in a right facing corner/groove turning a small overhang (peg) on the right to a peg belay on a small terrace.*

7a. 40m   (4/5)   *Continue up ice in the same line to a large terrace.*

8a. 55m   (2)   *A shallow gully leads to easy ground and the top.*

YPRÈS   330m   IV/V

Starts as for Western Gully but then breaks out along ledges to the obvious icy depression in the buttress to the right. This route was formerly call Go-Frit.

1.   100m (2)   As for Western Gully.

2.   60m   (2)   Traverse a snowy gangway on the right to belay at the foot of an obvious steep ice-groove.

3.   30m   (5)   Climb the groove with difficulty.

4.   140m (3)   Easier mixed climbing into the upper depression and the top.

ARCTIC FOX   250m   V

A poor route involving difficult mixed climbing which is essentially a direct start to Yprès which then finds an independent finish to the right. First climbed in very lean conditions (turf), it may improve under a substantial cover of hard snow. Start about 150m right of Western Gully on the broad sloping terrace above the initial ice-falls. A rightward slanting groove leads into a chimney blocked by a chockstone.

1.   40m   (5)   Climb the groove and chimney turning the chockstone on the right to a small bay (peg). Move up and right into the next groove and climb this to a belay.

2.   45m   (4/3)   A short corner leads onto a terrace. Cross diagon-

ally right up a shallow gully turning a chockstone on the left to belay at a large spike.

3.   20m   (3)   Climb into the base of the upper couloir and belay (nuts) on the left.

4.   45m   (5)   Climb up the right-hand side of the couloir past a jammed block.

5.   100m   (2)   Easier ground now to finish.

THE POLAR BEAR   350m   VI   **

A fine route, taking a very direct line up a system of grooves in the buttress midway between Yprès and The Somme giving sustained difficulty on steep, mixed ground based on the summer lines of Cannon Rib and Cannon Ball. The line takes little drainage and relies heavily on consolidated snow/ice or, more commonly, frozen turf. A variation following the exact summer line of Cannon Rib has also been climbed and involves some very hard climbing.

Start approximately 50m left of The Somme below the steepest part of the crag. Just right of the arête of the buttress is a rightward curving groove which gives the substance of the route.

1.   100m   (3)   Gain the large terrace by one of the many ice-falls or grooves.

2.   30m   (6)   Enter the V-groove and climb it to where it fades. Small stance and good nut belay.

3.   40m   (6)   Move right up a ramp; up again, then back left to follow the groove steeply rightwards to a hard exit onto a small ledge. Large spike belay 3m right.

4.   35m   (6)   The groove above the belay (hard) to a snow ledge. Traverse the wall on the right to a shallow runnel which is followed directly to a bay. Large spike belay on the left.

5.   35m   (4/5)   The continuation corner to a belay in a niche on the left.

6.   35m   (4/5)   Follow a runnel to the upper snow slopes.

7.   75m   (2)   Easier ground to the top.

TOPCAT   350m   IV/V

Takes a line about 30m to the left of The Somme, starting as for The Polar Bear, and using a rightwards-slanting, turfy ramp to breach the steep central section.

Start directly below the ramp where some ice streaks lead up to the main terrace on either side of a rock buttress.

1.   20m   Variously on ice to the top of the rock buttress.

2.   60m   A good ice pitch left of the buttress ahead leads to the huge terrace. Continue straight up to the start of the ramp.

3.   80m   Follow the ramp up rightwards in two pitches to the second terrace.
4.   190m   An awkward start leads to a line about 30m left of, and parallel to, The Somme. Follow the line to the top.

To the right and before the obvious bosses and ice-falls on the lower tiers of **Icefall Gully,** there is a very steep buttress with overhangs on its right. In good winters the area on the left of this buttress forms a number of long ice smears which all lead into a snowy ledge system about one third of the way up the cliff, above which the climbing eases somewhat. The generic route of this section is **The Somme** (formerly called **Lost Gully**), although its has a left-hand variation start and a short eliminate to its right (**Post War**). This area of cliff has numerous ice-falls (2/3) on the tier below the main terrace.

THE SOMME   350m   V   ★★★
Start below the lower tiers at a huge ice-fall in a well-defined groove/gully below and slightly left of the overhangs.
1.   45m   (3)   Climb ice in the steep groove to a large snow terrace. Spike belay high on the right below the overhangs.
2.   30m   Walk left along the easy terrace to belay beneath the left-hand and major ice-fall. A large rightwards slanting iced slab can be seen above.
3.   45m   (5)   Climb a steep groove with difficulty, then frozen vegetation to a pedestal stance below the ice-fall. Knife blade peg crack.
3a.   45m   (4)   Variation: Start 15m left and higher up in a sort of bay and follow a groove from the top of a pedestal rightwards to vegetated ground which joins the original route at the top of pitch 3. Easier, but considerably less good than the original way.
4.   45m   (3/4)   Step right onto the steep ice slab and climb to a balcony on the right at 20m. Step back left onto the ice and climb to exit right to a ledge at 35m. From this climb to the large snow terrace. Poor belays. A serious pitch.
5.   60m   (3)   Climb steeply up to the right then back left into the easy upper gully.
6.   125m   (1)   Straightforward snow to the top.

POST WAR   275m   V/VI   ★
Although this is really only a variation start to The Somme, it provides difficult and serious climbing up steep ice smears and grooves 10m to the right and directly above the first pitch of that route.
    Start on the large terrace below the steep buttress with the

overhangs and 10m right of The Somme's third pitch.
1.   30m   (5)   Climb thin ice to a rock belay in the groove.
2.   30m   (5)   Climb grooves above stepping left onto ice and continue to a belay on the left.
3.   30m   (5)   Climb directly above, then over easier ground moving left to belay as for The Somme on a snow ledge.
4.   185m (3)   Finish as for The Somme.

Immediately right of the steep buttress is a shallow but steep gully line which is *not* **Icefall Gully**! About 30m further right a series of ice-falls cascades down a blunt arête from a shallow, snowy upper gully eventually appearing as a stream on the slopes below. In lean conditions there are two distinct lines of drainage here, each of which may be followed, but the whole area becomes iced in a good winter. As this is the heaviest area of drainage on the crag and quite vegetated, it is the first to come into condition after a freeze.

ICEFALL GULLY LEFT-HAND   360m   III/IV   *
This climb starts up a wide area of slaby ice-falls directly below the upper gully.
1.   45m   (2)   Follow ice up to the right until it steepens somewhat.
2.   45m   (2/3)   Continue to the large terrace.
3.   45m   (3/4)   Above, the left-hand ice-fall follows grooves in a steep arête 6m left of an icy chimney and leads to a large ledge.
4.   45m   (3/4)   Climb an icy right facing groove above to easier ground. Peg and block belay on left.
5.   45m   (2/3)   One final short ice-wall leads into the upper gully.
6.   135m (2)   Slant leftwards up the shallow snowy depression to the top.

ICEFALL GULLY RIGHT-HAND   360m   IV   *
Follows a parallel line to the previous climb, some 10m to the right, and belays at the same level in each case until it converges above pitch 4. Pitches 1 and 2 are similar in nature and standard but in more of a gully on the lower slopes; pitches 3 and 4 are steeper (grade 4) and are chimney features.

Beyond **Icefall Gully**, the lower tier gradually merges into the terrace running below the main buttress. Here the crag lies back and offers numerous rather discontinuous lines. Whilst it is possible to climb almost anywhere in a good winter, only two climbs have been recorded and they follow ice-falls and grooves on either side of a prominent diamond-shaped rock buttress which is seamed with grooves and ribs. They both lead into obvious easy depressions higher up the cliff.

NIGHTFALL 220m III
A vague line taking ice-sheets on the left of the buttress.
1.   60m   Follow the best line up ice streaks over various slabby walls.
2.   160m   More easily up steep broken snow slopes to the ridge.

DAYBREAK 240m III
A similar line on the right side of the buttress.

To the right again is a steep blank rock buttress characterised by wide sloping terraces which cut across it. The next climb gains the broken ridge above the buttress from the left.

FINALE 250m III
Starts up Daybreak until ledges out right to gain the crest of the blunt ridge above the steepest rock. Follow the arête to the top surmounting a number of short walls and finishing near the summit of Carnedd Dafydd.

1.6 LLECH DDU

Grid Reference: 666636 (OS Sheet 115 Snowdon)
Altitude: 600m - 700m
Aspect: North
Climbing Conditions:
The crag is too steep to accumulate large quantities of snow, so any climbing which does exist depends on a build-up of water-ice from the predominantly light drainage. A period of very wet weather followed by a rapid freeze will therefore be needed to give good climbing conditions.
Approach:
As for The Black Ladders from Gerlan to the foot of Cwmglas Bach whence the right-hand side of the crag lies due south and may be approached directly, keeping to the left of the stream issuing from upper Cwmglas Bach.

This magnificent cliff, dark and brooding is the Carneddau's answer to Cloggy. It is therefore perhaps surprising that it has, to date seen little activity in winter. Its steep and unforgiving rock buttresses whilst often damp in summer, are ironically too dry in winter to produce ice in any quantity and its rather low situation often prevents favourable snow conditions from developing. However, there is much vegetation and given some snow and prolonged frosts, this is very much a crag for the future. It is here that the next step in winter climbing will be taken by those weary of slugging it out with frozen waterfalls. New winter routes on **Llech Ddu** will require exceptional conditions, a lot of imagination and plenty of talent!

The left-hand side of the crag, although vegetated is fairly continuous throughout its height, but moving rightwards into the centre, a wide area of easy, snowy, vegetated rakes leads up to a large terrace beneath the impressive **Central Wall.** Here the prominent chimney taken by **Skid Row** defines the left-hand margin and the summer line of **The Great Corner** stands out in the centre. Other smears exist, but wow!... Further right is the most impressive of the buttresses, **The Pillar**, which is actually separated from the bulk of the crag by a hidden chimney (**Pillar Chimney**). This is part of **The Pillar Traverse**, an exposed and wandering diagonal line from right to left across the whole of the main crag, linking the starts of the two climbs described and an interesting expedition in its own right. Right of **The Pillar** is the **West Flank** whose base is defined by the initial rising dyke of **The Pillar Traverse.** This is an area of alternate ribs and grooves, often lying back from the vertical, with **Y-Chimney** towards the right-hand side. Right of **Y-Chimney** is the icy unclimbed line of **West End,** beyond which the crag peters out into the hillside.

Descent:
It is possible to descend on either side of the crag. Both ways are steep and long with a certain amount of awkward loose scree unless well frozen/snowed up. From climbs on the Central Wall descend to the left (east), whilst from climbs on the West Flank it is easier to return to the right (west) into Cwmglas Bach.

The first route is approached via an easy rake which starts on the right of a little square bay at the left-hand side of the central vegetated area below the **Central Wall** in the middle of the crag.

SKID ROW   110m   V/VI   **

A technically difficult but well protected climb up an impressive piece of cliff.
1. 65m (2)   Follow the exposed rake up rightwards to the foot of the obvious icy chimney above the left-hand end of the level terrace.
2. 35m (6)   Surmount the first ice bulge and continue up the narrowing chimney (hard) to gain less icy ground leading to below the final overhang.
3. 10m (5)   Climb the overhang on the left to gain the top.

Y-CHIMNEY 100m V **
Start at the dyke at the right-hand end of The Pillar Traverse.
1. 25m (1/2)   Follow the dyke leftwards to the foot of the obvious icy chimnmey/groove.
2. 30m (5)   The chimney is awkward until an escape is possible to the right onto a platform with a large spike belay.
3. 20m (5)   A groove above the right-hand end of the platform leads to a series of ledges which are followed to a belay above the chimney.
4. 25m (5)   Follow the rib above to a groove which is climbed,with an exit right to broken ground.

1.7 CWMGLAS BACH

Grid Reference: 663634 (approx.) (OS Sheet 115 Snowdon)
Altitude: 650m - 950m
Aspect: North
Climbing Conditions:
The cwm is an excellent snow-holding area with conditions often persisting long into the spring given reasonably favourable weather. The climbing relies on the classic winter combination of snow-ice and water-ice, and its high altitude and northerly aspect, especially that of Craig Dafydd ensure that conditions are often good.
Approach:
Either approach from Gerlan as for Llech Ddu and continue up the cwm to the right of the crag (1½hrs.), or from Ogwen ascend Carnedd Dafydd up open slopes on its south flank from Cwm Fynnon Lloer, then descend Crib Lem (Grade I/II) until it is possible to cut down left into the cwm below Craig Dafydd (1¾hrs.). Although slightly longer this latter approach avoids the access problems at Gerlan, and in good visibility offers a dramatic descent into this wild, high mountain cwm.

The upper reaches of this wild and desolate cwm are one of the most inspirational settings in Snowdonia. What the crags lack in sheer size is more than adequately balanced by the remote feel and Alpine nature of the terrain. Soaring pinnacled ridges enclose hidden cwms and gullies, whilst impressive little buttresses pop up around every corner. For this area is the preserve of mountaineers, a place to explore and a refuge from the endless 'Climb when you're Ready's' of Idwal, or Craig y Rhaeadr.
   The cwm is almost completely enclosed by steep walls. **Llech Ddu** guards the gateway on the left, and from behind this impregnable

bastion the slender ridge of **Crib Lem** links its rocky top to the very summit of **Carnedd Dafydd** and divides **Cwmglas** into Mawr and Bach. At the head of the cwm, high on the summit slopes of **Carnedd Dafydd** lies **Craig Dafydd**, a collection of short, steep buttresses split by terraces and bounded on the right by another long ridge which defines the left-hand side of the upper cwm. Not perhaps as well defined as **Crib Lem**, it is nonetheless a striking feature. This ridge terminates abruptly at its lower end in **Craig y Cwmglas Bach**, an obvious triangular crag seamed with icy grooves and split on its left-hand side by the icy cleft of **The Gully**. Left of this is a very steep rocky tower, **The Pillar**, whose summit is easily accessible by scrambling round the back from the cwm. Below the foot of this crag is a large flat area above the initial steep step into the upper cwm, and a good place for gearing up and from which to survey what lies above.

Descents:
From above Craig Dafydd descend Crib Lem until it is possible to cut back down steep ground to the left into the cwm just below the crag. A safer but much longer descent involves descending the NW ridge of Carnedd Dafydd to a small col at 780m, whence a snowy couloir leads eastwards back to the foot of the cwm.

With the exception of The Gully, climbs on Craig y Cwmglas Bach are best quitted by traversing rightwards to gain easy ground well to the right of the crag. From The Gully traverse left behind The Pillar and descend the cwm.

CRIB LEM 450m I/II ★★
This narrow rocky ridge which is gained up broken slopes to the right of Llech Ddu provides an excellent outing, comparable with the best bits of Crib Goch and leads to the final summit slopes of Carnedd Dafydd.

CROSSOVER 150m III
More or less opposite the foot of Craig y Cwmglas Bach a shallow gully runs up to join the crest of Crib Lem crossing a rock barrier at mid height. If combined with the upper part of the ridge it provides an excellent mountaineering approach to the summit of Carnedd Dafydd.

1. 70m (1)   Easily up snow in the shallow gully to the foot of a narrow chimney in the rock barrier.
2. 10m (4) \ Bridge the awkward chimney until ice on the right wall allows a pull out right to be made to easier ground.
3. 70m (2)   More easily up the shallow gully via a couple of bulges to a notch on the narrow section of the ridge.

From here it is possibe to continue up the ridge, or reverse the lower section of the ridge, or descend steeply eastwards into **Cwmglas Mawr** and the foot of **The Black Ladders.**

CRAIG DAFYDD

The main buttress is on the left-hand side of the crag adjoining **Crib Lem**, and this is split by the obvious steep gully/groove lines of **David** and **Goliath.** To the right a short ice-fall crosses a rocky step into a snowy basin from which three obvious snowy lines appear from lower down the cwm, to radiate like the prongs of a trident. The left-hand line forms a sloping terrace above the finish of **David** and **Goliath**, and terminates on the upper part of **Crib Lem**. The middle line is **Central Trident Route**, and the right-hand line gains the right bounding ridge of the cwm, passing behind a steep buttress which forms the right-hand section of the crag, and which as yet, sports no routes.

DAVID 100m III

This climb takes the wide fault on the left-hand side of the main buttress, above a shallow chimney in a faint lower tier which leads to a wide, sloping terrace below the main fault line.
1. 50m (2)   Climb the chimney, and move diagonally right across easy ground to belay below the main gully/fault.
2. 50m (3)   Climb the gully, steeper than it looks, on frozen turf (or snow-ice if you're lucky!) to gain easy ground.

Traverse left to Crib Lem, or traverse right and reverse Left Fork.

GOLIATH 150m IV/V **

Right of David, a continuous icy groove cleaves the buttress and gives the line of this fine route. Approach up steep snow until progress is barred by roofs with an ice-fall on the right.
Note: This climb appears to coincide with the route shown as 27 in the diagram on Page 29 of the previous guide, suggesting that the bottom pitch may bank out completely under heavy snow/spindrift conditions!
1. 40m (5)   Climb steep thin ice for 15m, into a fine narrow groove of snow/ice which is followed to a belay on chockstones (difficult to reach) in a wide crack on the left, just below a steepening.
2. 50m (4)   Climb steep ice and the gully above to easy ground.
3. 60m (1/2)   Easy mixed ground leads to a traverse line, and a descent as for David.

LEFT FORK   250m   II

After the first pitch the rest is easy. Start below the centre of the Trident.

1. 10m   (2/3)   Climb the ice-fall to the huge snow basin.
2. 240m   (1)   Turn left and follow the wide snow slope, gradually narrowing towards Crib Lem. Various upwards lines are possible before this at Grade II or so.

CENTRAL TRIDENT ROUTE   200m   II/III

The central line leads directly to the summit of Carnedd Dafydd via a series of widely spaced pitches.

1. 10m   (2/3)   As for Left Fork.
2. 50m   (2)   Cross the snowfield and climb a short pitch through a rock barrier.
3. 50m   (1/2)   Another snowfield leads into more of a gully which steepens below an icy wall.
4. 50m   (3)   Climb the icy wall on the right and move up to below the final groove. Climb this to easier ground.
5. 40m   (1)   Easy snow leads to the summit slopes.

RIGHT FORK   200m   II/III

A rather indefinite line to the right of the previous route, and left of the obvious easy angled snow slope which leads from the snowfield above the first pitch, rightwards to the right bounding ridge of the cwm.

1. 10m   (2/3)   As for Left Fork.
2. 190m   (2/4)   Use a variety of ice-pitches to suit one's taste for adventure to link terraces, finishing near the top of the right-hand bounding ridge of the cwm.

CRAIG Y CWMGLAS BACH

The deep cleft of **The Gully** which separates **The Pillar** on the left, from the main mass of the crag to the right is a useful feature to work from. It also provides an excellent couple of pitches in the classic mould.

THE GULLY   100m   III/II   *

1. 30m   (1)   Easy snow leads to an ice-pitch.
2. 30m   (3)   Climb the pitch trending rightwards until the difficulty eases.
3. 40m   (1/2)   Easy now, but deeply enclosed to a snowy col behind The Pillar.

Either descend around to the left, or angle up rightwards to join the main ridge and follow this (I/II) to join the NW ridge of Carnedd Dafydd in a further 200m.

PETTICOAT LANE   185m   IV/V   **

A fairly serious line up the front of the main buttress. Start in a small bay to the left of the lowest toe of the buttress.

1. 40m (4)   Take the right-hand of two snowy grooves to a terrace on the right.
2. 40m (4)   Up the right-hand groove line to below the final steepening. Poor stance and belay on the left.
3. 20m (4)   Move back right and steeply up to exit on easier ground.
4. 40m (3)   Easier now to a large spike belay on the right.
5. 45m (4)   Up the rib on the right then step around to easier ground above the top of The Glass Wall.

THE GLASS WALL   110m   IV   *

On the right of the crag is an obvious wide gully with a steep finish (Straight Chimney). On the left wall of this a line of ice-falls develop in a prolonged frost.

1. 30m (1)   Easily up snow, moving left to below the ice-fall.
2. 35m (4)   Climb the steep ice which descends the left wall. Move right at half height, then up easy snow.
3. 15m (1/2)   Move up to the back of the snowfield. (Possible escape off right here.)
4. 30m (4)   In good years another steep ice-pitch develops on the left. Alternatively, a less steep snow-ice exit (3) is possible 10m to the right.

STRAIGHT CHIMNEY   60m   III

This is the well-defined short gully on the extreme right of the crag.

1. 40m (2)   Climb snow to beneath the final steepening.
2. 20m (3)   Up steep ice and frozen vegetation with no runners to a sudden exit!

1.8   CWM FFYNNON LLOER

Grid Reference: 662621 (OS Sheet 115 Snowdon)
Altitude: 700m - 930m
Aspect: E to NE
Climbing Conditions:
As most of the routes in this area are gullies in the easier grades, a good cover

of consolidated snow will afford the best climbing. In fact, the cwm holds snow particularly well and strips of old névé may be found in its deep gullies long after it has thawed from elsewhere. Care should be exercised after heavy snow-fall accompanied by strong W or SW winds as the slopes above the crags and in the W end of the cwm may become prone to windslab avalanche.

Approach:

Take the track past the new Glan Dena Hut towards Tal y Llyn Farm, turning uphill on a vague path before reaching the farm buildings. Follow an ill-defined footpath alongside Afon Lloer into the cwm (50mins.). Walk round the south side of the lake and approach the climbs in a further 15-20 minutes.

The cwm has an air of isolation well out of proportion to its distance from civilisation, and is rarely visited by winter climbers. It is none-theless an ideal spot for the more adventurous winter walker who wishes to learn some snowcraft in order to widen his mountaineering horizons.

The main area of crag forms the NNE flank of the ESE ridge of **Pen-yr-Ole-Wen**, and as such is best seen from the summit of **Carnedd Dafydd**. Most impressive at its west end, where the ubiquitous Kirkus left his mark on a fine rocky arête, the crag tails off to the east into a jumble of tiny buttresses. The quality of the lines at the right-hand end is somewhat marred by the inevitable escape onto tedious snow slopes before the summit of the mountain is reached. For those who need neither summits nor secrets, ignominious escape is possible to the right, but the true mountaineer will stay the course and be rewarded with an enteraining 'through route' in the rock band just below the summit ridge. Further left, the climbs finish on the ridge below the summit, and those of wavering resolve and heaving lungs will probably be tempted to turn left and return to the bottom of the cwm in search of another 'tick'!

Descent:

Climbs to the right of Broad Gully allow a traverse right to The Headwall whose Grade I slopes lead back to the cwm. Alternatively, continue up to the ESE ridge which either leads easily to the sumit and hillwalking, or back down via one short awkward section to the cwm.

Just to the west of **Ffynon Lloer** and at a slightly higher level, is a tiny lake. This lies at the foot of a vast, shallow depression which rises westwards towards the col between **Pen-yr-Ole-Wen** and **Carnedd Dafydd** and provides a straightforward ascent on snow (**THE HEAD-WALL, 250m I**). This also has obvious merit as a ski descent for the competent - or free fall for the incompetent!

To the right of **The Headwall** a broken buttress high up on the steep snow slopes offers a shallow gully line (**COL GULLY, 100m I**) which gains the summit ridge just to the north of the col and is reached by trending rightwards up the lower part of **The Headwall**. This gully line is often clearly visible from the A5 between Capel Curig and Ogwen. Beneath **Col Gully** and just above the lake, an ice-fall cuts through a steep lower buttress and gives **MOONFLOWER (5)**, a technically difficult pitch on water-ice.

Climbs are now described **from right to left** starting from **The Headwall**.

The first buttress to the left (**Western Buttress**) is the steepest and cleanest, and offers few prospects for genuine winter climbs, although **Kirkus' Climb** is a summer classic. Immediately left of this buttress a broad snow slope slants rightwards and divides into a pair of better defined gullies leading out onto the blunt spur to the left of **The Headwall**.

RIGHT-HAND Y GULLY   80m   I/II
The lesser of the two branches, it may contain a couple of steep bulges in lean conditions. A shallow V-groove on the left gives a more interesting variation near the top and prolongs the climbing a little.

LEFT-HAND Y GULLY   130m   I/II   *
The left-hand branch leads onto snow slopes higher up the spur, and contains a steep awkward step in its upper reaches. A long narrow runnel runs up to the left hereabouts and provides a more sustained finish (3).

Left of the **Y Gullies** is a buttress (**Eastern Buttress**) split by a wide snow shelf running up to the right from near the foot of the huge gully (**Broad Gully**) to the left.

MOONGROOVES   150m   III/IV   *
A fine natural winter line spoilt by the half-way terrace. Pitch 1 takes the obvious narrow snow-filled groove on the right-hand side of Eastern Buttress (the summer line of Central Route), and the continuation grooves above the terrace.
1. 75m   (4)   Climb the fine groove in two pitches until a very steep ice-bulge leads to the large sloping terrace.
2. 75m   (4)   Follow the grooves above, starting from the right and working leftwards until funnelled into a steep exit corner. This, or the steep vegetated buttress to the left leads to easy ground.

BROAD GULLY 220m I/II ★★★

Bounding Eastern Buttress on the left, this is the most obvious line in the cwm. It is wide and direct and finishes high on the summit ridge. In lean conditions the lower section may contain some ice; indeed, a short ice-fall some 20m to the right may be used as a rather indirect, but technically interesting (2/3) start.

HOURGLASS GULLY 180m I

More like two connected snow-slopes than a true gully, it offers a straightforward ascent through the 'narrows' and on via the upper reaches to the ridge.

1.9 BRAICH TY DU

Grid Reference: 650620 (approx.) (OS Sheet 115 Snowdon)
Altitude: 400m - 950m
Aspect: West
Climbing Conditions:
Unfortunately, only the upper section of the face really ever gets into true winter condition with consolidated snow, although extended periods of frost will produce water-ice in the main stream gullies.
Approach:
Parking is something of a problem as Ogwen is rather a long way away and the lay-by some way down the A5 is perhaps a little too low. Parking on the A5 is both expensive and dangerous - but the intrepid explorer will doubtless find a way round this minor problem! Approach the climbs by an unpleasant scramble up the steep, rather loose hillside. Following the frozen stream of your choice will add interest to the approach.

The massive west face of **Pen-yr-Ole-Wen** is a complex series of ridges and gullies rising some 500 vertical metres to the summit. The scale of the face can only be appreciated by being in the middle of it, and in true winter conditions it has a distinctly Alpine feel. All of the major gully lines (there are about eight of them!) will provide some interest, although it tends to be more in the way of short pitches followed by long easy sections than anything continuous. The climbs are described from RIGHT to LEFT as one encounters them from Ogwen.

Descent:
From the plateau, either head north following the mountain wall down the broad ridge of Braich Ty Du until well beyond the crags and then cut down to the A5 or, if the car is at Ogwen, go over the summit of Pen-yr-Ole-Wen and descend the long and tedious South Ridge. If descending directly to the A5 to

the north-west of Ogwen, it is longer, but considerably easier to follow the mountain wall right down to its bend at 641639 and gain the path below, which contours easily back down to the road at 642627.

About 1km down the road from Ogwen, at the far left-hand end of the crags just above the road (taken by the summer rock climbs) is an area of steep, short ice-falls descending a rather scruffy bit of crag (Buttress 9 in the CC's Carneddau Guide). These are best approached from Ogwen, and may be quitted above the steep section by traversing to easier ground on the left.

WINTER ROSE   70m   IV
The left edge of the crag is bounded by a slabby wall with sharp cut overhangs, and this route(?) takes a line up the ice in the recess just to the right. There are several icy possibilities in this area, none of which is particularly independent, although the actual climbing is worthwhile.

There are a number of deep gullies hereabouts, but they seem to lack both interest and continuity and would probably only be worthwhile in exceptional conditions of heavy, consolidated snow cover.

Some 500m further down the A5 a long gully may be seen leading up towards the summit, above a prominent, steep ice-fall some 100m above the road. The big gully line on its right, PETERS GULLY II, also offers some good, short ice-pitches (3) in its lower reaches, but it rather peters out higher up! However, the main gully to its left is very worthwhile.

GRUGOG GULLY   600m   II   **
A superb mountaineering outing which is best done when the stream is frozen down to the road, and there is consolidated snow high up. Probably the longest route in Wales? The first pitch is Grade 4, but can be avoided, and above are eight pitches of Grade 2/3, finishing virtually on the summit, enjoying any beneifts of the late afternoon sun.

High above the eighth milestone from Bangor are a pair of deep gullies of which the next route is the right-hand and longer of the two. The gully may be recognised by the prominent scree fan which curves rightwards from its foot and descends the right-hand side of a blunt spur on the hillside below.

TWLL DU GULLY   350m   II
Start from the lay-by and scramble up the hillside and stream bed into

59

the gully proper. About four pitches of Grade 2/3 over chockstones and icy steps lead to easier ground where the gully opens out into a wide basin just below the ridge, from which various exits are possible. It is generally more interesting and longer on the right.

TWLL DU LEFT HAND   200m   I/II

The left-hand gully starts higher up and is deeper and shorter than its neighbour. Good consolidated snow is needed if an ascent is to repay the long and unpleasant approach.

1.10   OUTLYING FALLS AND CRAGS
PENMAENMAWR QUARRIES

Grid Reference: Square 7075 and surrounds (OS Sheet 115 Snowdon)
Altitude: 300m - 400m
Aspect: Various, but generally North.
Climbing Conditions:
Another low-lying area close to the warm sea which requires exceptional conditions to produce the water-ice which is needed for climbing.

The extensive area of quarries above **Penmaenmawr** on the coast some 6km west of Conwy are reported to contain a number of short ice-pitches, but little is documented. An area, perhaps for the man or woman who's done everything else, or for the incurable explorer.

ABER FALLS

Grid Reference: 668700 (OS Sheet 115 Snowdon)
Altitude: 200m - 300m
Aspect: NNW
Climbing Conditions:
Obviously an extended period of severe frost at low level is needed, but if there is also lying snow with strong winds the falls are swept by spindrift which dramatically increases the rate of build-up, and generates softer ice which is more amenable to axe and crampon.
Approach:
From the A55 between Bangor and Conwy, a minor road turns off at Aber and follows a narrow valley up to a car park after 1½km where the valley divides. A well-trodden tourist track leads up the main, right-hand valley for 2km to the foot of the falls (40mins. from the car park).

'Climb Aber Falls?' someone said after the first ascent in 1985. 'It'll never freeze again - not worth recording.' Ascents in 1986 and 1987 have confounded the sceptics, and lead one to speculate on how many times it may have been frozen in the past; and no one bothered to go and have a look. In 1985 it was the 'ultimate': in 1986 everyone was there, with upward of 20 people clinging to its frozen tears at any one time.

The Falls themselves offer about four lines, although it is possible to climb anywhere on either side of the central water shoot, which itself looks unlikely to freeze completely. A girdle traverse could be the last great problem! The three right-hand lines all lead into the upper stream bed, but the left-hand line joins the traversing descent path. Full descriptions are thought to be inappropriate due to the lack of independence of the climbing. **Ice-screws are necessary for belays on all the routes on the main fall.**

Descent:
From the top of the falls, cut across to the left and traverse a steep slope above trees. Sometimes this is very steep, hard snow and should be treated with caution (keep crampons on and beware of balling up) - it was the scene of a tragic accident in 1986. Continue traversing to gain the lower part of Aber Gully which is descended steeply to the foot of the falls.

Running up into the hillside some 30m to the left of the falls above a steep snow fan is a narrow twisting snow gully. This is:

ABER GULLY 150m I/II
Steep snow leads into the gully which is followed until it peters out on the hillside well above the falls, and easier ground leads rightwards into the upper stream bed. Descend this and escape as for climbs on the main fall - or continue into the Carneddau, and over to Cwm Dulyn, perhaps?

The next two routes are on the left-hand side of the main fall:

FOUNTAIN OF YOUTH 140m IV *
Takes a direct line up the left-hand side of the fall, disappearing into the trees to join the descent path. As it steers well clear of the water it is recommended for aquaphobes!

WELL OF LONELINESS 130m IV ***
The line of walls, grooves and pillars on the arête just left of the wet central abyss gives a superb outing. Waterproofs and a can of de-icer are essential! Climb to a prominent clump of trees and escape rightwards into the stream bed.

The remaining routes lie to the right of the waterfall

THE ANGEL'S TEARS   130m   IV   ★★★
This is the mirror image of the previous route on the opposite side of the fall, and follows a long groove in the middle section.

WHIPPERSNAPPER'S ROUTE   140m   III   ★
An indirect version of the previous climb, it avoids the central groove by a diagonal line out to the right to belay below the crag which bounds the fall on the right, before slanting back left to finish in the same place as The Angel's Tears.

Some 400m to the right of the main falls is another long fall, which although not as impressive, gives sustained ice climbing at an easier grade.

RHAEADR-BACH   II/III   180m   ★
Approach along a footpath from Aber Falls and follow the frozen stream - steepest in the middle section - until it is possible to gain the hillside to the right for the descent.

DOLGARROG GORGE

DOLGARROG GORGE   600m   2/4   ★★
Grid Reference: In Grid Square 7667 (OS Sheet 115 Snowdon)
Altitude: The steepest section lies between 50m - 200m
Aspect: East
Climbing Conditions:
Starting as it does, almost at sea level, a long spell of extreme cold is needed and the climbing will then be exclusively on water-ice.
Approach:
The stream Afon Porth-Llwyd passes under the B5106 west Conwy Valley road at 769678 just north of the town of Dolgarrog, and access is straightforward.

The gorge which is a popular venue for local outdoor centres in its normal wet state, provides a great day out in rare icy conditions. It isn't really a climb as such, more an extended winter scramble with optional pitches to suit all tastes. The first section is a narrow, horizontal gorge with a short pitch at the end: there follow three major falls with lots more scrambling until a large upper pool is reached with some interesting chimneys to explore in the steep buttress to the right (This has a line of bolts leading up it, but no ice!).

Most, if not all of the difficulties can be avoided by gaining paths in the trees on the right, but if all the falls are taken directly, there are several sections of (3/4), with the first and third major falls being the most difficult.

HEALTH WARNINGS:
1. There are some very deep pools underneath the ice - make sure that it's safe before venturing across them.
2. The water is dam controlled and in, or after torrential rainfall (poor ice-climbing conditions!), it may flood catastrophically without warning. Normally, a siren sounds...!
3. There are many section of easy angled water-ice immediately above big drops. This is no place for anyone who is in the least bit unsure of, or unpractised in the use of crampons. A rescue from within the gorge would be very problematic.

Descent:
Paths lead down through the trees on the north side (true left) to gain a steep metalled road which leads back to the valley.

CRAFNANT VALLEY

Grid Reference: Grid Square 7360 (OS Sheet 115 Snowdon)
Altitude: 300m - 400m
Aspect: Various, but generally SE.
Climbing Conditions:
The climbs described are all on water-ice which will only develop in the coldest of winters.
Approach:
A narrow minor road leads into the valley from Trefriw on the B5106 in the Conway Valley, but this may be difficult, or impossible to negotiate in snowy conditions. The first climb is up on the left of this road before the lake is reached, but the others are at the head of the valley on Clogwyn yr Eryr, past the lake and beyond the end of the road. Cars may be parked immediately beyond the first gate (740603) where the road becomes a farm track. Do not drive farther as this irritates residents, and gains little. Both ice-falls may be seen from here, if they are in condition.

The crags may be reached in a further 20-30mins. by walking along the track until it ends at a house. By-pass this via a gate on the right and go up to a forest road. Clear-felling operations are currently under way, so don't be confused by the non-existence of trees in the forest! Turn left and follow the road to a hairpin where a path carries on into the open ground beyond. Follow the steep bouldery ground by the edge of the (ex?)forest directly up to Forestry Falls. For Craig y Dwr Falls, follow the traversing path leftwards beneath crags for a further 10-15mins, passing the formidable undercut SH Wall, a rock climber's haunt of some convenience!

Alternatively, mountaineers may approach from the Post Office at Capel Curig via a good track which leads over into the Crafnant Valley via the bwlch to the east of Crimpiau. This takes about 1 hour to the crag, and is probably as quick if approaching from the Llanberis/Ogwen side.

This low-lying, pastoral valley with more than a touch of the Lake District about it, is an unusual place to find any ice-climbing, and whilst it is certainly not a major area, it provides a couple of interesting water-ice climbs which may appeal to those who want a little solitude in beautiful surroundings.

Descents:
These are described for each climb.

The first climb is seen on the craggy hillside on the left before reaching the lake, and is situated at approximately 758618, above a disused quarry. It is really two ice-falls separated by a broad terrace.

LOWER FALLS   50m   2/3
Climb the two-stage falls with a short walk in between each section. Descend well to the right to gain a track running below the crag.

FORESTRY FALLS   30m   5
The prominent iced groove directly above the edge of the forest on Forestry Buttress at 735606. It is just left of a prominent rock pillar. A steep, exciting pitch. A path leads off to the left and descends beneath a two-tiered buttress.

CRAIG Y DWR FALLS   70m   III/IV   *
The central section (taken by Routes I and II in summer) of Craig yr Dwr (this is the crag where the hard summer climb Crash Landing is situated) accumulates a mass of ice in a good winter, and gives a worthwhile outing. There are two steep sections separated by a bay, and if tackled direct, each probably warrants Grade (4). However, judicious traversing reduces this grade somewhat. Descend around to the right.

Dave Langrish above the difficult section of the first pitch of GOLIATH (IV/V), Craig Dafydd, during the first ascent. Photo: Malcolm Campbell.

2. GLYDERAU

The north-east side of the long watershed, which reaches its climax in the high plateau of the Glyders and includes Tryfan, that most elegant of appendices, is no stranger to ice. Its dark precipices of bare rock bear witness to the relentless attritional power of ancient saw-toothed glaciers: its circular cwms sculpted by the ceaseless cycle of freeze and thaw. Filled with the snowfall of centuries, these frozen wombs dispatched their icy offspring in a crumbling, toppling cascade to join the great white river gouging its mighty groove deep into the Nant Ffrancon and bound for the frozen ocean.

But perpetual winter has long since relinquished its icy grip on these cwms and returns but rarely, its spidery fingers now scrabbling for grip in cracks and crevices it once enclosed; a brief reminder of former glory. Twelve cwms in all and each with its own winter secrets.

And what then of the ice? Kicked and stabbed, hacked and chopped by hordes of steel-clad warriors: graded and recorded, consigned to a guidebook; its secrets spilt.

Cwm Idwal lies at the heart of these wintry places; the birthplace of Welsh ice-climbing. J.M.Archer-Thompson once scaled the frozen cascade which tumbles into the black abyss at the back of the Devil's Kitchen. Devil's work too, with coal hatchet and such. It took 8 hours: it was 1895. Nowadays, the cwm abounds with axemen: hard men who shun the place in summer. But in winter they clamour and queue. For this is the natural home of winter climbing in Wales: the

CASCADE (V) on Craig y Rhaeadr. Terry Storry leading an easy, but serious first pitch, whilst Lindsay Griffin offers encouragement from below. Photo: Terry Storry collection.

white 'black hole' to which everyone gravitates; the honeypot which ensures that the other eleven cwms remain places of snowy solitude for mountain lovers.

More than any other area, perhaps, the Glyders has acquired a familiarity which has enshrined its more common features in folklore: Adam and Eve, the Cantilever Stone, the Devil's Kitchen, the Idwal Slabs, the Nameless Cwm, Tin Can Gully, the Tea Shack (R.I.P.)... the list is endless. And perhaps it is this familiarity which recommends the area, for in truth its winter climbing, with one or two notable exceptions, rarely lives up to expectation. So much steep ground but so few good, natural, continuous lines; it is a place for wandering at will on steep, mixed ground; for exploration of outlying cwms; for scrambling its fine ridges. Or for joining the queue to hack away at a hundred feet of bleeding ice, dodging dinner-plates and hooking holes.

But maybe this is too critical, for there is much that is magnificent about Ogwen in winter and just to climb in its cwms, so steeped in history and tradition, is to drink of a heady draught indeed.

2.1 GALLT YR OGOF

Grid Reference: 692596 (OS Sheet 115 Snowdon)
Altitude: 400m - 500m (Main Cliff)
Aspect: North
Climbing Conditions:
The main cliff, although north facing, is very low, and a period of very cold weather is needed to develop the water-ice needed for Maria. The rather heathery nature of the gullies demands substantial firm snow cover, which is rare, although Summit Gully being much higher, is often in condition.
Approach:
The cliff is readily seen from the A5, from which a path at 690602 (west of Helyg) leads across the streams to the steep hillside below the crag, the foot of which may be reached in 20mins. from the road. Alternatively, approach via the farm Gwern Gof Isaf, some 500m to the west, where parking is available.

The summit of **Gallt yr Ogof** is on the main spine of the Glyders, but it casts a rocky spur north-eastwards between the **Nant yr Ogof** and **Nant y Gors** valleys. This spur ends abruptly some 1km from the summit at the **Main Cliff**. The cliff is split by a steep rake which rises diagonally from left to right, and is obvious as a watercourse in wet weather (in this case, thoughts of ice-climbing on the crag may be safely forgotten!). Below and to the right of this rake is the **Lower**

Cliff, which as yet contains nothing of interest to the winter climber, whilst above and to the left is the **Upper Cliff** with its tall, dark cave from which the mountain derives its name, and by which the crag justifies its inclusion in this book. The left-hand side of the Upper Cliff is defined by a long, vague gully, **Old Gully**, and further left the crag sprouts a couple more buttresses before turning the corner into the **Nant y Gors** cwm. **Summit Gully**, as its name suggests, is high up at the head of this cwm.

Descent:
If it can be located, the rake splitting the crag forms the most convenient way off, but it is always possible simply to head westwards down easy ground into the Nant yr Ogof.

The first climb is located high up (around 600m - 700m) on the north-eastern flanks of the summit, at the head of the **Nant y Gors**, and is readily seen as the left branch of a snowy 'V' from the A5 just west of Capel Curig.

SUMMIT GULLY 120m I
A wide, easy-angled gully which gives a straightforward ascent on snow.

Just left of a long, easy-angled ridge which bounds the left-hand side of the **Upper Cliff** is the most continous gully on the **Main Cliff**.

OLD GULLY 150m II/III
Worthwhile under heavy snow conditions, which are rare, it can be quite awkward otherwise!
1. 45m (2) An icy groove leads up past a steep wall on the right. The groove may be avoided by climbing the heathery rib on the left.
2. 45m (1) Easier now to a sort of amphitheatre where two alternatives present themselves.
3. 60m (3) The left-hand branch leads steeply to easier ground which is followed up to the top.

The tall, dark cave on the **Upper Cliff** *may* contain an icicle within its murky depths. This can be seen from the road, and may suggest the existence of the following climb! The cave is approached by some nerve-wracking scrambling up vertical heather and snow.

MARIA 65m V ★★★
A superb and unlikely gem - when in condition. It is impossible to see whether the slab on pitch 2 is iced until it's too late! Start at the foot of the icicle from a belay on the left beneath roofs.

1. 20m (4)   Step right and climb the steep iced wall on the right to a ledge. Easier ground leads to a belay in a cave.
2. 45m (5/6)   Climb the icicle above, sometimes through an ice-window, to gain the undercut slab on the left. Precarious tip-toeing up thin ice, or back-and-crampon technique, (runners in the groove -perhaps!) leads to a steeper groove with thicker ice and the top. A magnificent pitch, which can be quite trying.

2.2 TRYFAN

Grid Reference: 664594 (OS Sheet 115 Snowdon)
Altitude: 700m - 900m
Aspect: ESE
Climbing Conditions:
Tryfan being such a slim, elegant peak, lacks the necessary catchment area to provide either the drainage or the spindrift needed for quality winter climbing. And its fabled East Face has just enough south in its aspect to allow the sun to get at any snow which may accumulate in its superficially promising gullies. Consequently these gullies are rarely in condition and the best sport (it would be inappropriate to call it snow or ice climbing, even though it may be winter climbing!) is usually to be had on the buttresses with a copy of the summer guide and a sense of humour!

Approach:
The climbs on the East Face all start from the Heather Terrace which is obvious from the A5: a rising fault cutting across the face beneath the steeper, upper crags. Its lower (north) end may be reached either by cutting up to the left beneath the Milestone Buttress from one of the lakeside lay-bys on the A5 and by crossing the north ridge, or from the east via a stile and path leaving the road opposite the prominent copse at Glan Dena. This gains the terrace at the top of a shallow gully from which scree emerges.

The Heather Terrace may also be gained at its higher south end, from Bwlch Tryfan by an almost level traverse, although this can be difficult to locate in bad weather.

Thought by many to be the most attractive peak in Snowdonia and certainly one of the most popular, it is especially disappointing that Tryfan fails to match its winter climbing to its reputation. As in summer, the best climbing is to be found on the **East Face** (although in a cold spell, short ice-pitches can appear to the right of the **Milestone Buttress**) and with exception of the fine **North Ridge**, all the climbs described are to be found there. Above the **Heather Terrace** the face is split into three main buttresses (North, Central and South) by **North Gully** and **South Gully**. To the north of **North Buttress** are a number of other gullies which stand out clearly when seen from a distance.

Descent:
The fastest return to the Heather Terrace, if not the easiest, is to descend into the amphitheatre of North Gully (which is just north of the summit) and follow the easy section of the gully until a subsidiary gully on the right, Little Gully, leads with a couple of awkward steps down to the terrace. This avoids the diffi-culties at the foot of North Gully proper. A useful descent in high winds as it allows shelter to be reached almost immediately on leaving the summit.

The commonest descent is via the South Ridge, over the South Peak to a col (NOT Bwlch Tryfan) whence a short descent to the east followed by a traverse to the north regains the Heather Terrace. Or continue over the Far South Peak to Bwlch Tryfan and follow the Miner's Track westwards past Llyn Bochlwyd towards Idwal Cottage. The brave may wish to round off the day by descend-ing the North Ridge!

Before describing the major lines, all of which start from the **Heather Terrace**, a number of ice smears to the right of the **Milestone Butt-ress** are perhaps worthy of mention. Low down on the **West Face**, and reached directly within 15 minutes, they are easily visible from the A5. Immediately to the right of the **Milestone Buttress**, in the region of the descent gully are three problem pitches. Ascend scree into the bottom of the gully.

WAY OFF ROUTE   45m   2/3
The left-hand branch goes into a deep cleft beneath the hanging icicles on the next route, but escapes easily.

DIRETISSIMA   10m   5
Climb the great hanging icicle, having first established its integrity!

DOWN CLIMB   50m   2
The right-hand gully is straightforward ice and snow.

The descent from these three pitches is rather problematic and best achieved by abseil - or just climb down **DOWN CLIMB!** If neither option appeals, continue uphill and make an enormous traverse across towards the North Ridge.

About 100m to the right of this area an ice smear runs down slabs just to the left of a faint gully. Climbing it is a

TRIVIAL PURSUIT   45m   2
Follow the smear and disappear rightwards into the gully. Descend heather ledges across to the right (south).

DEAD END SLAB 45m 3
Another 100m up to the right is a rocky rib with a couple of trees growing on it. Just to the right and before the huge gully is a large expanse of iced slab which gives a good pitch. Unfortunately, descent is tricky and it is best to continue up easy ledges to the right to gain another rocky rib which is crossed into the huge gully.

The climbs on the **East Face** are described from **right to left** as one meets them when ascending the **Heather Terrace.**

THE NORTH RIDGE 600m II ***
A superb outing under firm snow, but worthwhile in all conditions. The difficulties increase gradually as one gets higher, but nearly everything is avoidable if necessary. Although a straightforward scramble in summer, in true winter conditions (and the northerly aspect sometimes allows this), the upper section may be very icy and if the crest is followed religiously it can be both exposed and awkward.

Start from the end of the Heather Terrace and climb to the summit -jumping from Adam to Eve in crampons is not recommended.

The first shallow gully along the **Heather Terrace, NO GULLY, 100m I** is straightforward and undistinguished. Further along, the first steep rocks rise above the Terrace as a twin buttress beyond which is a deep gully:

BASTOW GULLY 150m I
The start lies between square-cut walls and the gully is fairly uniform-angled although the boulder-strewn nature of its bed requires a good covering of snow for comfort. It gains the North Ridge just below the interesting ascent to the North Tower and this makes a fine, natural continuation.

NOR' NOR' GULLY 150m II
The next gully along, some 50m away, beyond another prominent buttress, is a steep-sided corridor with three short pitches in the lower section. The first, The Tombstone, is a large block wedged across the gully a little way up. Higher up it opens out into a wide slope, but flagging interest can always be revived by poor route finding!

The next gully defines the right edge of **North Buttress**, and was shown incorrectly as **North Gully** on the diagram in the previous guide. Climbers who were unable to find Adam or Eve on the North Summit shouldn't believe everything they read in the Bible!

GREEN GULLY 150m III/IV *

Although it appears less than imposing from the Heather Terrace where the gully is more of a shallow slabby runnel, higher up it becomes a deep, dark cleft in the finest traditions and four short chimneys provide much sport and amusement - and not a little difficulty - before a grateful, if not graceful, exit can be achieved over jammed boulders. The start is just left of a big corner topped by a square overhang some 6m right of the start of Grooved Arête, which is sadly obvious from the large 'GA' scrawled on the rock.

DEFFING OUT THE BEN 150m IV *

This curiously named route follows an astral highway up the North Buttress via a series of excellent and logical winter pitches, many of which have probably been climbed before, but not recorded. Its exact relationship with the summer climb, North Buttress, is unclear, albeit meaningful! Exceptional conditions are necessary for a complete ascent - warm, dry rock and EB's don't count!

1. 40m (4) Follow the direct start to North Buttress (the right-hand and deepest of two V-grooves) for 12m, then continue up icy grooves above to a belay in a niche. When in condition, the first groove should be cloaked in ice.

2. 15m (4) Follow the groove above to a steep section leading in a few moves to a good belay.

3. 30m (1) Easy climbing on snow to the bottom of an icy slab.

4. 20m (4) Follow the slab and steeper ground above to an exit and easier climbing up to the left.

5. 45m (2) Go diagonally up left and finish up the gully.

NORTH GULLY 250m II/III

Possibly the best of Tryfan's gullies in its lower reaches, although it can be quite hard in marginal conditions.

Start below the obvious gully running up to the right of the summit, left of the grooves taken by the first pitch of the previous route. For keen traditionalists, there is a cave pitch just below the Heather Terrace for a warm up!

1. 40m (3) Two short pitches with snow leading into them.

2. 60m (1) Steep snow leads to the foot of a vertical corner.

3. 15m (4) Climb the corner which is hard when verglassed.

4. 85m (1) Steep snow leads into a wide amphitheatre, from which it is possible (cheats!) to escape up left to the summit and lunch.

5. 50m (1) True mountaineers will continue up the narrow upper gully to emerge smugly on the summit ridge beneath a fine natural arch.

LITTLE GULLY 250m I/II

Probably the easiest way up (or down) the main section of the face, this 'offspring' follows a vague line starting some 10m to the left of North Gully and joining the parent gully in the amphitheatre above the main difficulties.

SOUTH GULLY 200m III

The last major gully defining the left edge of Central Buttress, it is wide with a steep left wall. Quite reasonable when well banked up, but with less snow, skirting boulders and chockstones can prove trying. In these conditions, which are normal, it is well worth its grade.

1. 65m (1)   Easy snow leads to the first problem.
2. 65m (3)   A succession of short pitches around the various chockstones.
3. 70m (1)   Easily to beneath the final wall which offers options in all grades.

2.3 GLYDER FACH

Grid Reference: 656582 (summit) (OS Sheet 115 Snowdon)
Altitude: 750m - 950m
Aspect: NNW
Climbing Conditions:
Although this is not an unduly wet area there is sufficient draginage to allow good ice to form in the lower sections of the gullies. However, good firm snow conditions are also required if the ascent of these gullies is to be fully appreciated.
Approach:
Approach Llyn Bochlwyd *EITHER* from Ogwen Cottage (649603) via a path which joins the outflow stream from the lake, just below a steep section; *OR* from the large car park (659602) below the Milestone Buttress, following a path up to the left of a prominent, slabby buttress (Bochlwyd Buttress).
   From Llyn Bochlwyd:
for **Bristly Ridge**, follow the Miner's Track SE to Bwlch Tryfan:
for **Main and East Gullies**, follow the same track for some way before cutting back right to the foot of the cliff:
for **Central Gully** and routes further right, follow the feeder stream for about 700m into the upper cwm to a tiny pond which is a useful reference point, assuming it is not covered!
Allow 1¼-1½ hours to the foot of the climbs.
   The location of climbs on this mountain is particularly difficult in mist - the use of compass bearings taken from a 1:25,000 map is recommended.

Under true winter conditions, the impressive back wall of **Cwm Bochlwyd** which extends from **Bristly Ridge** on the far left, through the massive north face beneath the summit of **Glyder Fawr**, right round to the steep and broken east flank of **Y Gribin** on the far right, has an Alpine feel about it. For over 1km there is no real breach in the wall, although it is possible to imagine climbing it almost anywhere. Indeed, even the lines described - and they are the most logical - are none too compelling; there is plenty of scope for self-expression on Glyder Fach, even within the confines of its vague and shallow gullies. But it is reassuring to feel that even if you're not sure whether you've located the right gully - or whether you're still in it - it is almost always possible to proceed upwards to the summit plateau without running into insurmountable difficulties! Clean, steep little buttresses will keep looming out of the mist, but it's usually possible to sneak round the side: route finding ability and instinct will be more valuable here than climbing skill.

The centrepiece of the wall is the **Main Cliff**, which is almost due north of the summit of **Glyder Fach**, and **Main and East Gullies** each find a way through here - although one might debate their separate identities. Further right, beyond the steepest of the rock, **Central Gully** (called **West Gully** in summer, just to confuse!), which is undoubtedly the best and most popular route on the face, rises from just above the tiny lake. Further right, the angle eases as the face swings round beneath the prominent skyline buttress of **Castell y Gwynt**, the Castle of the Winds; then on, still steep, past the col at the head of the cwm and so to the slopes of **Y Gribin**, where one may wander at will (almost!) with axe and crampons, although not without confidence in their use and certainly not without exposure!

Descent:
Although the most difficult sections of most of the routes are low down, the majority of climbers will appreciate the necessity of continuing to the summit as any quick way off will almost certainly be more difficult than that which has already been climbed. From the summit a descent via the ridge of Y Gribin to the west is recommended. In the upper section keep well to the left (west) of the crest until 'The Football Pitch', a large flat area at 800m is reached. However, in bad weather, a certain facility with map and compass may be necessary to locate the starting point from the plateau. From 'The Football Pitch' it is possible to make for Lllyn Bochlwyd directly following an offshoot spur or to continue more easily down the ridge. Avoid the crag at the end (the Gribin Facet), either well to the left or right, to regain the path to Ogwen Cottage.

An alternative is to traverse to Glyder Fawr (½hr.) and descend to the top of the Devil's Kitchen and follow descents for that cliff. This too will require careful navigation in white out conditions if an unscheduled visit to the Llanberis valley is to be avoided! It is also possible to descend steep scree/snow slopes just east of Bristly Ridge to gain Bwlch Tryfan.

The first climb is approached from **Bwlch Tryfan**, and if combined with Tryfan's **North Ridge**, gives a superb outing for those with mountaineering ambitions.

BRISTLY RIDGE 200m II ★★★

The classic summer scramble is a sterner test in full winter conditions, with some great situations on the upper pinnacles. Approach by following the wall up from the bwlch until it abuts the ridge. Carry on steeply up the east side of the ridge until an awkward icy chimney/gully gains access to the crest. Follow the fine ridge to the plateau over some exciting pinnacles.

The area to the left of the **Main Cliff** can be tackled almost anywhere at about II, but just left of the cliff a fairly obvious gully/groove, followed by a series of short steps and terraces provides a recognisable, if undistinguished route, **FAR EAST GULLY, 220m II**. Right of the superb, clean, grey pillars of the **East Buttress** on the **Main Cliff** a rake slants up rightwards above the **Alphabet Slab**, the obvious triangular slab lower down. This rake is the entry to:

MAIN GULLY 260m II

The lower 120m provides the major interest; thereafter a broad depression leads easily up to the plateau. The steep entry pitches of East Gully, some 100m to the right are skirted in favour of a devious, but easier approach.

1. 100m   Follow the rake across the top of the Alphabet Slabs, almost horizontally until the main gully line is reached.
2. 100m   Directly up the gully, usually little ice, to a chockstone and cave; go around this to the right and enter the easier upper snow basin.
3. 60m   Anywhere - harder on the right - to the plateau and the Cantilever Stone for lunch (or dinner!).

EAST GULLY 60m III/IV ★

This is really the true, direct start to Main Gully, and is very steep. The amount of ice in the chimney varies greatly, but when it is choked it provides a fine steep ice-pitch.

CENTRAL GULLY 250m II/III ★

A fine winter climb, slightly flawed by the width of the gully and all the possible variations. The first 100m provides the technical interest if taken direct, but the faint-hearted will find soft options just to the right.

Start from the tiny lake and traverse 200m across the boulder-strewn slope before moving up for 50m to the mouth of the gully.

1. 65m   Climb easily for a few metres, then climb a steep ice-pitch, or the easier chimney and slab to the right.
2. 30m   Up the wide, square-cut gully to the next steep pitch.
3. 30m   Take the steep groove in the left-hand corner direct, or climb a long way round on ledges to the right.
4. 60m   Cross a rock band into an amphitheatre and follow the gully as it dog-legs to the left and joins a sharp little arête.
5. 65m   The arête up to the right has some delightful scrambling amongst huge blocks before merging into the summit slopes.

200m to the right and directly up the fall line of the slope behind the tiny lake is an area of easy angled slabs which receives good drainage and becomes iced after a long period of frost.

PLAQUES ROUTE   200m   II/III
A pleasant, if rather vague climb which uses the iced slabs to gain access to broken snow slopes. A long haul finds the plateau above.

WESTERN GULLY   130m   II
To the right, but before the face begins to swings round is a vague and undistinguished line which becomes more so as it rises. However, the initial stages provide a snow groove of fair interest. It is parallel to the next route and some 30m away. Either start directly below the line or traverse in from higher up to the right, just beneath a line of rock walls.

In the back left-hand corner of the cwm a vague gully line runs diagonally up to the left to finish hard under the rocky walls of **Castell y Gwynt.**

GULLY OF THE WINDS   75m   I
A buttress looms at the back of the cwm as things begin to steepen, so veer up the shallow corner to the left, keeping one hand on the rock to the right all the way!

Just to the right of **Castell y Gwynt** is a fine slab with a steep corner on the right - I wonder whether it's been climbed in winter? But further right again is a less demanding line:

COL GULLY 70m I

The slope and gully direct to the col at the rear of the cwm provide a straightforward route to the plateau.

Further right, the flanks of **Y Gribin** are steep but featureless, although a steep clean buttress high up is a landmark. Numerous lines are possible for those with imagination and a desire to get away from it all (temporarily, one hopes!).

2.4 CWM CNEIFION
THE NAMELESS CWM

Grid Reference: 647583 (OS Sheet 115 Snowdon)
Altitude: 800m - 960m
Aspect: The cwm faces North, with climbs having aspects between NE and
   NW.
Climbing Conditions:
This is certainly the best snow-holding area in the Glyders, with old snow patches often lying until well into the spring. Indeed, conditions here can remain quite wintry long after thoughts have turned to warming rock in the valleys. It is also a wet place and the ice which forms readily can combine with the snow to give classic winter climbing conditions.
Approach:
Perhaps the most interesting approach is by **East Wall Gully II,** beside the Idwal Slabs, but a more straightforward route from Llyn Idwal takes a rising traverse up the lower west flank of Y Gribin, leaving the lakeside about 200m south of the footbridge over the outflow stream. The aim is to pass above Sub-Cneifion Rib, the prominent, isolated, whale-back spur, from which only a little more height has to be gained to enter the lower cwm. Or pass beneath the rib and then climb steeply up its south side to gain a lower, slightly rising traverse line. 1-1½ hours from the road should suffice.

This magnificent high-mountain cwm nestles right under the summit of **Glyder Fawr**, surrounded on all sides by rugged cliffs. Impressive but not foreboding, it still possesses a certain charm and softness in its grassy bed. The cwm is long (almost 1km) and narrow, bounded on the left by the broken face of **Y Gribin** with its curious ribs and towers and by the shorter but steeper **Seniors' Ridge** on the right. The floor has two levels: the lower one flat and marshy; the upper one gently sloping and more barren. Between the two is a broken step, some 60-70m in height, over which two streams cascade and which is a superb area for novices to try out their newly acquired hardware on the real stuff: some is steep, some less so, but it's all good fun. For those who have no time to stop and play, the easiest line through lies on the left.

The main business of the cwm is situated in the back, right-hand corner, and can prove very elusive in mist: **Clogwyn Ddu**, the Black Cliff, is not so black in winter, but is nonetheless dramatic, with unlikely little icicles appearing from nowhere to adorn its impregnable central section. Winter climbers will be repulsed to its flanks, although **Pillar Chimney** starts in the centre, beneath the black roofs, before wriggling fearfully into the icy recess behind the huge, detached pillar on the right of the crag. The crag is best seen from the top of **Y Gribin**, but you've got to get there first! Further left, on the headwall and on the flanks of **Y Gribin**, there is nothing so grand, but the routes hereabouts have considerable merit for those of modest ambition, with a love of wild places. The lower slopes at the back of the cwm arc fine places for novice and expert alike to learn or practise their snowcraft.

Descent:
The descents from the plateau are the same as for Glyder Fach - routes finishing on Y Gribin offer the option of continuing up the ridge, or turning downhill if time is pressing, or strength and interest waning. The fastest return to the cwm is via **Easy Route,** but care should be taken here to accurately locate the point of departure in mist, lest a more exciting descent be discovered! The broad gully to the right (north) of Clogwyn Ddu may also be descended, if it can be located, as may the eastern flanks of Seniors' Ridge from the shoulder at the top of the upper cliff of Glyder Fawr.

Climbs on the left of the cwm, on the west flank of **Y Gribin** are concentrated in two distinct areas and are described first, whilst the ridge itself provides a pleasant winter scramble in good conditions.

THE GRIBIN RIDGE 150m (vertical interval) II **
Starting from 'The Football Pitch' at 800m, the ridge gradually narrows and steepens and may be tackled easily on the right (I), although it is most interesting (II) close to the crest. However, the plunging drop - even just the view of it! - into Cwm Bochlwyd on the left may be too much for those of a nervous disposition. Wobblers will take succour from the gentle zig-zag 'path' over to the right!

Above the traversing path which leads from the top of **Sub-Cneifion Rib** into the cwm, a broad, triangular, slabby pinnacle stands out clear of the snows (or screes in lean conditions). **Pinnacle Gully** takes the deep, easy gully on its left side, but the first route takes a shallower gully in the face to the left.

SHALLOW GULLY   80m   I

Head up towards Pinnacle Gully but as the ground steepens make a rising traverse leftwards to the foot of a shallow gully, some 40m to the left, which cleaves the broken buttress above. The gully is straight and straightforward.

PINNACLE GULLY   100m   I

Easy snow slopes lead into the deepening gully which fans out just below the level of the top of the Pinnacle. Either continue around to the left, or more interestingly, go up rightwards to the little col behind the Pinnacle. From here, easy mixed ground quickly leads to the ridge just below 'The Football Pitch'.

The right side of the Pinnacle also has a wide, shallow gully, but this seems of less interest. Further right, beyond a broad, broken slope and just inside the cwm, a very prominent rib with a slabby left side and a short, steep right side emerges from the hillside and gives:

CNEIFION ARÊTE   150m   III   **

Although it rarely ices up, the arête gives a fine climb under good snow, in a superb position. Most of the difficulty lies in the first pitch, which is purely rock climbing, and which may be avoided by climbing the slabs to the left. Thereafter, life can always be made easier by moving left away from the crest. Start at, or just right of the arête.
1.   30m   (3/4)   A groove leads to the crest, where a little chimney on the left gains easier ground.
2.   120m   (2/3)   Delightful mixed ground with good belays leads to the ridge - more difficult, and certainly more exposed on the crest.

Right of Cneifion Arête is another parallel, but less prominent rocky rib, whose middle section consists of a huge, flake tower. Immediately right is bow-shaped gully curving gently up to the left around the flake.

FLAKE GULLY   200m   I/II

A straightforward climb on snow leads to 'The Football Pitch', although two chockstones in the middle section could provide interest in lean conditions.

BROAD GULLY   150m   I/II

50m to the right a wide, open snow slope gives an easy exit from the cwm, although in conditions of little snow it contracts to a narrower, shallow gully line with a step leftwards through broken ground.

CURVER   150m   II   *

Immediately right is a slabby buttress with a rightward-facing, curving corner in the centre, formed by the overlapping slab on the left. This excellent climb tackles the corner directly in three pitches.

CURVER II   150m   I/II
Some 15m to the right a parallel curving corner offers a similar, but inferior alternative.

The crag now degenerates into steep, featureless hillside, but some 200m further right (above the level of the rocky step in the bed of the cwm), a prominent buttress with a pinnacle on its summit, **The Tower**, has a well defined and continuous gully on its right side. This, and the following four climbs all finish on the plateau to the right (SW) of the top of **Y Gribin**.

TOWER GULLY   150m   I/II   *
Probably the most obvious winter line on this side of the cwm.
1. 60m (1)   A very shallow snowy gully lead up to below The Tower.
2. 50m (2)   The gully narrows and deepens and may contain an ice-pitch near the bottom.
3. 40m (1)   A minor buttress splits the gully just below the ridge and escape can be made to either side.

TOWER SLABS   160m   II/III   *
The slabby buttress right of Tower Gully is often a mass of ice on its right-hand side. Start about 20m right of the gully.
1. 100m (2/3)   Starting at a prominent shallow chimney/gully, various lines of ice lead in two long pitches to a terrace.
2. 60m (1/2)   Scramble up leftwards to gain the blunt arête bounding Tower Gully, and follow it easily to the top. Endless variations are possible to sustain the interest.
It is possible to descend back to the foot of the route by following snow down right from the terrace above the first section. (Grade 1/2).

The next broad buttress to the right is split at half height by a wide snow terrace, and the following climb cuts through this buttress near its right-hand end.

NAMELESS GULLY   120m   II
1. 50m (1)   A broad, snowy gully with one steeper step leads through the lower tier to the terrace.
2. 70m (2)   The narrower gully above the terrace leads to easier ground and the plateau. An alternative line exists some 5m to the left.

NAMELESS FACE 140m II
Right of the two-tier buttress, an area of iced slabs gives an entertaining climb on snow, ice and rock.
1. 80m (2/3)   Various lines up the ice bulges chosen to suit one's ambitions or courage, lead to a steeper area with less ice.
2. 60m (2/3)   Interesting route finding and delightful mixed climbing leads by a variety of short steps, ledges and traverses to the top.

CORNER GULLY 80m I/II
A straightforward wide snow gully in the back, left-hand corner of the cwm, which may have a corniced exit. The gully splits at a little buttress just below the top, and the left-hand finish is probably more worthwhile.

The slabby backwall of the cwm can be climbed in any one of a number of places at Grade I/II, but the next climb is the most logical and pleasing escape. It is also a useful descent in good conditions.

EASY ROUTE 150m I *
A companion route to Corner Gully, although longer, better defined and more popular, it takes the snowy depression in the back right-hand corner of the cwm. The initial slope is wide but becomes slightly more confined as it slants up towards the summit cornice.

HIDDEN GULLY 100m II **
From some way up Easy Route, which is the normal approach, a narrow little gully can be spotted running off up to the right, just to the left of the black mass of Clogwyn Ddu. It is steep and tight and is a little gem.
1. 50m (1)   From a short way up Easy Route, move diagonally right to the narrows.
2. 50m (2)   There is often a pitch in the narrow section and a steep, corniced exit. In lean conditions a couple of chockstones can prove trying.

CLOGWYN DDU

PILLAR CHIMNEY 90m IV/V **
This runs from left to right to gain a chimney behind a huge flake which leans agains the crag at two thirds height. It requires a substantial build-up of ice to ease the passage, but even then is steep and awkward.

1. 40m (3)   From directly below the centre of the crag follow a snowy fault diagonally right past two short, steep chimneys, to a platform below the pillar.

Variation (3):   Start just left of Clogwyn Ddu Gully LH and climb iced slabs leftwards to gain the normal first pitch below the pillar.

2. 20m (5/6)   Climb the thinly iced, steep wall on the left of the pillar. This is very awkward as the chimney prevents a clean swing of the axe and the ice choking the exit (crux) may have to be hacked away in order to reach a belay on the other side of the Pillar.

Variation (4):   Traverse the front face of the pillar, finishing with a short, difficult slab and climb the icy chimney on the other side to the belay. This reduces the overall grade of the climb to III/IV but avoids the main issue.

3. 30m (3)   Climb the ice wall on the right, steep (and often mixed) at first, then up the leftward slanting slab to the top.

Starting from a snowy bay at the right-hand end of the crag is a deep, narrow gully which is very obvious when in good condition. Just to the right is a parallel, though less well-defined line, which starts as a shallow groove in a broken buttress. These are the two **Clogwyn Ddu Gullies,** and the left-hand one in particular gives a fine winter climb.

LEFT HAND BRANCH   120m   IV   ***
One of the best climbs in the area and one of the most frequently in condition. It is often an almost complete strip of ice and snow/ice.

1. 35m (2)   The narrow twisting gully leads to a stance below an icy rib with sheets of ice cascading down the wall on the left.

2. 30m (4/5)   Bridge between the rib and the wall on the left until it is possible, even if undesirable, to commit oneself solely to the steep ice-fall. Continue strenuously until the angle eases as one gains the upper gully.

Note: It has been traditional, although illogical and certainly not easy, to climb the right-hand branch by making a hard move right from 6m up this pitch to gain a shelf which leads into the upper section of that gully. The authors take the view that anyone who has got thus far will wish to continue up the better, left-hand branch (assuming it to be in condition), and thus an independent start is described for the right-hand gully.

3. 35m (2/3)   Up over a chockstone and steep snow to belay below the final chimney.

4. 25m (3)   Climb the chimney past a spike to an exit onto steep snow. A short step leads to the top.

Variation (3):   The final chimney can be avoided by climbing steep, iced slabs on the left to gain a rising diagonal line which trends leftwards towards the top of Pillar Chimney.

RIGHT HAND GULLY DIRECT 100m III ★
Start about 10m right of the previous route beneath some snowy grooves.
1. 45m (3)   Climb the shallow snowy grooves and steps directly into the narrow central section of the gully. The traditional start arrives from the left hereabouts.
2. 45m (3)   Up the narrow chimney to a cave below a jammed boulder. Go over this (crux) and traverse right to an open gully.
3. 10m (3)   A chockstone pitch at the top of the gully concludes the difficulties.

To the right the flanks of **Seniors' Ridge** offers a few short gullies and iced slabs which are perfect for beginners but little remains for hardened campaigners.

2.5 GLYDER FAWR - THE IDWAL SLABS

Grid Reference: 645589 (OS Sheet 115 Snowdon)
Altitude: 400m - 600m
Aspect: NW
Climbing Conditions:
Although there are several major drainage lines, and the angle of the slabs is sufficiently gentle for snow to accumulate, the relatively low altitude ensures that this famous training ground remains the preserve of the masochistic rock climber in all but the hardest of winters when a number of frozen watercourses may provide entertainment.
Approach:
A time-honoured and well-worn track leads from Ogwen Cottage to the gate by the NE end of Llyn Idwal at the entrance to the Nature Reserve. The track continues along the east side of the lake to the foot of the slabs. (½ hour from the road.)

The north face of **Glyder Fawr** extends from the left edge of the **Idwal Slabs** (which continue above as **Seniors' Ridge**) to the **Idwal Stream** (which is described under **Clogwyn y Geifr**) and comprises two major sections. Low down on the left is the clean sweep of the **Idwal Slabs** themselves, topped by a number of steeper, tiered walls which gradually diminish in height as **Seniors' Ridge** proper is reached. Across to the right from **Seniors' Ridge** and above an easy-angled snow bowl in the centre of the face, is a complex area of leftward-slanting slabs and grooves which is loosely termed **The Upper Cliff.**

The **Idwal Slabs** may, of course, be climbed in all the same places as in summer, albeit with greater difficulty. Indeed, they often are and many a happy day can be had in Dachsteins and big boots, sweeping snow from the holds of **Faith, Hope** and **Charity**, and the like. But you won't need this book to tell you how to do that and the climbs described herein take the few *natural* winter lines which exist. The upper walls will also have felt the scrape of steel from time to time, but it would be rare for **genuine** conditions to exist on these steep, clean faces, so nothing is described. Don't be put off if you want to teeter your way up **Lazarus**, or **Groove Above** or whatever - you may find it harder than **The Devil's Appendix** and you may even find it more enjoyable! In that case, Tom Leppert's wonderful Climber's Club guide to **Ogwen** will serve you in good stead. But if it's grooves and gullies, dirty, wet and vegetated that you're after, then read on!

Descent:

The normal descent path takes the line of least resistance up to the left from the large terrace some 160m up the slabs where the routes end beneath the steep upper walls. A number of short pitches, which may be quite awkward under snow and ice, leads in about 100m to a shoulder overlooking the start of the gully section of East Wall Gully. It is important to climb high enough here before attempting a descent, as starting down to the left too early could result in an unscheduled flight down Suicide Wall. This is as steep and uninviting as its name suggests! In any case, even the true descent is far from easy and it can often warrant the use of the rope, and may even necessitate a *short* abseil.

From the gully, either descend close to The East Wall, or more easily, follow tracks out onto the hillside, and pick a line well away from the crag. But be warned - there have been many accidents to parties attempting to use this descent.

An alternative is to climb rightwards (ledges, and a couple of V Diff rock moves) from the terrace at the top of the routes, beneath the prominent, straight crack/groove of Javelin Buttress into a short, overhanging corner. A very awkward move up the short wall on the right leads to easy ground, whence a careful diagonal descent leads to the stream above Introductory Gully. Now cross the rib on the far side and descend a short gully to snow/scree just above the path to the west of the foot of the slabs. Although initially quite hard (stay roped up for a bit), this is a much faster and safer descent.

The first climb follows the frozen stream issuing from **Cwm Cneifion** above, starting some 100m left of the edge of The Slabs.

THE NAMELESS STREAM   200m (vertical interval)   III/IV   ★
In cold conditions the stream may be followed all the way from the path into Cwm Cneifion but the difficulties are concentrated in the upper section, where it runs in a steep, narrow slit. This provides a

couple of excellent pitches before the angle eases to allow access to the upper cwm. An alternative, at a similar grade, is to follow the lesser frozen stream some 10m to the left.

Either continue up routes in Cwm Cneifion or descend to the left via the traversing path described in the approaches to The Nameless Cwm.

The next climb makes its way beneath the left edge of the slabs and **Seniors' Ridge** and as well as showing **Suicide Wall** at its awesome best, it offers an interesting natural approach to **The Nameless Cwm** above.

EAST WALL GULLY   200m (vertical interval)   I/II

1. 130m   (2/3)   Zig-zag up easy slabs to a shallow chimney groove which leads eventually to the base of Suicide Wall, a steep and well named piece of rock! A very awkward short chimney, right beneath the wall provides entertainment on the way to the start of the gully proper. Here the way off from the slabs descends a short wall to join the gully. This point can be reached more easily by scrambling up alongside the streams to the left (NE).
2. 70m   (1/2)   Follow the gully which is often mixed, to emerge suddenly on horizontal ground in the bottom of The Nameless Cwm.

ORDINARY ROUTE   165m   III

The central trench on the main sweep of the slabs starts easily with numerous spikes, but peters out after an awkward steeper section (3/4). A difficult traverse (3) across the foot of a tower to the large ledge on White Hope holds the key; then an easy pitch up ledges to the large terrace. But there *are* other ways...!

WHITE HOPE   165m   III   *

This, the only true winter route on the slabs themselves, follows the drainage line which the summer climb of Charity fails to avoid! It is a prominent line of leftward-facing corners near the centre of the crag. Start at the foot of the corner just to the right of the previous route.
1. 45m   (3)   Climb the corner, then the slab on the left before belaying on a broad ledge in the corner on the right.
2. 45m   (3)   Climb the next corner until a traverse can be made with difficulty across the slab on the left. Go up to a shallow overlap and follow its curving edge to a ledge at the foot of a deep V-groove.
3. 45m   (3)   Climb the groove with a difficult exit onto a large ledge.
4. 30m   (2)   More easily up ledges above to the terrace.

SUBWALL CLIMB 140m IV

This climb takes the curving, shallow corner formed by the right edge of the slabs where they abut the steeper West Wall. Although there is plenty of drainage in the lower section, the water does not follow the line of the corner higher up; a fact which may lead to the redundancy of crampons and axes in an only averagely extreme winter!

1. 40m   (3)   Climb the iced slab to the terrace.
2. 30m   (4)   Follow the slab on the right until forced left (with difficulty, unless well iced) beneath the impending wall to a grass ledge.
3. 45m   (3/4)   Continue in the same line up thin ice in the groove beneath the wall.
4. 25m   (3)   Go up leftwards to join the rightwards traverse into the overhanging corner on the right and the way off (see section on descents).

A short distance to the right, a black cleft with a curiously pocketed, overhanging wall on its right, and an iced staircase on the left, gives the next route. Although it is easy-angled, it is frequently pure water-ice and demands caution. An excellent direct approach to the **Upper Cliff.**

INTRODUCTORY GULLY 100m II *

A splendid outing up the icy treads of the Idwal Staircase, easing as it rises to eventually peter out into a snowy little valley beneath the towering Upper Cliff, which longs to make your acquaintance after the introductions below. So read on...

2.6 GLYDER FAWR - THE UPPER CLIFF

Grid Reference: 643585 (OS Sheet 115 Snowdon)
Altitude: 650m - 850m
Aspect: N
Climbing Conditions:
Ideally, a good covering of consolidated snow is best as there are few water-ice lines, but the abundant vegetation when frozen, can permit worthwhile ascents at a somewhat higher grade, under cold conditions with only a little snow.
Approach:
Go past the Idwal Slabs for 100m or so until a long, wide scree or snow gully leads tediously up to the foot of the cliff. A better approach is by Introductory Gully, or some other route on the slabs followed by a judiciously chosen, rising traverse to the right (not recommended in mist). The direct approach will take about 1 hour from the road at Ogwen Cottage.

The crag is best considered in sections: from **Seniors' Ridge** rightwards, and just above a wide ledge system is a broken, tiered area of cliff which terminates in a wide band of slabs before the slim, soaring pillars of the **Grey Group** protrude from the anonymity of the background. **Narrow Gully** and **Square Furrow** define the junction between these slabs (**Square Slabs**) and the **Grey Group**. Right again, beyond the clean pillars and square grooves is the first of two large, prominent corner/gullies in the centre of the crag. This is **East Gully**, with the **East Buttress** to the right. Further right is the second large corner/gully, **Central Gully**, which defines the left edge of **Central Buttress**. Finally, a shorter, but less well-defined fault, **West Gully**, concludes the parade. There is an air of isolation up here, rare indeed in Idwal and the climbs have position and tradition to recommend them - they may not be instant classics, but then, Nescafé isn't everyone's cup of tea either!

Descent:
The climbs finish on a broad terrace which slopes gently up to the left, some 500m from the summit of the mountain. Either follow the top edge of the cliff leftwards and descend the upper section of Seniors' Ridge, until gentle slopes give access to The Nameless Cwm to the east; or, more easily, follow the broad terrace down to the right until it becomes a stream valley which leads to Llyn y Cwn, the lake above The Devil's Kitchen cliffs. The continuation of both these descents are described elsewhere in the book under the relevant crags.

The first climb is at the extreme left-hand end of the crag, indeed it might better be described as belonging to **Seniors' Ridge**. It starts from a ledge system some 50m below and just to the left of a huge quartz vein (if visible under snow cover!) and is best approached directly from below, rather than by traversing from the main cliff.

OBLIQUE GULLY 120m II
A deep gully which is frequently in condition as it takes a lot of drainage and catches plenty of snow.
1. 50m (2)   A couple of steep pitches lead to a more open, easy-angled area where the gully splits.
2. 20m (1)   Both branches are interesting, the right-hand one perhaps the more so and easy ground leads up to a steep chimney.
3. 50m (2/3)   Climb the chimney which can be awkward in lean conditions, to easier ground and a saddle on Seniors' Ridge. Descend into the Nameless Cwm or continue up the ridge.
Variation: *An ice-fall forms on the buttress between the two branches and gives a good pitch (3).*

To the right is a wide area of slabs, bounded on the right by an obvious gully.

NARROW GULLY 120m II/III
Start just right of a smooth, gently sloping glacis some 20m long and to the right of the lines of chimneys above. An icy slab leads up to the left into the main line which is followed with interest to the ridge.

SQUARE FURROW 130m II/III
Some 25m to the right is a broken, left-facing corner line rising the height of the cliff and marking the left edge of the slender, slabby ribs of the Grey Group. Start at a shallow, square-cut chimney about 5m left of an obvious, steep wide crack.
1. 10m (3)   Climb the chimney to easier ground.
2. 40m (2)   Move right to climb the groove beneath the steep rock wall to the right and exit up icy slabs to a broad terrace.
3. 80m (1/2)   A shallow gully continues in the same line to the top.

GREY GULLY 130m II/III *
Just to the right of the first slim rib (Grey Rib) a short awkward wall (banked up in good conditions) gives access to a narrow hidden gully which slants leftwards through clean rock to join Square Furrow just below the broad terrace at the end of pitch 2. A good pitch. Finish as for Square Furrow.

To the right is a deep, square corner with the elegant **Grey Arête, HVS** above. At the right-hand side of the big slabby wall to the right are two parallel sets of cracks rising above a bay some 30m up the crag. A continuous line of drainage down the crag defines the next route.

PROCRASTINATION CRACKS 70m V *
Start at a shallow, left-facing groove below the snow bay.
1. 30m (2/3)   Climb ice on the left of the groove to belay in the bay. *This pitch may bank out in heavy snow.*
2. 30m (5/6)   Traverse diagonally left across a snow/ice slab to a shallow chimney. Climb this on thin ice, exit right to a sloping ledge. A shallow scoop leads rightwards into an icy V-groove above the right-hand set of cracks. Unfortunately, a poor belay has to be taken in this area if belays are to be reached at the top.
3. 10m (5/6)   Climb the V-groove, peg runner, and exit onto a snowfield. Belay well back.

THE TIME-WASTER FINISH 45m III
Not really a winter route, but logical and great fun. It takes the corner

and cave in the steep buttress directly above the finish of the previous route. Rucksacks may prove awkward!

1. 45m (3) Climb the corner beneath the cave formed by the huge jammed block until it steepens, then move awkwardly right up frozen vegetation. Now move back left and swarm up the slab beneath the jammed block and SQUEEEEEZE through. Another hole leads up to the next floor, whence an escape onto the rib on the left can be made. Owners of new Goretex jackets should not bother contacting the authors!

TWISTING GULLY 180m III *

Just before the deep cleft of East Gully, a narrow gully can be seen to start some 30m up the crag. The middle section is very steep and often contains much ice, although the upper pitches rather lack line. Start just right of Procrastination Cracks.

1. 30m (2) Scramble up from the left to a ledge at the foot of a steep, left-facing corner. In good condtions, a steep ice-fall (4) may be included in this pitch.
2. 45m (4) Climb the corner for 6m, then more easily up to a very steep groove which is bridged to easier ground after 10m. (Hard in thin conditions.)
3. 105m (2) The upper gully is followed past a chockstone, then it swings to the right to gain a shoulder, whence an easy-angled groove leads to the ridge.

EAST GULLY 200m IV *

The biggest gully on the crag, it is very wet, so can be climbed in a freeze with no snow. However, it is best with a good accumulation.

1. 30m (1/2) Easily to the foot of a steepening.
2. 20m (3/4) Climb the bulging wall above which can be hard and serious in thin conditions.
3. 150m (2/3) Initially the gully lies back, but it steepens once more before the easier upper section is reached.

CENTRAL GULLY 230m IV

Past the next rib and at a lower level is the other main corner on the crag; it is bounded by slabs on the left and is rather open and uninspiring. Heavy snow cover is needed if it is to 'go' at this grade.

1. 45m (3) Either climb the icy corner or a shallow icy groove in the slabs to the left, to gain a ledge.
2. 45m (3) Carry on in the same vein either on the slabs or in the corner, to beneath the huge chockstone, which one must hope is

well-buried and therefore invisible!

3.   6m (3/5)   There is a through route - sometimes! Otherwise the thinly iced slab on the left, or energetic jumping up and down must be employed.

4.   135m (2/3)   Continue, passing a few less problematic pitches to the top.

HIGH PASTURE 230m II *

An all-weather outing up the tilted field just to the right - '... where only goats will wish to browse'. In dry, cold conditions with the security of modern tools, it provides an exposed route up the cliff on perfect frozen vegetation. Any snow cover just gets in the way! Belays are scarce though.

WEST GULLY 125m III/IV

Shorter but steeper than its neighbour, it tackles the last remaining fault on the crag. It does sport one excellent pitch though.

1.   45m (2)   Start to the left of the fault line and climb slabs to a terrace beneath the obvious steep corner.

2.   30m (4)   Climb the steep chimney corner which often contains a lot of ice, into the bay above.

3.   50m (3)   Move across into the left branch and follow it more eaily to the top.

GRASS ROUTE 120m IV *

Another outing for the goats and their chacals! It takes a faint line in the steep right wall of the gully.

1.   45m (2)   As for West Gully to the terrace.

2.   35m (4)   Descend a little and climb a very steep vegetated groove in the right wall and exit left into the bay of West Gully.

3.   40m (4)   Follow the right branch of the gully to easier ground and the top.

2.7 CLOGWYN Y GEIFR - THE DEVIL'S KITCHEN CLIFF

Grid Reference: 638588 (OS Sheet 115 Snowdon)
Altitude: 600m - 700m
Aspect: NE
Climbing Conditions:
The climbing is mainly on steep water-ice (Grade 3 and above) and because of its relatively low altitude a period of hard frost is required to produce good conditions. However, the climbs on South Buttress do require a certain amount of snow build-up before they are worthwhile.

Approach:
From the car park at Ogwen Cottage follow the 'motorway' up to the gate by the outflow from Llyn Idwal, at the entrance to the National Nature Reserve. Follow the track on either side of the lake and reach the Kitchen via the boulder scree in about 45 minutes from the road.

This dark, wet and vegetated crag is transformed in winter to a sparkling playground dripping with ice and reflecting its glacial origin. The cliff extends from the stream crossed soon after passing the foot of the Slabs past the great cleft of the Kitchen itself and round to the broken ground to the right of the diamond-shaped **North Cliff**. In winter it benefits from substantial drainage from the large wet col between **Glyder Fawr** and **Y Garn**. Much of this drainage seeps along the dish-shaped strata of the syncline until it spills over the edge to freeze into the characteristic ice-sheets of the crag. **Llyn Idwal** below, when frozen, is a fine arena from which to view this icy amphitheatre.

Descent:
The main path descends the broad ramp on the Glyder Fawr side of the Kitchen above the ice-falls of The Ramp, The Screen and The Curtain, and it starts some distance to the east of the stream which drains Llyn y Cwn into the Kitchen. A more awkward and serious descent is down the same stratum on the west side of the Kitchen, passing impressively beneath The Devil's Appendix, the Jewel in Idwal's Crown. However, the start of this path (**The Goat's Path, I**), can be difficult to locate in mist.

The path from the base of the Slabs to the Kitchen crosses a prominent steep stream in a narrow, rocky V-shaped bed. When frozen, this watercourse **THE IDWAL STREAM, II (3/4) ★** provides any number of short, interesting ice-pitches on its way down from the extreme left-hand side of the col above the Kitchen. As most of these are avoidable this is an excellent outing for novices.

Right of the stream, and well above the path, the left-hand end of **South Buttress** has a prominent gully which encloses a waterfall in wet conditions. This is:-

SOUTH GULLY 140m IV ★★★

The classic route of its grade in Idwal. In lean conditions the main ice-pitch can be steep and long, whereas a good build-up of snow will lessen the difficulties.

1. 30m (3) From the foot of the gully climb the bulge on the right to the easy central section. Belay on the left.
2. 30m (1) Move up to belay on the right of the main ice-fall.

3. 40m (3/5)   Climb the ice-fall moving left to the overhanging left wall (rock runners), then back right over a bulge to gain the upper gully.

3a. *Variation:*   *SOUTH GULLY PILLAR 40m (5). Climb the steep ice-fall on the right directly to join the original route in the upper gully.*

4. 40m (2)   One further bulge leads to easy ground and the top.

CENTRAL ROUTE 85m III *

In good conditions which are fairly rare, this provides a continuous groove of snow-ice, but it is much harder with poorly consolidated snow.

Start: There are two shallow grooves in the wall right of South Gully, and this is the right-hand and more obvious of the two.

1. 40m (3/4)   Straight up the narrow snow groove to an easement and tiny spike belays.

2. 45m (3)   Straight on again, gradually easing to a gangway with poor belays. Scramble off the gangway to the left.

Right of **South Gully**, beyond the wall of **Central Route** a lesser gully runs up the cliff, trending right above the ramp which comes down from the left at half height. The lower section displays two distinct ice lines.

GRECIAN 2000 120m IV

A bit of an eliminate but enjoying some good climbing, it starts up the left-hand, direct start to Chicane Gully.

1. 45m (4/5)   Climb the hanging icicle direct and continue to belay on the ramp.

2. 45m (1)   Follow the ramp leftwards to belay beneath an obvious ice-fall coming down from a roof.

3. 30m (4)   Climb the ice-fall to the roof and move right into a corner which leads to the top.

CHICANE GULLY 120m III *

This provides two contrasting pitches: the first on steep water-ice and the second needing good hard snow to be in condition. The second pitch may be found to be quite hard in anything but perfect conditions.

Start below the prominent icicle which forms at the bottom of the gully.

1. 45m (3)   Climb a rightward leaning groove to the right of the icicle, then follow ice back left into the line of the gully and

continue to belay at the bottom right of the ramp.

2. 45m (2/4)   Move down right into the continuation gully and climb snow to poor belays. A very steep heather pitch in poor conditions.

3. 30m (1)   Easy snow leads to the top.

DEVIL'S PIPES 50m V

The last to form and the hardest of the Idwal Smears. A serious route.

Start to the right of Chicane Gully, a thin ice smear comes down a blunt arête. Start just right of the arête.

1. 50m (5)   Up rickety flakes to the icicle. Climb this steeply to the cave then traverse right and go up an icy groove to the top. (The pitch can be split in the groove after 30m.)

To the right of **Devil's Pipes** this section of the cliff tapers down, finally disappearing altogether just to the left of the Kitchen. The tourist path descends the broad shelf above the cliff and divides the lower **South Buttress** from the upper left-hand end of the **Main Cliff**. However, before it vanishes into the boulder field trampled by the passage of countless parties of apprehensive feet, the **South Buttress** yields three very popular short ice climbs. These are a good introduction to the style of climbing hereabouts and are often the first ice routes to come into condition after a few days of cold weather.

THE RAMP 100m III/II **

An excellent and justifiably popular little route which follows the obvious icy ramp slanting up to the left beneath an overhanging, bulging wall.

Start below a deep, V-gully beneath the bottom right-hand end of the ramp.

1. 30m (2)   Climb bearing left up slabby ice to a peg belay at the foot of the ramp proper.

2. 45m (3)   Climb leftwards up the ramp and swing steeply round to the right to belay on blocks in the easier gully above.

3. 25m (1)   Easy snow leads to the top.

THE SCREEN 65m III/IV **

Start just to the right and at a slightly higher level than The Ramp, below an obvious icy V-groove.

1. 20m (3)   Climb the pleasant groove to a ledge below the obvious, steep ice-fall. This section may be avoided by traversing in easily from the right (crag rats) - or the next section avoided in a similar way (cowards)!

2. 45m (4)   Climb the first steep bulge to an easier angled

section in 8m. Either move awkwardly right and continue up steep ice to the top, or follow a V-groove further back on the left (easier).

THE CURTAIN   30m   IV

To the right of The Screen and just before the crag peters out, another broad ice-fall forms in cold conditions and gives this short, technically difficult practice pitch.

1.   30m   (4)   Climb it - by a line that offers a suitable challenge! The faint hearted will probably attack from the right. Belay well back.

The tourist path intervenes now but above it lies the **Main Cliff**, gradually increasing in height towards **The Devil's Appendix**, then tapering again as the **Goats' Path** rises up above **The Band** and **The North Cliff** on the right. The next two climbs take the heavily iced triangular area just left of the first buttress outside **The Devil's Kitchen** itself. Two crack/chimneys at the apex of the triangle define the two exits, but the lower section may be climbed almost anywhere on ice and frozen vegetation.

DEVIL'S PASTURE   75m   III

The left-hand line. Start anywhere!

1.   30m   (2/3)   Climb ice on the left to the foot of a chimney.
2.   45m   (3)   The chimney leads to easier ground in the upper gully.

COLDHOUSE CRACK   80m   III   *

The right-hand line is better and a bit harder. Start below the right-hand crack.

1.   45m   (3)   Climb an icy slab until forced right by an overhang into a scoop. Go up and climb thin ice in a chimney/groove to a small spike belay.
2.   35m   (3)   A steep verglassed corner leads to the upper gully and the top.

THE DEVIL'S KITCHEN   30m   IV   ***

A magnificent climb when in condition. The powerful atmosphere derived from its setting at the back of the huge, icy cavern in the very centre of the cliff probably contributes more to the experience than the climbing itself - which is mercifully short-lived. Approach by scrambling to the very back of the cleft, tackling a number of short ice-pitches on the way. In 1979 it was possible to walk out the back, so banked out was it with snow! But in most winters, life is more difficult.!

1.   30m   (5/6)   On the right wall the ice is thickest and steepest

near the cave, so start further right and then move back left above the initial steep section. Now go up to a bulge which has to be surmounted (crux) before the freedom and daylight of the upper gully can be reached.

The next three climbs lie on the upper part of the Main Cliff above.

THE GOATS' PATH 200m I
A narrow terrace following the curve of the syncline and steepening towards the top. Although easy, it is exposed and icy.

DEVIL'S STAIRCASE 100m IV/V ★★
This is the obvious and compelling chimney line between the Kitchen and the Appendix ice-falls to the right. It is steep and enclosed and takes less drainage than some of the other clefts hereabouts, so only exceptional conditions, preferably with a build-up of hard snow, will produce good winter climbing. But in these conditions it is hard and superb with good runners and belays. Start 30m right of the Kitchen.
1. 25m (5/6) The chimney is thinly iced - and hard.
2. 15m (5) An icy wall on the left leads to an ice platform: or climb the difficult chockstoned chimney direct.
3. 20m (4) Up snow and a verglassed groove.
4. 40m (5) Gain the deep chimney on the right, squirm inside (interesting if full of soft snow!) and wriggle skywards avoiding chockstones, to emerge perhaps on easy ground.

THE DEVIL'S APPENDIX 130m VI ★★★
Wales' finest ice climb and as good as anything else in these Isles. The most obvious winter feature in the cwm, cascading over the vertical cliffs to the right of the Kitchen, it is easily visible from a number of strategic points along the A5. Unfortunately, the bottom icicle rarely joins up although the upper sections may be well iced. The impatient may then come in from the right - and miss the point.
1. 40m (6) Climb ice into a small cave at 10m (peg runners). The ice may form to the right or left of the cave, but whichever way it is, it has to be climbed! To the right it forms a free-standing vertical pillar which leads strenuously to a good ledge (peg belay).
2. 40m (5) Move out onto the ice slab on the right which leads up and left into an ice chimney. Climb this over a bulge to a tiny stance (poor pegs, one buried in the corner, one on the right rib).
3. 50m (5) Traverse horizontally right, exposed, to an ice-groove. Climb this left then right to a short gully. Go up mixed snow and ice on the right. Belay well back.

HANGING GARDEN GULLY 100m IV *
The obvious wide but steep gully well right of the Appendix. It needs a good build-up of snow ice and is rarely in condition. Start below it.
1. 30m   Climb the narrow strip of snow ice.
2. 30m   Climb easily to the back of the snow bay where an awkward chimney leads to another snow bay.
3. 40m   Climb a verglassed wall to a steep icy crack. Up this with difficulty into a snow gully which gains the top.

Below the **Goats' Path** as it curves upwards and left of the impressive diamond-shaped **North Cliff** is a steep section of cliff called **The Band.** It sports two obvious ice-falls in cold weather which are reached by heading for a curving terrace parallel to and below the **Goats' Path**.

THE STING 55m IV/V *
Although short, the left-hand fall is both hard and good. The ice-fall is usually quite wide so there is scope for variation.
1. 10m (3)   Climb an ice-slab into a small cave with a good thread.
2. 45m (5)   Tackle the steep ice-pillar and wall on the right. Climb a steep groove to the Goats' Path terrace. Spike at the back.

THE DEVIL'S CELLAR 70m IV **
This fine ice route crosses the terrace, so start below the left-hand end of the North Cliff. This is reached either by traversing in from the left or directly up a shallow gully.
1. 40m (4)   Climb the steep ice corner, then the icy slab to the right to the lower terrace. Poor belays.
2. 30m (5)   Traverse left and climb the steep ice-groove.
2a. Variation: (4) Climb the steep iced chimneys on the right, exiting left at the top. Slightly easier and more often in condition, although not as good.

So far, the imposing **North Cliff** has remained inviolate to the axe and crampon brigade, but it can surely only be a matter of time? To the right of the **North Cliff** is a broad area of steep hillside down which three streams trickle. After a good freeze these provide excellent practice grounds, particularly the central one which braids as it flows over an outcrop just below half height giving a wide band of ice. The left-hand stream hugs the edge of the **North Cliff** and swings round above into some steeper and more interesting ground below the ridge. This provides a good long training climb, getting harder towards the top. The right-hand stream enters a shallow gully higher up and is also worthwhile for beginners.

Over to the right of these streams is an attractive bit of mountainside which belongs neither to **Y Garn** nor to **Clogwyn y Geifr**, so as it is approached from the Idwal side we will include it here. A rocky spur juts out from the flanks of **Y Garn** and dominates the west side of **Llyn Idwal**, holding the promise of fine rock climbing, but proves to be disappointing on closer inspection. It is called **Castell y Geifr** (637594) and does hold some interest for the winter climber despite its apparently southerly aspect. Cutting a swathe beneath its rocky face is a wide (25m), flat-bottomed channel which is clearly shown on the 1:25,000 map.

THE TRENCH 250m I
Offers straightforward crampon practice when full of consolidated snow. The right wall near the top has some excellent short, vertical ice smears for the ambitious beginners! The slope emerges on the SE flanks of Y Garn and is probably the best ski descent into Cwm Idwal under good snow conditions.

Some way up **The Trench** a deep gully may be seen up on the right and occasionally a tempting line of ice smears wanders down steep rock on its right-hand side but is, as yet, unclimbed. However, the gully has been, and is

CASTLE GULLY 120m II/III
It holds a substantial stream and is therefore one of the first of the Idwal routes to come into condition in a frost. The main pitch is good, even with no snow after just three or four days of cold weather. However, it becomes easier as it fills with snow.
1. 40m (1/2) A rib splits the entrance to the gully. Climb either side of it to belay beneath the steep ice-pitch and the impressive right wall.
2. 25m (3) Climb ice at the back of the gully to easier ground.
3. 55m (1) Continue well up the hillside above before cutting left to rejoin the upper Trench, or carry on to the ridge above.

2.8 Y GARN

Grid Reference: 631595 (summit) (OS Sheet 115 Snowdon)
Altitude: 650m - 940m
Aspect: NE and N
Climbing Conditions:
The climbing is predominantly in wide, easy gullies, high on the mountain and

David Howard Jones tackling the final bulge on THE DEVIL'S
APPENDIX (VI) in Cwm Idwal. Photo: Dave Alcock.

is therefore only practicable in good firm snow conditions. All of the gullies described below are prone to dry slab avalanche after heavy snowfall and west or south-westerly winds. You are advised to examine the snow cover and retreat in unfavourable conditions. In addition, there can be corniced exits on any of the gullies.

Approach:
For Cwm Clyd gain Llyn Idwal from Ogwen Cottage and go round the north end of the lake and follow the steep stream issuing directly from Llyn Clyd, or more interestingly, scramble up the broken rocky rib on the left. Once in the cwm approach the gullies directly - a 1:25,000 map (on which the gullies can be identified) and a compass are useful in mist.

For Cwm Cywion approach from the hostel at 644604 on the gated road beyond the Idwal Cottage Youth Hostel. From here, a steady climb to the west into the flat upper cwm should take no more than ¾hr. The climbing is clustered around the SW corner of the cwm beneath the smooth concave north face of the mountain.

This fine, rather stately mountain is best viewed across a frozen **Llyn Ogwen** when the classic armchair appearance of **Cwm Clyd** stands out beneath the summit cone, its lofty crest frowning disapproval, perhaps, at the antics on the ice-falls of Idwal. Because this is a mountain for stumbling youth and reflective old age there are few attractions here for those in their performance-conscious middle age. Uh-Garn, Ogwen's gentle mountain, home of the elusive **Banana Gully** where long easy gullies can start you on your way and where rambling buttresses can, in later years, re-kindle inquisitive spirits and spent ambitions: a tale of two cwms.

Cwm Clyd, high and round, facing NE and embraced by two fine ridges and **Cwm Cywion**, lower and less well-formed, facing N and rarely visited, let alone embraced. The cwms are separated by the elegant NE ridge which joins the main spine of the Glyders some 200m north of the summit. When descending in mist, care should be taken to identify the correct ridge at the junction.

To the south and east of the summit the lip of **Cwm Clyd** swings round to terminate in the rocky spur of **Castell y Geifr**, but before it reaches the crag at the end, a subsidiary spur drops down to the NE towards the tiny lake nestling in the depths of the cwm below. This spur gives an entertaining scramble and was called the **North East Ridge** in the previous guide. To prevent confusion with the true NE ridge of the mountain it has been renamed the **North East Spur**.

Descent:
The routes in Cwm Clyd all finish somewhere near the summit, so the best

descent is via the well-marked path down the NE ridge which returns to the floor of the cwm. Alternatively, descend to the col above The Devil's Kitchen and return to Idwal as previously described. For climbs from Cwm Cywion, either continue to the summit or return to the cwm from the north side of the col between Y Garn and Foel Goch via an open snow gully.

CWM CLYD
NORTH-EAST SPUR 250m III **

The spur rises as a series of rocky steps to the left of the stream starting well below the entrance to the cwm. The first, rather steep step may be skirted on the left. At about 650m the ridge levels out and a curious square tower, over to the left, The Pinnacle, is passed. A steep section just above is the crux and its difficulty may be varied with the line of attack. Above is easy ground on the SE ridge.

There are four main gullies in the back wall of the cwm traditionally known as **A, B, C and D**. However, since the rumour was put about that **D Gully** was actually the obvious curving cleft of **Banana Gully** - which itself was formerly thought to reside on the other side of the mountain in **Cwm Cywion** - the labelling has gone somewhat awry. Despite extensive searching - fruitless searching some might say - of **Cwm Cywion**, it would appear that the elusive **Banana Gully** has gone to ground. It would therefore seem reasonable to permit **D Gully** to assume this auspicious title until she too, decides to quit in favour of some other snowy cwm. And God bless all those who flail in her!

On the left-hand side of the headwall of the cwm are a pair of snow gullies in a 'V' configuration: these are

A GULLY 220m I
The left-hand line gives a straightforward ascent.

and

B GULLY 240m I/II
The right-hand line is a bit steeper near the top and sometimes contains a pitch.

The buttress to the right is:

BC BUTTRESS 240m II
Take the easiest line, with the difficulties concentrated in the lower and upper thirds. Start at the fork of A/B Gullies, or with greater difficulty (III) from C Gully.

C GULLY 260m II *
The central gully on the face which finishes just left of the summit. It

has one steep section just above half way.

CD BUTTRESS 260m II
Climb the buttress starting near the foot of C Gully and finishing on snow slopes below the summit. The line is somewhat indefinite - luck and instinct playing a role in any successful ascent!

BANANA GULLY 280m I **
The shallow curving line which defines the right edge of the steeper ground. It stands out very clearly from a distance and gets easier as it rises. Other lines are possible, though less logical, to the left.

CWM CYWION
The area within the cwm of most interest to winter climbers is on the left-hand side as one walks in, on the northern flanks of the NE Ridge of **Y Garn**. Initially, an extensive but not very high band of rock beneath the featureless north face offers a number of steep practice ice-pitches, both in gullies and on slabs. As one gets closer to the back of the cwm this rock band abuts a steeper tower some 100m high. **Chicken Gully** takes the left side of the tower whilst the slanting overhung chimney on the right is taken by **Banana Split**. To the right the rock is still steep, but more broken and vegetated and forms the left wall of a very wide easy snow gully. This gully, in deference to tradition is called **False Banana Gully** and has four steep exits to the ridge above. It emerges on the NW ridge of **Y Garn** mid-way between the junction with the NE ridge to the left and the col at the head of **Cwm Cywion** to the right. The first three routes each start **above** the lower rock band and are described from left to right down the NW ridge.

SUMMIT GULLY 100m I
Just a depression in the face some 80m to the right of the summit of the NE ridge. Access is via a long slog up the face below, traversing above the rock band or via one of the short, harder ice-pitches through the rock band. The line of the gully is not obvious under heavy snow.

SPURIOUS GULLY 70m I
This defines the left-hand side of the small buttress which forms a slight spur some 100m further down the ridge from Summit Gully. It is slight, but hardly illegitimate! Approach as for Summit Gully.

SPUR GULLY 90m I/II
The gully defining the right-hand side of the spur gives a couple of good pitches beneath the steep wall on the left. The best approach is via Chicken Gully which leads directly to the start. Otherwise, a

similar approach as for Summit Gully should be used.

The following climbs start at a lower level in the cwm below the rock band which bounds the left side of **False Banana Gully.**

CHICKEN GULLY 75m **II**

The gully to the left of the steep rock tower starts from a recess immediately right of the end of the rock band. The difficulties ease beyond the rock band and easy ground leads up rightwards behind the tower for 90m to the foot of Spur Gully, or escape leftwards.

BANANA SPLIT 150m **IV** *

Some 30 to the right, this is the obvious overhung chimney line slanting up to the right, giving two long steep pitches. Some of the more difficult sections can be avoided on the right. Above the difficulties, turn up to the right and follow the crest of the blunt arête easily to the ridge.

The next four climbs are the exits from **False Banana Gully** described from left to right.

NO.1 GULLY 110m **III**

The right-hand edge of the broken vegetated buttress beyond Banana Split has a prominent groove which slants up right to a steep exit. Climb the groove to easier ground and a terrace, above which a further rope-length of broken ground leads to the ridge.

NO.2 GULLY 100m **I**

The obvious direct continuation of the main gully (False Banana Gully). It is more like a steep headwall than an enclosed gully. A short, narrow gully leading leftwards near the top can add interest.

NO.3 GULLY 50m **II**

This is a more enclosed gully on the right-hand side of the headwall, bounded by a prominent ridge on the right and starting about 60m below the ridge. It has a steep exit and may be corniced.

NO.4 GULLY 100m **III**

Across the ridge from No.3 Gully is a deep wide gully which steepens alarming and forks before gaining the ridge. The right fork is a steep narrow chimney.

A buttress to the right of the col on the **Foel Goch** side has a couple of short, easy-angled gullies, but they hardly warrant description and are left for solitary explorers to discover.

2.9 FOEL GOCH

Grid Reference: 628612 (OS Sheet 115 Snowdon)
Altitude: 600m - 800m
Aspect: North and East
Climbing Conditions:

The mountain, with the exception of one prominent area low down on the North Face which drains into Esgair Gully is relatively dry and needs consolidated snow cover to provide the best winter climbing conditions. Although many of the climbs are good when in condition, this is rarer than on some of the higher crags.

Approach:

For climbs on the North Face, approach directly up Cwm Bual from the minor road on the west side of the Nant Ffancon starting at 638623. For climbs on Creigiau Gleison and the East Face, follow the stream into Cwm-coch from the same road at 641612. 1 hour should suffice to reach either climbing area. As there is neither right of way nor path into either cwm and mountain walls and fences without stiles may be encountered, climbers are requested to keep a low profile until they reach open country.

This splendid mountain with its classic NE ridge seen in silhouette from Ogwen is totally inaccessible to walkers from the north and east. Its rugged north-easterly aspect is hardly breached throughout its 500m length and even its classic ridge has a few shocks in store for the ambitious scrambler. This ridge, **Yr Esgair** separates the Ogwen-facing **East Face** and **Cwm-coch** from the Bethesda facing **North Face** and **Cwm Bual**. Both are steep and in true winter conditions each has a serious, almost Alpine feel. Lines are vague and exposure is immense; there is a feeling of isolation up here, lording it over wild, deserted cwms and the climbing is intricate and thought-provoking, although rarely technical. Most of the routes described have much to recommend them and **The Curver** is probably the most striking line in the whole Ogwen valley.

As one approaches the **East Face** up **Cwm-coch**, a ragged line of crags rears up on the left. Described by J.M.Archer-Thomson as 'the most important addition to the climber's domain since the annexation of Craig yr Ysfa in 1900', and more recently returned to nature and obscurity, this is **Creigiau Gleision**, and its right-hand edge is defined by the obvious wide descent gully, **Easy Gully**. The convex **East Face** looms to the right, turning the corner into **Cwm Bual** and the **North Face** as if folded along the crest of the ridge of **Yr Esgair**. This **North Face** has few features, but a shallow depression running the height of the face on the right and an area of steep ice-falls low down on the left are convenient points of reference.

Descent:
Either descend Easy Gully into Cwm-coch or regain Cwm Bual from the col (626616) between Foel Goch and Mynedd Perfydd. If trying to locate Easy Gully in poor visibility do not follow the fence line but leave it on your right and follow the top of the crags around to gain a small col before the ridge rises slightly to the crest of Creigiau Gleision.

The first four climbs are on **Creigiau Gleision**

FUNGUS GULLY   150m   I
This is the wide snowy gully on the extreme left-hand end of the crag and is situated between two broken, rocky ribs. Sometimes called Eastern Gully, it is more obvious from the road than from its foot!

NEEDLE'S EYE ARÊTE   150m   III
The rib on the right-hand side of the previous route gives an interesting outing under exceptional conditions of heavy, consolidated snow. It is exposed with numerous blocks and pinnacles and may be started from some way up Fungus Gully.

BUTTRESS GULLY   100m   II
In the centre of the crag is a buttress which is more continuous than any of the others. This gully runs up the left-hand side of it, starting up ledges from the right and containing a couple of narrow steps.

BUTTRESS CHIMNEY   100m   III   *
To the right of the buttress is the best line on the crag - a deep rightward-slanting chimney with a chockstone which leads to an easier snow bay above. Although it holds little ice it offers a good mixed climb.

EASY GULLY   130m   I
In the corner between the East Face of Foel Goch and Creigiau Gleision is a gentle snow slope. It just about qualifies as a climb, although it is probably closer to the horizontal than the vertical.

RED GULLY   150m   I/II   *
The very deep twisting gully just right of Easy Gully is straightforward apart from a steep section near the top.

RED FACE   160m   II/III
The buttress to the right is easier-angled than it appears and gives an interesting climb under good snow.
1. 60m (2)   Start near the foot of Red Gully and follow an

obvious rake slanting up to the right onto the crest of the slabby buttress.

2. 50m (3)   Move up easier ground on the right then climb a steeper section.

3. 50m (1)   A uniform snow slope (avalanche danger) leads to the summit ridge.

THE CURVER 170m III ★★

A fine line curving up to the right in the centre of the face. It is readily seen from the A5, and fortunately is not as steep as it appears from the car! It is a shallow corner which gradually lies back as one proceeds. The first pitch is the most difficult, and as it holds little ice, an ascent should be reserved for a day when the snow is iron hard.

EAST FACE ROUTE 180m IV ★★

An expedition of great character linking the obvious snow-fields on the face left of the ridge of Yr Esgair. The exact line taken will vary with conditions and from leader to leader. Some skill at route finding would be an asset. Start right of and at a higher level than The Curver.

YR ESGAIR 180m II/III ★★

Probably the most eyed yet least climbed ridge in Snowdonia, it gives a fine outing in winter and should 'go' in any conditions. Approach the notch at the start of the 'up' part of the ridge either along the long, horizontal knife-edged arête (dancers) or via Esgair Gully from Cwm Bual (cavers). The upper section of the ridge is stoutly defended by the first 15m - a steep narrow fin of rock which rears alarmingly above the gully on the right and saves its crux for the top. Brave purists will ignore the advice given here and attempt it direct - and retreat! Others will tackle the steep icy slabs to the left - and fail! The wise will descend the gully on the right for 8m or so and climb a short, icy corner to gain a faint turfy ledge leading rightwards to easier ground. The ridge can be regained after a bit and followed directly without further difficulty (1/2).

ESGAIR GULLY 100m I ★

The gully which approaches the foot of Yr Esgair directly from Cwm Bual. It is deep and twisting and the steep ice smears plunging down the walls on the right add to the atmosphere. A fence leads directly into the gully from the bed of the cwm. Descent into Cwm-coch from the top of the gully is straightforward for those not wishing to carry on up the ridge.

THE NORTH FACE 200m I/II ★★
Connoisseurs of frozen vegetation will appreciate the effectiveness of modern ice gear on this all-weather route. Follow the obvious shallow depression to the right of centre, finishing just right of the summit.

2.10 CARNEDD Y FILIAST

Grid Reference: 623627 (OS Sheet 115 Snowdon)
Altitude: 550m - 800m
Aspect: East
Climbing Conditions:
The two gullies require consolidated snow, which is fairly rare, but The Ribbon is a drainage line which may be climbed after a period of hard frost.
Approach:
Follow the stream up into Cwm Graianog from Tai-newyddion (630635) on the minor road on the west side of the Ogwen Valley. The foot of the climbs may be reached in about 1 hour.

The climbing is situated in the magnificent east-facing amphitheatre of **Cwm Graianog** which has a unique character amongst these mountains. The slopes beneath the summit of **Carnedd y Filiast** are layered with the most unusual rock slabs; vast, rippled and feature-less. The largest of these, **Atlantic Slab**, is well-named! The angle is modest but the scale is massive. There are two major gullies: **The Runnel** high up on the left, with a blunt arête on its left and the smooth expanse of **Atlantic Slab** immediately on its right. To the right, beyond a prominent area of overlapping slabs is **Wave Gully**, a wide, easy-angled highway. There can be few finer places to be than high on this complex face as the feeble sun peers round the shoulder of **Pen-yr-ole-wen** on a frosty winter's morn.

Descent:
The fastest descent is to follow the top edge of the crags steeply down to the ENE from the summit to gain the road, but better perhaps, is to head SE to the col before Mynedd Perfydd and descend the spur to the east of the col, steeply at first, but with fine views of your climb.

THE RUNNEL 300m II ★
Easy ground following the stream bed leads into the steepening, narrowing upper section where the difficulty increases sharply. The temptation to escape onto the oceanic slabs to the right can usually be resisted!

Right of **Atlantic Slab** are a number of overlapping ribs and grooves. The next climb takes a tenuous line of ice which snakes down the slab to the right of the central of the three main grooves.

THE RIBBON   160m   IV   *
Scramble up to the terrace at the foot of the ice smear.
1. 80m   (2/3)   Climb the easy-angled smear with neither runners nor belays (unless it is exceptionally thick!) until it rejoins the groove on the left.
2. 80m   (2/3)   Continue, with less fear, up the groove to the top.

WAVE GULLY   250m   I
To the right the wide gully beneath the curious 'waved' slab gives a straightforward climb on snow - if it has snow in it!

Undoubtedly, in a good winter there would be a number of other winter climbs in this unusual area and it would certainly repay a day of quiet exploration under these conditions.

3. LLANBERIS

Beris, the town, lies at one end; a microcosm of Snowdonia with its past and present laid bare; a town of contrasts and conflicts, growth and decay: and at the other, a car park (a Youth Hostel and café too, of course - but mostly a car park). And in between, the Pass, THE pass; five miles of badly engineered road and a living record of Welsh Climbing.

From here the climbing chameleon can change his skin as he crosses the road: tights and T-shirt for the sun-kissed walls on the north side; gloves and gaiters for the frost-nipped facades to the south. Two worlds, two games, one Pass: Left Wall, Right Wall, Ice Wall: same day, somedays.

Low down on both sides the routes are uncomplicated; curtains of water-ice in sheets or columns, some steep, some less so; all obvious. But high on the flanks of Crib Goch and Crib y Ddysgl, that's where the real winter is. Rime-ice, snow-ice, water-ice: powder snow, wet snow, firm snow: winter-time, sometimes.

The Pass has everything. Not, it must be admitted, all at the same time; but keep coming back and its winter secrets will slowly be revealed. Fight for survival at the cornice of Parsley Fern in a storm; go on tip-toe up a slender Cascade with your heart in your mouth; squirm in the icy blackness behind the Jammed Boulder; or trace the slender ribbon of Bryant's Gully to its source amidst the rotting columns of Esgair Felen. Or just go ice cragging by the roadside.

Whatever your winter bent the Pass of Llanberis and its towering flanks can provide it. You only have to make the effort.

3.1 SHORT CLIMBS IN AND AROUND LLANBERIS

THE SLATE QUARRIES

The Llanberis quarries have many hidden and esoteric little ice-falls, the following being a selection of the better finds. Needless to say, their presence requires a prolonged spell of intense cold.

Up at the BUS STOP QUARRY (592612), an ice smear forms to the left of Scarlet Runner on the Rippled Slab. This is **THE TUBE**, (**4**) and serious. Around in the bay to the left lies another steep ice-fall, **UN-NAMED ICE-FALL** (**5**).

Down in the VIVIAN QUARRY the big bay that contains LOVE MINUS ZERO has a steep ice pillar in the back corner. **JUST ANOTHER UN-NAMED ICE-FALL** (**4/5**).

In the RAINBOW area, the watercourse of **FROGS** has been climbed at (**4**), as has a fall, **WHITEMATE** (**5**), that often forms in the LOST WORLD behind TWLL MAWR.

LLANBERIS

Llanberis itself contains a smart little gem in the shape of the **WATERFALL** (**4**), (578593) found by taking the *Cloggy* road from opposite the Victoria Hotel and following the signs. Needless to say the crux of the route is crossing the thinly-iced pool to start the fall (**7**)!

It should be pointed out that these ice-falls are often very short lived, and that falling ice is somewhat heavy...

3.2 LLANBERIS PASS - NORTH SIDE

The north side of the Llanberis Pass presents a very contrasting appearance to that of the south side. Catching any sunshine, more often found in winter than summer these days, the snow departs as quickly as it falls leaving the ice-falls and deeper gullies to gleam amidst the brown and green of the heather. The sunshine and the roadside nature of the climbing here obviously appeals to the 'Tremadog Set' and a cold weekend sees the hillside swarming with winter 'craggers' jangling with gear.

Altitude: 200m - 820m
Aspect: South West
Climbing Conditions:
Most of the climbs are at a relatively low altitude and in addition are subject to direct sunlight for the greater part of the day. The routes are thus only possible in sustained periods of very low temperatures. They form almost entirely of water-ice, although snow cover would add to the interest. The most attractive feature of the climbs is their roadside position. One or two of the easier ice-falls may even, on occasion, be started from the road.

In general, the routes take normally damp and broken gullies although some form where drainage lines weep over steep rock faces. All the climbs are worthwhile and the easier routes provide a good introduction to the vagaries of water-ice climbing. The harder, hanging ice-falls provide difficult test pieces although a minor Ice Age is required to bring all the lines into condition.

Approach:
All of the climbs are obvious from the road and may be gained directly up the hillside via the summer paths in some cases.

NANT PERIS WATERFALL   80m   III
(621580)
Reached by following the Ogwen path from Gwastadnant until level with the ice and then traversing across the hillside to the stream. This provides a couple of good pitches of ice before the angle eases.

CRAIG DDU
Grid Reference: 618574 (OS Sheet 115 Snowdon)

The most westerly of the crags and the first one encountered when driving up the Pass from Llanberis. Damp and treacherously slippery in summer, the cliff often sports a conspicuous set of ice-falls on its left-hand side.
Descent:
From the top of the crag, traverse well over to the left (W) before descending to arrive easily at the foot of the left-hand end of the crag.

SHORT TREE CHIMNEY   60m   II/III
The ice forms down both sides of a prominent small buttress at the left end of the crag. The left-hand is formed more often: both falls leading to a ledge and tree belay (3). Finish as directly as possible and belay well back (3).

CROWN OF THORNS   50m   IV   **
This fine ice-fall lies a few metres to the right of the previous route,

and follows a line to the left of the summer route. Climb up to gain a ledge on the right at 15m (belay possible) before climbing steep ice to pass an overlap via a chandelier of ice (4). Above a short ice-slab leads to a tree belay.

An alternative finish can be made by following the summer line rightwards to the top. This can be easier or harder depending upon prevailing conditions.

Some 15m right of the previous route, ice streams over a small roof high on the crag, spreading out to form a broken sheet and petering out into mixed ground near the bottom. This provides a strenuous and precarious climb which is rarely in condition.

TERMINATOR 70m VI
Start just left of a vague bay and climb rock and ice past grassy ledges to gain a short crack leading to a niche and peg belay (5). Continue up right, then left, to reach the ice-fall proper by a very hard series of moves (poor protection). Climb the ice directly over the roof to reach ice-slabs and the top (6).

CLOGWYN Y GROCHAN
Grid Reference: 620572 (OS Sheet 115 Snowdon)

This large crag lies directly above a point on the road where there are lay-bys on either side of the road. It is divided into thirds by Goats' Gully on the left and Central Gully on the right and is bounded on each side by deeper clefts.

Descent:
This is best achieved by walking up and over to the left (W) to reach a large ramp running down above the left-hand end of Craig Ddu. Alternatively, go right (E) with care on a sheep track which crosses Short Gully near the top to gain the Carreg Wastad descent screes.

ARCTURUS LEFT-HAND 50m IV

ARCTURUS RIGHT-HAND 50m IV
The steep ice that falls on the left side of the Descent Gully provides two lines that climb up to reach tree belays. Non-David Bellamys will abseil off!

DESCENT GULLY 140m II *
This is the deep left-hand bounding gully of the crag. Follow ice steps directly into the depths, the final section providing a steep and interesting crux (3). A good route.

GOATS' GULLY 110m V
This hanging gully, bounded on each side by steep rock, may contain

the mythical ice-fall that provides entry to the upper gully. It probably appears just as the beer in the Padarn Lake Hotel freezes up!
1.   50m   Climb the ice on the right wall and continue up steep ice until it eases and a tree belay is reached.
2.   60m   The easier upper gully would require snow fill to be worthwhile.

CENTRAL GULLY   50m   V   **

This is the deep stepped gully right of the last route, again requiring a period of hard frosts to form. However, this very good climb is in condition a lot more often that GOATS' GULLY and is worth waiting for.
1.   15m   (3)   Climb straightforward ice into the back of the gully.
2.   35m   (5)   The ice forms on the right wall which is climbed first rightwards, then back left over very steep ice to gain the upper gully. A fine exposed pitch.
3.   70m   (4)   The upper gully is followed over several short ice-pitches. Snow fill would again provide a more pleasant finish.

BROADMOOR   50m   V/VI

In the centre of the right-hand of the crag a hanging corner weeps a large icicle which provides the substance of this difficult little route.
1.   30m   (6)   Start below the corner and climb icy rock to the overhang. This is passed (with an aid point on the first ascent) to gain the ice wall above. Belay high on the right.
2.   20m   (5)   Gain the main ice-fall and climb the right-hand side to reach a tree belay. Abseil off, unless exceptional conditions allow you to 'boldly go where...'

CAULDRON GULLY   120m   II   **

The right-hand bounding cleft of the crag provides another fine stepped ice-fall. The stream can be started as low as the ice permits - from the road on occasion - although the true gully starts at the point where it narrows and steepens. From here a number of ice steps are climbed, steep if taken direct, to reach a well positioned final steep pitch which finishes suddenly on the hillside above.

The ice-fall on the left wall at two thirds height can be climbed to give a much harder (4) finish, but care should be taken to establish the integrity of its attachment to the rock beneath.

CARREG WASTAD

Grid Reference: 625571 (OS Sheet 115 Snowdon)

Although this orange-tinged crag boasts no winter routes, it is a good reference point for the two climbs that lies to either side. It is directly across the road from Ynys Ettws, the Climbers' Club hut.

SHORT GULLY   100m   II   *

This frozen watercourse lies a little to the left of the large scree runnel that bounds the left-hand side of the cliff (and provides the descent path). It is similar to Cauldron Gully, being a series of ice steps, but is more open and the steepest parts can be avoided. The best line takes each step as steeply as possible!

BRYANT'S GULLY   500m   II   **

The gully that climbs into the deep split 30m to the right of the crag is the starting point for this interesting line. It is rarely in condition over its whole length, as this would require both consolidated snow cover higher up and water-ice lower down.

1.   130m   The frozen stream enters a stepped gully which can be quite hard if taken directly. This section is worthwhile on its own.

2.   170m   The lower gully pays out into a snow trough climbing the open hillside.

3.   200m   The true continuation, the rocky right-hand branch runs up to the right of the crags of Esgair Felin above.

3a.   200m   The left-hand branch runs up to meet Esgair Felin where the either of the twin gullies of Tweedledum and Tweedledee may be taken to provide a deep finish.

DINAS CROMLECH

Grid Reference: 629569 (OS Sheet 115 Snowdon)

This impressive fortress of rock, characterised by the open book formation of Cenotaph Corner with its Left and Right Walls, lies above the lay-bys at Pont Y Cromlech (next to the famous Cromlech Boulders). The winter climbs lie to either side of the main crag and start much lower down.

Descent:
From the next two areas it is best to descend the hillside to the left of the ice-falls, whilst easy ways down can be found anywhere from Finger and Thumb gullies.

CROMLECH ICE-FALLS   50m   2-4

This is the wide band of ice-falls that are obvious from the road. They can be tackled anywhere according to taste, although care should be taken with loose rocks at the top. It is an excellent area for introducing novices to ice-climbing; the steepest sections usually sport an ego-tripper pleading for a top rope rescue!

FORTRESS GULLY 70m II/III *

Towards the right-hand end of the ice-falls lies a deeper and more distinct gully slanting up to the right. This provides two or three good pitches before petering out on the hillside above, the middle section being quite steep.

Across on the right-hand side of the Cromlech and running up from the flat valley bottom above Pont Y Cromlech are two streams that provide a good introduction to crampon technique. There are also a number of short steep ice-falls on the hillside inbetween.

FINGER GULLY 200m I/II

The left-hand stream gully of the two.

THUMB GULLY 200m I/II

The right-hand stream gully which passes the rock pillar of the Thumb.

LLANBERIS PASS - SOUTH SIDE

In contrast to the north side, climbing is possible on the south side of the Pass from the first frost until the last snows melt on Crib y Ddysgl. The whole area faces generally north and ranges in altitude from 250m to over 1,000m, providing an excellent selection of climbs of all difficulties. A series of routes starting on the lowest crags and culminating on the summit of Crib y Ddysgl would provide a superb 'Alpine day'.

3.3 CRAIG CWM BEUDY MAWR

Grid Reference: 630555 (OS Sheet 115 Snowdon)
Altitude: 500m - 600m
Aspect: NE
Climbing Conditions:
A good spell of cold weather is needed and some consolidated snow will help to fill-out the naturally icy lines, although some sport can be had on the water-ice alone. The crag can be seen from the road and the presence (or absence!) of an ice-fall on the right-hand side will give some indication of conditions.
Approach:
Either approach from **Pont y Cromlech** (629566) by walking 300m up the road and following one of two parallel streams into the cwm or follow the PYG track from **Pen y Pass** to within 100m of **Bwlch y Moch** before heading down to the right for 250m to the foot of the crag.

Cwm Beudy Mawr contains a number of small crags of which only the highest is of interest to winter climbers. Despite its proximity to the PYG track it is rarely visited and for this reason alone it deserves the attention of anyone

who aspires to climbs in the middle grades and wants to get away from the
crowds. It's not a hugely impressive crag but the climbs are pleasant, undaunt-
ing and set at a civilised angle. 'Tickers' will probably complete all the routes
on one visit whilst mountaineers will use the crag as a warm-up on the way to
the vast and complex **East Face** of **Crib Goch** above.

The crag is roughly fan-shaped, with an area of overhangs on the left,
bounded on the right by the excellent **Dodo Gully**. This is a very obvious icy
V-groove running the full height of the crag. To the right the rock is more
broken although a number of drainage lines offer pleasant, if slight, routes in
good conditions. Right again, a long, broken rib separates this area from the
deep, icy gully of **Pterodactyl**, with its prominent hanging ice-fall on the right
at the top.

Descent:
The rib to the right of **Pterodactyl** affords an easy return to the foot of the
crag.

DODO GULLY 100m III *
The obvious V-shaped gully just right of the overhangs on the left of
the crag is climbed directly with an escape to the right at the top to
easier ground. The first half forms an excellent ice-runnel but the
upper section needs a little snow.

DODO BUTTRESS 100m III
Some 15m to the right a line of ice smears descends the buttress in a
series of grooves and ledges and provides some interesting mixed
climbing.

To the right, a broad rake slopes up above a small broken buttress
before running into the broken rib to the right. The next two climbs
start from this rake.

GOGO GOCH 90m II/III
A line up iced slabs some 20m right of Dodo Buttress.

GOGO GULLY 90m II/III
The gully bounded on the right by the long broken rib at the top of the
rake.
1. 45m (2) Easily up ice-bulges in the shallow gully to a fork.
2. 45m (3) The left fork leads easily to the top of Gogo Goch but
keep right, passing an interesting chockstone by an iced wall on its left
to gain the easy upper gully.

PTERODACTYL 100m II/III *
Beyond the long rib and starting lower down is a deep gully with an
obvious ice-fall high on the right. This provides the major drainage
line on the crag.

1.   65m   (2/3)   Pleasant ice-bulges in the gully lead to a fork, above which there are three options.

2a. 35m   (2)   The right branch is short lived and straightforward.

2b. 35m   (2/3)   The better left fork leads to the top via an iced V-cleft beneath the vertical ice-fall.

2c. 30m   (4)   The ice-fall itself may be climbed by bridging up the cleft and swinging rightwards. The further one goes up the cleft the easier it becomes!

3.4   CRIB GOCH

Grid Reference: 625553 (OS Sheet 115 Snowdon)
Altitude: 921m

A fine mountain with two interesting ridges and a magnificent traverse. A number of fatal accidents throughout the years underlines the seriousness of this mountain in winter conditions. The routes 'go' under virtually any conditions but fresh snow or névé would be best.

EAST RIDGE   I   *
Gained from the PYG track at Bwlch y Moch (the col overlooking Llyn Llydaw), this provides the easiest approach to the summit. The ridge steepens to provide some good mixed climbing before easing slightly to the top.

EAST FACE   I   *
This face, often in condition, can be gained by traversing across from the PYG track or directly from the top of Craig Cwm Beudy Mawr. A variety of lines can be taken and the face has an Alpine feel about it. Be wary of stonefall though, especially when the ridges are crowded.

NORTH RIDGE   I   *
Approach from Pont y Cromlech around either side of Dinas Mot, or from Cwm Beudy Mawr, to gain the steep initial slopes. Near the top the ridge narrows and the final 100m can be tricky especially when verglassed.

CRIB GOCH - CRIB Y DDYSGL TRAVERSE   I   ***
From the summit of CRIB GOCH the traverse to CRIB Y DDYSGL provides a classic expedition of great quality, although serious and often underestimated in winter. Interest is sustained beyond the classic 'knife-edge' between the summit of Crib Goch, with further

difficulties occuring on the descent from the Crib Goch Pinnacles to Bwlch Goch and on the iced rocks leading to the final ridge of CRIB Y DDYSGL, an accident black spot.

The only feasible escape from the ridge is north or south from Bwlch Goch and both these ways are initially very steep and can be serious in genuine winter conditions. The descent into Cwm Glas to the north is the easiest from here, although escape from the upper cwm itself is never easy in bad weather, or with a lot of ice on the ground.

CRIB Y DDYSGL - CRIB GOCH TRAVERSE I ***
Although simply the reverse of the previous route it contains an additional navigational hazard. Parties have come to grief by mistakenly following the upper part of the Clogwyn Y Person Arête down into steep terrain. The wrong ridge is deceptively easy at first, 50° magnetic, and leads onto hard icy slopes. The TRUE path, rocky, runs east on Magnetic Bearing 105°. The main difficulties are the icy rocks leading from Crib y Ddysgl down to Bwlch Goch, and later on crossing the Crib Goch Pinnacles.

As with the east-west traverse, escape from the ridge is problematic.

CRIB GOCH: NORTH WEST FACE

Grid Reference: 623552 (OS Sheet 115 Snowdon)
Altitude: 760m - 920m
Aspect: NW

The face above Cwm Uchaf is somewhat featureless and routes could be forced anywhere in good conditions. However, the following climbs are worthwhile. Being shallow features, the first two are difficult to identify under heavy snow.

ARCHER THOMPSON'S ROUTE 150m III
This takes the shallow gully in the centre of the face left of Crib Goch Buttress.

CARR'S ROUTE 150m III
A shallow depression just left of Crib Goch Buttress is followed with interest.

CRAZY PINNACLE GULLY 100m II/III
A short route in the weakness between Crazy Pinnacle Buttress and the main crag. Easy snow leads left to the foot of the gully, which is followed with the crux at the chockstone.

3.5 DINAS MOT

Grid Reference: 625563 (OS Sheet 115 Snowdon)
Altitude: 300m - 430m
Aspect: North
Climbing Conditons:
Although low in altitude, the crag receives considerable drainage from the hillside above and in very cold conditions several good ice-falls develop. Some are openly visible from the road; others lurk deep in clefts that cleave the hillside; almost all are worthwhile.
Approach:
Any route can be gained from the Cromlech car park in 15 minutes. Wet feet can be avoided by using the stile at Pont y Cromlech!
Descent:
The safest way down is by heading left (SE) around the hillside above the main section of the crag until a broad scree/snow slope can be gained running back towards the road. This can be followed to the base of the crag. Do not attempt to descend any of the steep gullies passed on the way. The alternative is to traverse a long way around the hillside rightwards (NW) until the large gully between Dinas Mot and Craig y Rhaeadr can be located and followed down, with care, to easy ground. This descent is best for climbs right of Black Cleft unless a return to the foot of the main crag is contemplated.

The most obvious feature of the crag is the Nose, a smooth sweep of rock, roughly triangular in shape, that dominates the steep rock buttresses on the left-hand side. In the centre is the large slanting break of Jammed Boulder Gully just left of the split of the Black Cleft. To the right the crag appears more broken, but a number of ice smears can be made out before the crag fades into the hillside left of Craig y Rhaeadr.

STAIRCASE GULLY 100m III
This follows a curving line up the left-hand side of the East Wing on the extreme left of the crag. Start up and left of the lowest rocks of the Nose.
1. 45m The lower section contains a number of good ice-falls which lead to where the gully steepens.
2. 55m The gully steepens to the right and contains less ice. Hard at first, easing towards the top.

Across the sweep of the Nose and separating it from the main mass of the West Wing behind, is a parallel-sided, slanting break, which is commonly used as a summer descent from climbs on the Nose.

WESTERN GULLY 80m III
With good snow cover this gives an entertaining mixed climb with an often difficult start. Start below the gully.
1. 20m (3/4) Usually, either of two short ice-falls can be

climbed to reach the base of the gully.
2. 60m (3)   Mixed climbing up snow-covered, ledged rock leads to the summit of the Nose.

The Eastern Gully, defining the other side of the Nose, provides a problematical descent (abseil?), the combination being a good outing.

A short technical problem has been climbed up the ice smear that forms on the steep black slab to the right of Western Gully; WHITE TRASH, 40m (5), abseil off from pegs at the overlap.

The first major break in the crag, 200m to the right of the Nose and starting at a higher level is:

JAMMED BOULDER GULLY 110m III **
An interesting and popular route which is best after hard frosts. Start after gaining a ledge leading to the bottom of the gully from the right. Take care not to wander too far up the gully as roping-up is not easy once the ice has been engaged!
1. 45m (2/3)   Scramble easily to the start of the ice, and carry on up icy ledges to reach a tree and stance beneath the huge chockstone.
2. 20m (4)   Either up the groove on the right steeply until it is possible to step left onto the top of the chockstone, or, with amusement and not a little difficulty, climb the 'through route' under the chockstone to reach the same ledge. Interesting in deep snow!
3. 45m (2)   The easier upper gully leads to the open hillside.

JAMMED BOULDER BUTTRESS 95m IV/III *
A serious route on brittle and often thin ice taking the iced slabs to the right of Jammed Boulder Gully. Start at the foot of the gully.
1. 50m (4)   Climb the ice to the right of the gully to reach a ledge with a small tree above the level of the chockstone.
2. 45m (3)   Follow the best line steeply up to the left to reach an exit onto easy ground which can sometimes be awkward. Good belays well back.

Right of the last two routes and above the approach path is a deep, dark gash in the crag,

BLACK CLEFT 90m IV/III **
The dank gully is often thinly iced and gives some awkward moments. However, when in condition, it gives a classic outing. Start at the base of the gully and climb easily into the depths.
1. 25m (5)   The initial problem is a steep chimney corner, poorly iced which gains a ledge.
2. 20m (4)   Thin ice on the right wall is climbed over a bulge to a

large stance.
3. 45m (3) Short ice steps lead up right, easing towards the top.

Right again is the steep rock of Plexus Buttress which eventually breaks back into an open bowl of broken vegetated ground bounded on its left by a shallow gully containing a number of small trees in its snowy upper part and ice-slabs below.

The descent for this and the remaining routes on Dinas Mot is the rightward (NW) alternative, following ledges around towards the foot of Craig y Rhaeadr.

SAPLING GULLY 130m III
A pleasant climb which requires both hard frosts and some snow to fill the upper gully. Start slightly right of the line of the upper gully at an area of steep iced slabs.
1. 35m (2/3) Climb the slabs and trend leftwards to the foot of an obvious slabby ice-filled groove.
2. 15m (2) Climb the perfect groove to the foot of the gully proper.
3. 80m (3) Climb the gully over various bulges, chockstones and trees, with more interest than is apparent from below.

In the centre of the bowl a large ice-sheet sweeps in two steps from easy broken ground and leads to a hidden, left-slanting ice-filled gully.

WESTERN STEPPES 130m II/III
A disjointed route, but offering some interesting short pitches. Start below the obvious stepped ice-sheets.
1. 10m (3) The first step.
2. 15m (3) The second step.
3. 80m (1) Scramble to the foot of the hidden, left-slanting gully.
4. 25m (2/3) Climb the icy runnel, fairly easy-angled, to reach snow and the top.

Right of the bowl there are more steep rocks. However, high in the centre of this final buttress is a deep V-gash containing a fine 30m ice-fall which forks near the top. It is directly above and easily seen from Ynys Ettws.

THE CHUTE 40m III/IV *
An elegant pitch in a fine situation again requiring hard frosts. Start below the gully.
1. 10m (2) Climb a short step trending leftwards to a tree belay.
2. 30m (4) Move up to the ice in the back of the deep gash and

climb it to the fork. The steeper left-hand branch will appeal to some, but most will continue up the right branch with relief.

Beneath this area large slabs of easy-angled ice form with some steeper steps, and provide a good area for the novice to try out crampon techniques.

3.6 CRAIG Y RHAEADR

Grid Reference: 620561 (OS Sheet 115 Snowdon)
Altitude: 460m - 580m
Aspect: North
Climbing Conditions:
In a hard winter this normally repulsive looking crag is transformed into a superb white mesh of ice-falls, and provides the stage for some of Snowdonia's most spectacular and popular hard ice routes. The routes are described with respect to the Pedestal, the large triangular rock at the centre of the base of the crag.
Approach:
The routes can be reached by the main Cwm Glas path and then across left to the crag, in 30 minutes from the road.
Descent:
Go well back and around to the right to return to the foot of the cliffs.

CHEQUERED WALL   100m   VI   *

This difficult route takes the ice-streak to the left of the Pedestal, passing to the left of the upper overhang. It is less frequently complete and usually much less thick than the main falls to the right, thus offering a more serious proposition.
1.   30m   Start just to the left of the Pedestal. Climb up left on thin ice, then back right steeply to a stance on the Pedestal summit.
2.   40m   Move up to gain an ice-ramp leading up left to a short groove. Mixed climbing up this leads to a step onto the ice which is followed to a stance at the left end of the overhangs.
3.   30m   Step left around the overhang and move up and right along a snowy ramp to gain a short corner which leads to easy ground.

CENTRAL ICE-FALL DIRECT   100m   VI   ***

This superb climb is only in condition in prolonged cold spells and provides steep climbing with a spectacular and well-positioned climax.
1.   35m   (5)   Start at the centre of the Pedestal. Climb the very steep ice-streaks up the front face of the Pedestal (possible belay), and then up rightwards to a ledge and belays.
2.   35m   (6)   Traverse back left onto the ice and climb it trending

left to a stance under the left side of the overhangs (shared with Chequered Wall). A very sustained pitch.

3. 30m (6)   An icicle may descend from the roof to reach the steep ice below. If it does, move right with an awkward move to get established before climbing steeply to easier ground the top - an outstanding pitch. If it doesn't, a grappling iron may be of some use!

On recent ascents the belay at the end of pitch 2 has often been taken to the right of the icicle. This will depend upon the formation of the ice and the amount of in-situ gear left by previous teams.

WATERFALL CLIMB 135m IV **

Despite being overshadowed by the more direct routes, this is an interesting excursion which weaves its way up the cliff, taking a reasonable line through impressively steep terrain. Start at the right-hand side of the Pedestal.

1. 30m (3)   Climb the groove behind the Pedestal, steep initially, then leftwards up the ramp to belay below the main ice-fall.
2. 15m (5)   Steeply up the ice-fall to a good ledge and belay along on the right.
3. 25m (3)   Continue right across the next ice-fall along the break and belay on its far side.
4. 40m (4)   Climb mixed ground steeply up to the right, then a spiky wall to the right again leads to frozen turf and so to a poor belay.
5. 25m (3)   Up frozen rocks and turf more easily to the top.

CASCADE 110m V ***

Another fine route which takes the right-hand ice-fall. Popular, but the price of incompetence should be obvious. The first pitch is last to form, often thin and difficult to protect.

1. 25m (5)   Start right of the Pedestal below the ice-fall. Straight up the ice to reach a niche at 15m, rock peg. Up again to a ledge and move right to belay.
2. 15m (5)   Move left and up the ice steeply again to the next ledge. Belay on the right.
3. 50m (5)   Regain the ice-fall and climb directly, easing all the time, to a belay on ice-screws at the end of the rope.
4. 20m (3)   Carry on to the top.

CASCADE RIGHT-HAND 100m V *

The narrower, but grooved ice-fall just to the right of Cascade may be followed to give a somewhat more difficult ascent of the ice-sheet. In good conditions it is possible to maintain an independent line all the way to the top, but ice-screw belays will probably be required. Otherwise, return to the parent route for stances.

GROOVED SLAB   100m   IV
50m right of Cascade, beyond two minor buttresses split by a dry groove is an open, left-facing system of corners. To its left is a broken area of vegetated slabs hanging above a steep wall. A ramp and icy runnel on the right provides access to these slabs and the corner is followed to easier ground and the top.

On the right of the crag a number of possibilities exits. A steep chimney rises above a 6m vertical ice-boss and gives interesting mixed climbing above. This is **BOTANY BAY, 80m, IV,** whilst on its right, at the top of a snowy gully, an ice-stream on steep slabs gives another possibility;

MORTUARY SLAB   45m   V
This follows the ice-streak on the right wall of the short open groove and gives a serious pitch. Move right at the top, climb a bulge to easy ground and walk off right.

3.7   CYRN LAS

Grid Reference: 613559 (OS Sheet 115 Snowdon)
Altitude: 550m - 730m
Aspect: North
Climbing Conditions:
The main crag provides little of winter interest unless unusually plastered in snow as it receives only slight drainage. However, the wetter courses to the left and right are often in condition and very popular.
Approach:
Approach to the area is by the main Cwm Glas path beside the stream up from Blaen y Nant.
Descent:
All the routes finish in Cwm Glas, and in order to return to the foot of the crag it is necessary to descend the steep, broken hillside between Sargeant's Gully and the stream to its left (E) which issues from Llyn Glas. This descent can be awkward in icy conditions and crampons should be kept on even if there is no snow on the ground.

SARGEANT'S GULLY   200m   II   **
The main stream from Cwm Glas to the left of the crag freezes into a series of steps of continuous interest. Start by cutting across from the main path to the first obvious ice-fall. This first fall is the steepest but can be turned easily, as can many of the problems (2-4). Taken direct it is a superb introduction for the ice novice, the gully eventually

paying out into the flatter base of Cwm Glas. Although technically much harder, it offers an ideal approach to Parsley Fern Gully or one of the other routes above.

Up on the right, above the upper part of Sargeant's Gully, the top section of **THE CHASMS** often holds snow, **(II)**, but little ice. These are gained by traversing out right across slabs to gain the first of two deep chimneys separated by a terrace.

THE GREAT GULLY 150m III/IV

Unfortunately rather dry with little ice, this climb requires consolidated snow to permit a winter ascent. However, when in condition it is quite a good climb. The gully is the obvious deep gash slicing through the left side of the main crag. Start by climbing the rake to its foot.

1. 35m   Up the snow to below the steepening.
2. 45m   A hard wall leads to easier ground and a cave above.
3. 70m   Turn the chockstone on the left and climb the chimneys which can be very hard in poor conditions.

Two of the three gullies on the right-hand side of the main crag, **SCHOOLMASTER'S GULLY, 85m, III/IV** and **YELLOWSTONE GULLY, 80m, II/III** have had winter ascents, but are not popular as they are rarely in condition. The central gully of the three, DOUBLE CAVE GULLY may also have been climbed in winter, but no record of this exists.

GWTER FAWR   150m   I   *

This is the deep ravine well right of the main crag and under snow gives a good simple climb. From about half height a gully leads off to the right to join the upper, easier pitches of the next route and provides the opportunity to enjoy the delightful upper section of that route without the rigours of the steep ice below.

FACE ROUTE   300m   IV   **

The buttress between Cwm Las and the right-hand bounding ridge of the cwm provides a popular route as drainage from the upper gully forms pleasant ice-falls on the lower crag. Start at the lowest point of the buttress.

1. 70m   (3)   Follow the drainage line over the lower buttress to gain a snow ramp slanting up from the right. This can be used (1) to avoid the lower ice-steps in lean conditions. Go up to belay below the steep ice-falls.
2. 70m   (4)   Climb the central fall directly over a bulge before

following the ice leftwards into the gully on the left.

3. 80m (3) The gully is drier and snowier. It has an interesting chockstone higher up which is turned on the right, before gaining the delightful summit ridge (Gyrn Las Ridge).

4. 80m (2) Follow the ridge in a fine situation to the top.

From the shoulder on the ridge at the top of Face Route, climb up for 50m or so before turning east to descend the right-hand side of the blunt spur which leads down into upper Cwm Glas. This descent is often icy.

On the smooth facet right of Face Route called THE EQUATOR WALLS, improbable looking ice smears often form. Although they do not usually reach the top of the crag, or the bottom, rumour has it that they've been climbed (6). Perhaps they lead to a bolt...?

3.8 CRIB Y DDYSGL

UPPER CWM GLAS

Grid Reference: The cwm lies in Grid Square 6155 (OS Sheet 115 Snowdon)
Altitude: 750m - 1,065m
Aspect: NE to NW
Climbing Conditions:
Together with those on Clogwyn y Garnedd, the climbs from Cwm Glas provide the most consistently good snow conditions in Snowdonia, offering reliable climbing on both snow and ice for a number of weeks each winter. The climbing concentrates on the cliffs of the Clogwyn y Person Arête, and the cwm to its right, upper Cwm Glas.
Approach:
Approach from near Ynys Ettws in the Llanberis Pass (623568) by following the path on the north-west bank of the stream draining Cwm Glas Mawr, into the flat bottom of the lower cwm beneath Cyrn Las. From here, the easiest approach to the upper cwm is via the steep and often icy hillside to the left of Sargeant's Gully (see Cyrn Las) and to the right of the stream draining Llyn Glas. Upper Cwm Glas consists of two shallow depressions, each containing a small lake, and separated by a rounded ridge which is the downward continuation of the Clogwyn y Person Arête. The lake on the left (Llyn Glas) is the larger of the two and has a small island with a few stunted trees growing on it. Once flat ground is reached, it is a simple matter in poor visibility to locate either Llyn Glas to the left, or the flat upper section of the stream above Sargeant's Gully to the right. For Parsley Fern Gully, follow this stream to the back of the cwm in a straight line to the SW until it changes as if by magic, into a winter climb! On this course, the tiny lake (Llyn Bach) will not be encountered as it lies some 50m off to the left beneath the right-hand side of the Parson's Nose.

Descent:
Descent into the cwm can be tricky. From the top of Parsley Fern Gully, go north down easy slopes on the ridge (watch out for cornices on your right) until after 300m or so, one can turn SE, either with great care, or a parachute, and descend the side of the cwm to the flat bottom. Parsley Fern Gully can provide a descent for the competent and a much faster one for the incompetent. Those who are still unsure can descend to Llanberis following the railway, a useful handrail in a storm.

The cwm is dominated by the imposing rocky spur of the Clogwyn y Person Arête, which is like some miniature version of Tower Ridge on Ben Nevis. It is terminated by the aptly named 'Parson's Nose', a smooth, partly-detached triangular buttress with gullies on either side; rather reminiscent of the Douglas Boulder. To the left, the crags are steep and repulsive with unclimbed ice smears; further left, the snows of the funnel-shaped Fantail Gully mark a deterioration into broken hillside which continues all the way round to the north face of Crib Goch.

To the right of the Parson's Nose, the left wall of the main cwm is initially steep, rocky and dry. This is the superb Clogwyn y Ddysgl - superb that is for rock climbing, as it rarely holds sufficient snow or ice to excite readers of this guide. Further right, there seems to be more possibilities as the crag degenerates into broken hillside terminating at length in the classic snow gully of Parsley Fern at the back of the cwm. The other side of the cwm is but a poor relation with easy-angled snow and ice which may be tackled at will.

The first climb lies on the left of the Parson's Nose where an icy rake, the Parson's Progress leads SE under the steep, repulsive cliffs. 300m along this is a broken snow gully.

FANTAIL GULLY   150m   I
This broad gully can sometimes be quite icy and leads out onto a fan-shaped snow-field above.

The fine arête above the nose is taken by:

THE CLOGWYN Y PERSON ARÊTE   200m   II/III   **
An interesting mixed climb in a fine position. It can be quite difficult, though always possible in poor conditions. Start by taking either the East or West Gullies, the latter being somewhat easier to gain the bridge of the nose via a short chimney section (3). From here, tackle the right-hand side of the ridge where problems between ledges provide interest. These last for about 150m. Above, the ridge widens and eases, and eventually joins the Horseshoe Path to the summit trig point of Crib y Ddysgl.

The huge cliff of Clogwyn y Ddysgl to the R of the nose contains some rock routes that have been ascended in winter, but these appear to remain rock climbs in poor condition, rather than true winter routes. However, one line in the centre of the cliff holds snow well enough to merit description.

CHURCH BUTTRESS 175m IV

Start at the foot of the summer climb Fallen Block Crack (an obvious cleft marked by the eponymous block).

1. 45m (5)   Climb the chimney, technically difficult but safe, to reach a belay high on the right.

2. 30m (4)   Step down to gain a ramp line leading up right-wards. Follow this past one hard section to a spike belay below another difficult step.

3. 45m (3)   Continue in the same line over a crevasse to reach a large jumble of blocks, The Vestry.

4. 25m (4)   Traverse right with difficulty to gain a deep square-cut chimney/groove, the right wall of which is climbed to a terrace.

5. 30m (3)   Take the continuation line past one steep section to reach the crest of the Clogwyn y Person Arête.

Running up beneath this area of the crag is the next winter line:

THE RAMP 450m II *

A wide, easy-angled ramp runs up beneath the foot of the main cliff and above the lowest, slabby rocks. This is followed, on snow, up rightwards for mile upon mile, linking a number of snow-fields and finishing near the summit of the mountain, crossing the next three routes. An interesting excursion which can be varied by heading up leftwards through steep broken ground from high up to gain the ridge somewhat left of the summit.

WATERSLIDE GULLY 155m IV **

Not often in condition, this is the steep gully in a corner to the left of the rightmost buttress of the cliff, and is gained by following The Ramp up to below the gully, which can be seen to divide higher up.

1. 15m   Climb up to the start of a steep gully/chimney.

2. 35m   Ascend the very steep chimney with difficulty, particu-larly if thinly iced, then go right up an icy groove.

3. 105m   Follow the gully up right to the ridge.

Variation: The left branch of the gully can be taken, but the rock is appalling higher up, so good conditions are required.

INFIDELITY 335m IV **

An interesting line up the right-hand margin of the crag, giving sustained climbing up thinly iced grooves and walls. It may prove easier under heavy snow. Start at the foot of the lower buttress, some 80m below and well to the right of the foot of Waterslide Gully, at a snowy groove which leads up to a wider shallow gully above.

1. 40m (3) Climb the groove to where it opens out.
2. 30m (2) Follow the open gully above to a sloping terrace. A shallow chimney arrives here from the left.
3. 45m (3) Move leftwards down the terrace for 5m and climb icy grooves and frozen vegetation leftwards to a larger terrace. Go up a short step to belay right of a blunt, slabby arête. (This point is 50m right of Waterslide Gully, on The Ramp, and may be reached by that route.) A more direct line to here via a long, right-facing corner further left would give a better, more logical start, but was insufficiently iced on the first ascent.
4. 50m (5) Follow a narrow ledge around to the left to reach thinly iced grooves. Follow these, sustained, to easier ground and a good thread belay.
5. 45m (4) Take easy ice over a couple of bulges to reach a steepening ice-fall. This is climbed, old ring peg out on the right, to a belay on the right.
6. 45m (4) Move back left and follow the steep ice-runnel past a jammed block to easy ground.
7. 80m (2) Up easy mixed ground to the ridge.

SINISTER GULLY 220m III **

Although slightiy disjointed, this provides the best line through a rather broken area of the cwm. It is very popular and contains a couple of excellent pitches. Start some 50m up and left of the bottom of Parsley Fern, above the obvious left-hand moraine groove.

1. 35m (2) A fine, wide ice-groove leads to belays on the left.
2. 60m (2) A short, narrow iced groove leads out onto snow which is followed up to below an ice-fall.
3. 20m (4) Climb the surprisingly steep ice-fall directly into the upper gully. (A poorer alternative is to climb mixed ground on the left to the same point if the ice-fall has not formed.)
4. 105m (2) Follow the gully line, narrow and icy at first, out onto snow-fields and so to the ridge at a prominent notch just left of the summit.

The area to the right of Sinister Gully has been the subject of a number of new route 'claims', but as there are few natural lines, and it is possible to weave one's way skyward almost anywhere at around Grade III, the area has been left in its wild and unreported state for climbers bent on exploration and adventure.

PARSLEY FERN GULLY 250m I ***

A classic of its grade, taking the most obvious feature of the cwm and easily visible from the road. In condition if anything is, it provides a fine climb and will even 'go' when mostly water-ice in poor conditions (II). Ascend to the true start of the gully, between rounded buttresses. The gully is followed directly with an icy section usually present at half height to the right of a thin buttress which divides the gully. Belays can be taken against the left wall. The final slopes steepen up and the lip is often corniced.

PARSLEY FERN LEFT-HAND 300m II **

A worthwhile variation, somewhat more difficult than the parent route. Begin by following the ordinary route for 100m or so until a break in the left-hand bounding rocks can be crossed and the left-hand gully gained. This contains a good section of ice and leads to steep snow which is taken directly to the summit.

The broken buttress to the right of Parsley Fern is taken by:

CHARLIE'S COLLABORATION 300m II/III

This takes the left-hand of two gullies in the buttress to a snow-field, followed by a groove and an ice-pitch on the left. This leads to more snow which is climbed to a final 6m chimney leading to the ridge.

SHALLOW GULLY 150m II

Below and 100m right of Parsley Fern a line which starts below a prominent gully/chimney through a steep band at one third height, often holds ice. Above the ice, snow-fields can be followed to gain the lip of the cwm.

The broad slope to the right of the last route sports many short, easy-angled ice smears, providing a good practice area for novices. This should be bourne in mind when descending this slope from the ridge in poor visibility and care should be taken not to dislodge ice or rocks.

3.9 CWM GLAS BACH & CWM HETIAU

Grid Reference: 610565 (middle of the cwm) (OS Sheet 115 Snowdon)
Altitude: 300m - 800m
Aspect: N or NE
Climbing Conditions:
Although much of the climbing would benefit from a plastering of hard snow, and indeed become easier, all of the routes described are possible in the more

common water-ice only conditions and the gradings given are based on these. There are many substantial drainage lines which often produce copious quantities of ice in prolonged cold, yet not extreme weather.

Approach:
These cwms lie immediately to the west of the more popular **Cwm Glas Mawr**, and may be approached either directly up the outflow stream from the bridge at 614576, or from **Ynys Ettws** by contouring around the foot of the spur which divides **Cwm Glas Mawr** from **Cwm Glas Bach**, keeping above the walls and sheepfolds, and below the crags of **Clogwyn Mawr**. This second approach passes directly below **Forgotten Gully** and **The Squeeze**. Climbs on **Railway Buttress** and above **Cwm Hetiau** are reached in about 1 hour from the road.

Although it lacks the grandeur of its bigger brother, this is still a fine winter cwm - some would say finer, given that solitude is almost guaranteed - and in a cold spell it sports a remarkable quantity of ice, much of it at a reasonable angle. **Cwm Hetiau** - the Cwm of the Hats - a curious name, whose etymology is even more curious, being derived, it is said, from its accumulation of millinery, plucked by the winds from the hapless (or hatless?) clients of the Snowdon Railway above. **Cwm Hetiau**, whose little pool is in such a delightful spot; tucked away in the southernmost corner of the cwm, a deserted stage in a frozen theatre of cascading ice. Ice which promises much, yet on closer inspection, lacks commitment and line: a wonderful playground nonetheless for novices and ice-boulderers, with problems to suit all tastes. Across to the right and slightly lower down is a crag which is loose, vegetated and scruffy in summer, but which in a cold spell, sports a number of well-defined lines of water-ice which are clearly seen from the road in the Pass. This is **Railway Buttress**, for want of a better name, as it lies directly beneath the Snowdon Railway some 200m north of **Clogwyn Station**. Here are two fine steep, technical pitches and a long, relatively easy gully.

Cwm Glas Bach will never have the draw of its senior partner but life's more relaxed up here: you can climb if you want and not 'when you're ready'. Or you can just enjoy being away from it all.

Descent:
The quickest descent to the bed of the cwm is to head due north from **Clogwyn Station**, following a steep slanting rake diagonally down to the foot of **Railway Buttress**. Alternatively, descend **Gyrn Las Ridge** (I/II, and awkward), or follow the railway path for about 300m past the station before heading across left to the lip of **Cwm Glas** at 611558 and descending easily into the upper cwm.

Snowdon and the Trinity Face in winter.
Photo: Andy Newton.

The first two climbs are actually on the crags of **Clogwyn Mawr**, which is the blunt end of the **Gyrn Las** spur which divides the two **Cwm Glas's** and are passed when approaching from **Ynys Ettws**. The first route is high up at the back of an amphitheatre in the middle of the crags of **Clogwyn Mawr** and is characterised by a short, vertical pillar of ice which forms at its base.

FORGOTTEN GULLY   135m   III
A straight gully which is easily seen by looking back from the road west of Craig Ddu.
1. 15m   (4)   Climb the vertical pillar for 6m to enter the gully proper.
2. 45m   (2/3)   Follow the gully on ice over various bulges to belay below a steep iced wall on the left, which bars further progress.
3. 45m   (3)   Climb the bulge by the iced wall to exit into the easier upper section.
4. 30m   (1)   Either follow easy snow to the top, or more interestingly (3), pursue the ice as it slides into the gully from the right.

Either descend eastwards across the ridge on the left into **Cwm Glas Mawr**, with good views of the antics on **Craig Rhaeadr**, or go down a broad, easy rake to the foot of the next climb which starts just uphill of a long wall that traverses the whole width of the cwm.

THE SQUEEZE   150m   III   *
This is the line of one of the main drainage streams from the cwm above and is seen as a pair of narrow, parallel gullies in a wide fault cutting through the steep crag above. The ice crosses from one gully to the other at mid-height and gives two excellent pitches.
1. 30m   (3)   An iced slab, a short wall and easy ground leads up to the steep right-hand ice-fall.
2. 30m   (3)   Climb steep ice and squeeze under the chockstone (problematic if the ice is thick!) into the easy-angled stream bed above.
3. 40m   (4)   Move across left and climb the steep, iced corner to escape.
4. 50m   (2)   A few more bulges remain before a walk off to the right into the main cwm.

The next two climbs are much higher up on the **Cwm Hetiau** face of the upper buttress of the ridge of **Gyrn Las**. They are visible and may be approached directly from the top of the previous route.

Spindrift on second pitch of GOLIATH (IV/V), Craig Dafydd during the first ascent. Dave Langrish is the climber. Photo: Malcolm Campbell.

GYRN LAS RIDGE   Section betwen 670m - 800m   I/II   *

This is really a continuation of the North Ridge of Crib y Ddysgl and this section is narrow, rocky and steep, giving an enjoyable scramble under winter conditions. Difficulties, of which there are several, are usually turned by chimneys on the right.

GYRN LAS GULLY   190m   II/III

The obvious gully splitting the face some 30m to the right of the ridge holds a lot of ice and is worthwhile. Start at iced slabs above a prominent scree or snow cone.

1. 70m   (2)   Iced slabs then easy ground leads up leftwards to the foot of the gully proper.
2. 50m   (3)   An iced corner, a bulge and a steep chimney lead up to an easing of the angle.
3. 25m   (2)   Easily up iced slabs leading leftwards.
4. 45m   (2/3)   Back right now and steeper, to gain the open hillside above. Either continue up to join the top of the ridge on the left, or make a rising traverse off rightwards to the railway.

To the right is a mass of ice which rises directly above the small llyn in **Cwm Hetiau**. There are maybe four or five reasonably continuous lines running for about three or four rope-lengths up the back wall of the cwm. Of these, the left-hand line is probably the best, at about Grade 3, whilst to the right of the central gully and its iced slabs (2), an interesting and difficult (4) series of pitches can be linked up grooves in the steep rock buttress above the llyn.

Railway Buttress can be seen in profile from here, lower down and across to the right. On the extreme left-hand end of the crag, a wide expanse of ice comes down the vegetated hillside and gives a steep but unrewarding pitch or two at Grade 3. Further right is a very steep ice-fall. This is:

THE FLYING SCOTSMAN   50m   IV   *

A fine pitch taking the right-hand section of the fall (5). Move up right to gain a narrow ramp leading leftwards beneath an icicle fringe. Above this, move steeply up to the right and climb a faint groove until the ice runs out just below the heathery top. Fear not, as a step round to the left allows the vegetable cornice to be avoided! Belays are a problem. Continue (1) up to some easy ice leading in a shallow gully (2) to the top, or traverse off to the left with difficulty.

RAILWAY GULLY   250m   II/III   *

The obvious central line which splits the crag above its lowest point gives an enjoyable outing for beginners, with all the difficulties being short-lived. Ice-screws should be carried for belays, as any rock which appears is decidedly suspect.

1. 25m (3)   A short, steep wall and left-slanting groove lead to easier ground.
2. 45m (1)   Easily to the foot of the gully proper.
3. 10m (3)   An ice-pillar bars entry to the gully - climb it!
4. 45m (2)   Easy-angled ice in the gully.
5. 10m (2/3) Steeper ice leads across to the right.
6. 45m (2)   As for pitch 4!
7. 70m (2/3) One more steepish groove, then it's Grade 1 all the way.

THE IRISH MAIL   100m   IV   ⋆

The first ice-fall to the right of Railway Gully gives another enjoyable route via two steep but short, free-standing ice-pillars on the first pitch (4). The second pitch is easier (2/3).

To the right there are a couple more ice smears, but they don't seem to lead anywhere. Right again is a shallow and wide easy gully which might be worthwhile in hard snow (Grade 1).

4. YR WYDDFA

4.1 **THE SNOWDON HORSESHOE**
4.2 **LLIWEDD**
4.3 **CLOGWYN Y GARNEDD**
4.4 **CLOGWYN DU'R ARDDU**
4.5 **MOEL EILIO**
4.6 **SNOWDON - SOUTH SIDE**

It is fashionable to knock Snowdon. Tryfan, Crib Goch and Cnicht are all popular contenders for the title of 'My Favourite Welsh Mountain', whilst Yr Wyddfa slumps sadly on the scrap head, discarded in the eyes of many on the basis of its lack-lustre performance in summer. Beefburgers and beer, tourists and trains, lemmings and litter: where is the attraction in all that? Well, maybe, but crunch over the crisp névé to the summit of Crib y Ddysgl as the sun disappears into a steel grey and yellow ocean, then gaze across towards that perfect pyramidal peak. Just feel the power emanating from the vast face of Clogwyn y Garnedd and picture yourself fighting your way off the mountain in the gathering gloom, having misjudged the scale of it. Or stand out in the centre of frozen Glaslyn as the early morning sun lights up the towering triangular face which dominates the cwm. No other mountain in Snowdonia can evoke such a response.

And what of the other peaks and crags which cling to Snowdon's coat tails? Like mighty Lliwedd, whose East Face is the biggest crag south of the border? Or the legendary Cloggy, whose black and sombre buttresses continue to hold the rock climber in their sway? They surely take pride of place on this proud winter mountain? Well, maybe - but maybe not. Impressive as they undoubtedly are, they are still beneath Yr Wyddfa, this top of Wales. But you must form your own opinion, and whatever that is, agree on one thing: that grouped within this section are some of the finest winter mountaineering experiences which Wales has to offer. Savour them, and then come back for more.

4.1 SNOWDON HORSESHOE

SNOWDON HORSESHOE I/II ★★★
Distance: 12.8km
Ascent: 1,000m

This superb expedition, unrivalled in Snowdonia cannot be too highly praised. However, it is long, arduous and can be very serious. The descending sections especially, call for great care and concentration. The party should be fit, competent and well-equipped. ICE-AXES ARE ESSENTIAL and CRAMPONS ARE HIGHLY RECOMMENDED.

   Pen y Pass to **Crib y Ddysgl** has already been described. From **Crib y Ddysgl** it is an easy walk past *The Finger Stone* at Bwlch Glas and up the railway line to **Yr Wyddfa** (Snowdon Summit). The descent to Bwlch y Saethau crosses steep rock strewn slopes, often of hard icy snow and should not be underestimated: it is a notorious accident site. Head down the ridge SSW at a prominent cairn and zig-zag diagonally leftwards down the slope to the welcome level area of the Bwlch. A more difficult descent follows the SE ridge directly down from the summit cairn above the NE face.

   From here the ridge up to **Lliwedd** provides good, interesting scrambling. Staying on the crest is most exciting but provides the most difficulty. The descent to Llyn Llydaw and The Miners' Track leaves the ridge just after it levels out and often has bands of water-ice lying across its steeper section.

4.2 LLIWEDD

Forming the southern arm of the **Snowdon Horseshoe**, this fine cliff provides a clutch of superb and difficult climbs of the old-fashioned kind. Serious and elusive, even the best lines becomes confusing high up on the crag and a good nose for finding the way is a distinct advantage.

   If in the course of a day on this steep face one feels that Lliwedd is a gripping place, spare a thought for those pioneers of yesteryear who rock climbed routes in not dissimilar conditions in their quest for Alpine training.

Grid Reference: 623533 (OS Sheet 115 Snowdon)
Altitude: 610m - 890m
Aspect: North
Climbing Conditions:
The crag, although greasy and wet in summer, does not receive much drainage and so a very good snowfall followed by freeze-thaw action is required to bring the routes into condition. Even the gullies are comparatively dry and many of the routes involve teetering about on iced slabs and rocky ribs, assisted by judicious use of that classic Welsh climbing medium, frozen turf. All the climbs are hard and involve mixed climbing, combined with a lack of adequate protection and sound belays. The major gullies provide the most popular climbs and are the best landmarks on a mountain renowned for its route-finding difficulty. Those teams with a summer knowledge of the cliff will find it an advantage.
Approach:
Cars are best left at Pen y Pass and a fast simple walk-in leads along the Miners' Track to Llyn Llydaw. From here, a faint rising path, running around to the east of the lake leads to the foot of the cliffs. In poor visibility, there are few positive features and care should be taken to avoid climbing the well-marked summit path. The approach path passes below a long line of rocks and 300m beyond these, steep snow/scree can be climbed to reach the Central Gully area. Care is needed here in bad visibility as it is easy to go too far and arrive at the rocks below Slanting Gully. A good point of reference, known appropriately as The Reference Rock, is a 10m rocky rib amidst the screes some 60m below the centre of the East Buttress.
Descent:
From the summit area the best descent is to follow the ridge ESE then NE to where the Horseshoe Path drops down the hillside back to a junction with the Miners' Track at Llyn Llydaw.

An alternative for those who have never had enough, is to follow the Horseshoe Path NW down to Bwlch Ciliau and on up to Snowdon Summit. The less energetic teams heading in this direction will take the Watkin Path down from Bwlch Ciliau!

The cliff is divided into four parts by the three main gullies. **Central Gully** halves the cliff, **East Gully** bisecting the left-half whilst **Slanting Gully** cleaves the right portion. Between East Gully and Central Gully lies the **East Buttress**. Between Central Gully and Slanting Gully is the **West Buttress**. **Slanting Buttress** lies to the R of Slanting Gully.

The buttresses are indented by smaller gullies, corners and ledges, all of which hold snow in good conditions, so making it possible to climb almost anywhere. This is probably fortunate, given the route-finding difficulty and the likelihood of finding oneself anywhere!

EAST GULLY 215m IV *
The left-hand of the three main gullies.

Start up steep snow to reach a snow groove leading into the main gully.
1.   30m   Iced slabs and snow leads into the gully.
2.   35m   Up and left following a series of iced cracks leading to a good ledge.
3.   30m   Continue up the gully, via iced rocks on the left, crux, to reach the broader amphitheatre.
4.   120m   Up snow to reach the summit ridge.

The upper sections of the next three climbs may well coincide in places, and conditions will generally dictate the route chosen in each case. They each find their own way through the ground below the Great Terrace, but all finish on the crest of the buttress in the region of Terminal Arête.

EAST PEAK VIA THE HORNED CRAG 290m IV/V *
Start beneath the right wall of East Gully.
1.   65m   Follow the general line of weakness up the middle of the gully wall to a break and take the chimney groove above to reach a snow-field on the right. This is approximately the line of the summer route. The Runnel.
2.   45m   Break up the steep right wall to reach its top.
3.   105m   Now follow Horned Crag Route up grooves to the Horned Crag; two huge, leftwards slanting pillars just left of the crest of the buttress. The crack splitting the crag is hard if fully iced.
4.   75m   Follow Terminal Arête to reach the summit.

EAST PEAK DIRECT 285m V *
Scramble up to the left-hand end of a heathery ledge and move right to start in the first small gully/groove to the right of East Gully, as for the summer route Yellow Slab.
1.   40m   Follow the gully with its icy right wall to a stance with a large spike.
2.   70m   Move out to the left edge of the gully and follow this to gain a traverse line leading diagonally right above the gully. Take this to reach an easy snow ramp leading back left.
3.   65m   Follow this ramp to a similar ramp leading up right to below a steep section.
4.   35m   The steep section is tackled directly via a shallow couloir.
5.   75m   Continue as close to the crest as possible to reach the East Peak.

Another somewhat indeterminate route climbs directly up the East Buttress:

WHITE DOVE   300m   V   *

The climb starts below Birch Tree Terrace, directly above The Reference Rock, in the centre of the buttress. Climb a steep groove/chimney to the left-hand end of Birch Tree Terrace and continue in the same line above. This is the line of the summer climb called Central Chimney and leads to slabs which are followed first rightwards, then back left, to reach the crux wall and groove of Avalanche Route. This is followed to the Great Terrace. From here a groove at the back left of the Terrace is climbed before joining Terminal Arête for the final 70m.

SHALLOW GULLY   300m   IV/V   *

A difficult climb unless conditions are very good. Start as for Central Gully.

1.   75m   As for Central Gully pitches 1 and 2 to the Bowling Green.

2.   30m   Traverse the Bowling Green leftwards to enter the gully. Cross to a ledge and belays on the left.

or with greater difficulty (V), follow the steep lower section of the gully up icy grooves to gain this point directly.

3.   65m   Continue with difficulty up a series of corners and shallow grooves to the Great Terrace.

4.   130m   Climb a chimney from the right-hand extremity of the Terrace, and continue to the top more easily.

CENTRAL GULLY   265m   V   ***

The large Central Gully emerges from a slabby recess in the centre of the crag. A direct ascent is guarded by the very steep snow-ice groove of Central Gully Direct, and this is avoided by an excursion leftwards to the Bowling Green, which is above the steepest section. The climb is not well protected.

1.   30m   Climb the right-hand side of the slabby depression to belay below Central Gully Direct on the Quartz Ledges.

2.   45m   Traverse left along the ledges, then diagonally left and climb steeply up an icy rib, or shallow gully to reach the Bowling Green.

3.   35m   Traverse right to the rib and climb (crux) up into the gully, which is followed to belays. This pitch can be very hard and it may be necessary to resort to aid.

4.   155m   The main gully continues steeply, the middle 90m

having no obvious runners or belays, giving sustained climbing. The final 30m is taken easily on the left. (A hard variation is to take the narrow left-hand branch of the gully via the Great Chimney.)

CENTRAL GULLY DIRECT 60m VI ★★★
This climbs the very steep entry to the upper gully and is usually very thin, only coming into condition in the hardest winters. It is HVS in summer!
1.   15m   Climb the groove to reach a belay.
2.   45m   Continue up the sustained groove to reach the upper gully; the crux is passing the overhang at half height. An outstanding pitch.

CENTRAL GULLY ARÊTE 285m IV ★
A line up the West Buttress starting from Central Gully and following the arête on the right. Start below the steep groove of Central Gully Direct.
1.   45m   Traverse right across the snow ledge to the arête. Climb this then go diagonally right to ledges.
2.   50m   Climb a 6m wall to another ledge and move right across snow banks and walls to a shallow chimney, slanting to the rib.
3.   30m   Another groove slants left to a ledge which is followed left again.
4.   30m   Climb the steep spiky wall until the angle eases and one overlooks the main gully on the left.
5.   130m   It is possible at this point to descend into Central Gully, but it is easier and safer to continue on the buttress, zig-zagging to avoid difficulties and generally trending rightwards.

THE WEST PEAK 275m IV ★
This route is based on the summer line of Bilberry Terrace Route. 'In thick cloud, gives good orienteering with limitless chances to get lost and into difficulties'. If found, the climb may be found to be easy for IV - but who's going to find it!
   Start below the end of the terrace about 50m right of Central Gully.
1.   25m   Climb iced rocks steeply to the left end of the Terrace.
2.   45m   Follow the snow ramp easily rightwards.
3.   75m   Climb a series of short corners diagonally up to the right.
4.   130m   Another series of snowy corners and grooves just left of the crest lead straight up to the summit.

SLANTING GULLY 250m V ★★
The pitch out of the cave can be very difficult, as can the top chimney,

but the rest of the route is of a more reasonable standard.

From the foot of Central Gully, traverse across the steep snow for 300m until it is possible to gain the lower part of the gully, obviously slanting up to the left.

1. 50m (2)   Climb the snow to reach a steep groove/chimney on the left. A harder alternative lies to the right.
2. 80m (4)   Take the left-hand chimney, steep for 10m, and the easier gully above to belay in the cave.
3. 30m (4/6)   Traverse left out of the cave on to the icy(?) slab (no protection, but easy *if* in condition) and teeter up to reach the top of the cave; or surmount the dubious chockstone and climb the groove (harder, but safer) to the same place. The amount of ice on the slab dictates the difficulty: a fine pitch.
4. 90m (4/6)   Continue more easily up snow, and a deep chimney (hard in normal, lean conditions) to reach the top.

COOL WATER SANDWICH 240m IV *

This takes a line up Slanting Buttress and is better protected than usual for these crags.

Start some 20m right of Slanting Gully.

1. 85m   Climb iced slabs moving left to belay in a snowy recess beneath the central of three V-grooves.
2. 35m   Climb the iced back of the groove, directly past a cave and up to a well-positioned belay.
3. 45m   Up left and follow the arête to where it meets the steep upper wall.
4. 25m Climb diagonally right on a rampline to a quartz block, then steeply up to the foot of a groove. Good belay on the left.
5. 50m   Take the groove on the left, then right past a big spike to a move right around a corner onto a snow slope. Climb up this left, to a step left back around a rib into more snow. Up this to finish through a notch on the right.

Well below and to the right of the start of Slanting Gully is a subsidiary buttress split by a prominent gully.

SKIVER'S GULLY 150m III

Follow the gully, turning a large chockstone on the right, or by a spur on the left, to gain the large sloping terrace to the right of the start of Slanting Gully.

A logical continuation of the above line may be found above:

WESTERN GULLY 100m II

This is the large gully well to the right of Slanting Gully, starting at a much higher level at the top of the terrace. It curves round to the left like a miniature version of Slanting Gully before gaining the summit ridge just above the col.

Higher up in the cwm a rocky ridge, **Y GRIBIN, 100m, I/II ***, leads from the Miners' Track at the outlfow of Glaslyn up to Bwlch y Saethau. It provides a good, often neglected outing in a fine position.

4.3 CLOGWYN Y GARNEDD

The magnificent face below **Yr Wyddfa** (Snowdon Summit, 1,085m) has become one of the most popular winter climbing areas in Snowdonia. The very reliable snow conditions, combined with a finish on the highest summit in England and Wales, have ensured that solitude is not on the agenda over a winter weekend.

A good range of lower and middle grade climbs, sometimes complete with an escalator of steps (and commuters), make it feel not too serious. However, in poor weather, the distance from the road is well felt and the summit regains its remote and lofty ambience. This is no place to left familiarity breed contempt; it is not unknown for very experienced teams to fail to find their objective.

Grid Reference: 610546 (OS Sheet 115 Snowdon)
Altitude: 850m - 1,085m
Aspect: North
Climbing Conditions:
This large face is seamed with sprawling gullies and snow-fields, and its height and aspect are virtually unrivalled in Snowdonia. The climbs will 'go' in almost any conditions, but a good cover of névé is ideal. Cornice collapse and avalanche risk are very real, so snow conditions should be thoughtfully examined before attempting a climb.
Approach:
There are a number of ways to reach the face. The fastest is to park at Pen y Pass and walk in along the PYG Track (preferably), or the Miners' Track, to reach the bottom of the face, just above the area of mine-workings. Beware of some lethal snow bridges over deep holes. A small llyn, often frozen, provides a handy landmark. It is possible to drop down the Zig-Zags from the Finger Stone at Bwlch Glas (literally, so great care and crampons are needed at this accident black spot) to reach the base of the face from the Tourist Track to Snowdon Summit, or from a route in Cwm Glas.

From the frozen pool head SW across the floor of the cwm and climb up to reach the Central Trinity approach to the Spider, an eponymous snow-field from which the Trinity Gullies all start.

Descent:
As all the climbs culminate very close to the summit of Snowdon, or on the Tourist Track/Railway, detailed descriptions are not necessary, and any of the usual paths can be taken.

The most helpful will be to follow the Railway back down to the Finger Stone, marking the top of the PYG Track, and thus a return to the start via the Zig-Zags. Despite recent footpath work here, crampons are still necessary in a number of places.

The most obvious feature on the face is the Spider, a large snow-field with radiating legs forming the climbs in the Trinity area of the face. To the left the Terrace rises gently from the lower left-hand side of the Spider to peter out just before reaching Great Gully, the bounding feature of the left-hand side of the face. To the right of the Spider the face is more rocky and gashed with deeper clefts containing Ladies' and Cave Gullies. It gradually decreases in size as the valley floor rises, to finally peter out in the broken area below Bwlch Glas. The upper part of the face above the Trinity area is rather featureless and one can head up almost anywhere.

The first route described is actually around on the **East Face**, and is reached by scrambling across steep snow and the frozen stream from the junction of the PYG and Miners' Tracks to below the very steep face.

THREE PITCH GULLY 150m III
Neither popular nor easy to find, although in good visibility it is clearly seen from the PYG track on the walk in, bounding the left edge of the face, and showing a marked dog-leg at mid-height. An easier, shorter gully (**GLASLYN GULLY I**), stikes off leftwards from the same point to gain the ridge just above Bwlch y Saethau.

Climb snow and difficult iced walls to reach the foot of a steep narrow chimney. Climb this and move right above on a snow ledge to reach a snowy groove which is followed to reach the ridge well below the summit.

THE NORTH FACE

GREAT GULLY 230m II/III **
Well viewed from the approach, this is the large gully running up to join the bounding left-hand ridge of the face. A well-positioned route. Start by heading towards the Spider, but cut across leftwards below the lowest rock and drop slightly into the base of the gully.

1. 60m (3) The gully is blocked by two or three iced boulders, the passing of these providing the crux of the route. They can be very

140

difficult. The gully leads into a small bowl.

2. 30m (2)   The gully is blocked by a short, steep ice-fall (3) which most teams will by-pass by climbing up left into the upper gully.

3. 60m (1)   Carry on up the snowy gully, steepening as it closes on the ridge. In poor snow the broken ridge on the left can be followed.

4. 80m (1)   The easy broad ridge leads up right to the summit in a fine position.

INTRODUCTORY GULLY 220m III

A mediocre route, starting midway between Great Gully and the approach to the Trinity area. Start by climbing snow to reach a short, easy groove. Scramble up this to gain a snowfield above which the going becomes trickier. Time for the rope!

1. 60m   Head upwards via icy groove and ribs until a snowy ramp break up and left to reach the left-hand end of the Terrace.

2. 60m   The indistinct gully leads up on the left and is taken in a couple of broken pitches.

3. 100m   Easy snow gains the summit ridge.

MISTAKEN IDENTITY 180m V/VI

This is a bit of a non-route, as it manages to avoid most of the obvious feature which it attempts to climb! However, the main pitch brings the crag screaming into the 80's!

About 25m left of Snowdrop is a continuous thin groove of snow-ice which finishes in an icicle fringe above a shallow cave on the left-hand end of the terrace. In truly exceptional conditions it may be possible to gain and climb the groove directly at around Grade IV - in which case it would rank in quality with its more famous neighbour. It is seen clearly from the tiny pool below the face and may easily be mistaken for Snowdrop, being a better defined line from this viewpoint. Approach as for Introductory Gully.

1. 35m (4)   Start just right of the cave on the terrace and move diagonally up left heading for a couple of enormous perched flakes about 2m right of the main line above the cave. An awkward groove on the right-hand side of the blocks leads to a good belay.

2. 45m (6)   Move left into the main line and climb a short, steep ice-wall leftwards into the continuation of the groove line. Go up this, narrowing and steepening, until a flake crack on the right wall provides good runners. At this point it ought, in exceptional conditions, to be possible to continue up the groove (4?) but on the first ascent the ice was in dangerous condition. This would also avoid the

drama of the next 25m! Gain the flake crack by difficult mixed climbing and continue up the steep wall using turfy ledges to make progress. Reach the rib on the right and continue, still with difficulty, to belay on a huge, detached block on easy ground.

3. 110m (2) More easily to gain the summit ridge.

SNOWDROP 185m III/IV ★★

Although the interest is concentrated in one pitch, this is one of the best routes on the face.

Start by traversing the Terrace past the ice-falls of Little Gully to the point where further progress becomes more difficult below a steep chimney V-groove, capped by an overhang. An alternative and more interesting approach may be made up the steep broken ground directly below the groove, but this is not recommended in poor visibility.

1. 40m (4) Climb the right-hand wall of the groove boldly on good snow/ice and turn the final bulge on the right. Good thread below this, the crux. Continue up left to two large blocks.

2. 55m (2) Carry on up the gully and follow it steeply upwards to reach the easy summit slopes.

3. 90m (1/2) Easily, anywhere, to the top.

LITTLE GULLY 185m II/III ★

This takes a distinct snowy ice-fall that tumbles down to meet the Terrace, and is best gained by traversing about 50m leftwards along this terrace from the left-hand Trinity approach.

1. 20m Climb up to the foot of the obvious corner.

2. 60m Take the hard icy corner (or leftwards up a snow ramp) to reach easier broken ground.

3. 105m Up the snow-field to the summit.

The climbs in the Trinity area share common starts and radiate from the large central snow-field, the Spider. From the base of the cwm, a shallow snow-filled trough leads up towards the Spider. There are two broad snow lines gaining the Spider, about 50m apart and separated by a blunt rocky rib. Both are very easy and the left-hand start is better when attempting routes from the Terrace.

LEFT-HAND TRINITY 220m I/II ★

Interesting climbing which is somewhat more serious than its Central neighbour.

1. 60m Easily up to the Spider.

2. 30m Halfway up the Spider a narrow groove, often iced, breaks up leftwards to reach the Fly, a small triangular snow-field.

3. 30m   Carry on up the snow groove from the top of the Fly.
4. 100m   Easier broken ground leads up to the summit. Care should be taken here as the belays are poor and the climbing can be awkward.

CENTRAL TRINITY 220m I/II ★★★

A classic snow climb, marred only by the line of bucket steps and procession of climbers often found in situ. Queue early on sunny weekends. The upper part of the gully can contain an icy surprise in some conditions, and although the main objective danger is tumbling incompetents, it is one of the first areas to avalanche in poor conditions.

1. 60m   Easily up the snow to the *The Spider*. Often this is marked by a well trodden track.
2. 80m   Straight up the gully leaving the top left-hand corner of *The Spider*. The gully narrows, and may contain some icy steps, before paying out onto the easier steep snow of the summit slopes.
3. 80m   Easily to the ridge, some 50m right of the cairn.

TRINITY BUTTRESS 150m III

A short route, but quite worthwhile.
   Start at the top right-hand arm of the Spider, below the obvious gully.

1. 50m (3) Climb the steep snow until the gully gets more difficult, then move up and L over steep ground to reach a small snow-field. If the gully is followed until it closes, a much more difficult traverse left has to be made.
2. 100m (2) Straight up over easing broken ground to gain the ridge.

RIGHT-HAND TRINITY 150m II/III ★★★

A nice route with interesting climbing that can be difficult in the middle section.
   Start at the top right-hand corner of the Spider, below the entry to Trinity Buttress.

1. 40m (2) Take the snow rightwards and up into the better defined gully.
2. 80m (3) The steepening gully provides good sport in passing various obstacles and is hard in lean conditions.
3. 30m (1) The gully peters out into snow slopes leading up to the ridge.

SNAKEBITE 195m III

Best attempted in good snow conditions, this pleasantly open route

143

breaks up right of the Trinity area.

Start at the break in the rocks some 30m to the right of the right-hand approach to the Spider.

1. 45m   Climb snow, then more broken ground to reach a snowy gully on the right.
2. 45m   Follow the steepening gully to arrive on a snow-field across a large rocky couloir.
3. 45m   Traverse right and climb mixed terrain to below a well-defined groove slanting up L.
4. 60m   Take the groove which leads to easier ground and the ridge.

FALL OUT   175m   IV/III
This takes the steep direct entry to the snow-field on the previous route, to finish up that line. Good conditions are necessary.

Start 30m right of Snakebite, where an icy groove cuts through steep rocks.

1. 80m   (4)   Climb the groove to beneath the overhang. Surmount this and continue up the icy groove above to break slightly leftwards to gain the snow-field.
2. 95m   (3)   Follow Snakebite pitches 3 and 4.

LADDIES' GULLY   165m   III   *
This takes the obvious straight shallow gully which starts at the foot of Ladies' Gully, bearing leftwards to gain the right-hand end of the prominent snow-field of Snakebite and Fall Out. The line is obvious from the Zig-Zags.

1. 70m   (3)   Climb steep snow in the gully to the terrace.
2. 95m   (3)   As for Fall Out.

EQUAL OPPORTUNITIES   150m   III
This eliminate climbs a series of indefinite grooves on mixed ground and is based on the slim rib between Ladies' and Laddies' Gullies, and offers continually interesting climbing. Start some way up Ladies' Gully just as it steepens.

1. 40m   (3)   Climb the groove on the left side of the rib, on the left of the gully, to its end. Move left and up snow to a flat block.
2. 40m   (4)   Move right and climb the right-hand of two grooves. Keep right at the fork and belay at the foot of a steep tower.
3. 70m   (2)   An easy groove on the right leads to an elegant snow arête. Keep left of the rocks to finish.

LADIES' GULLY   180m   III   **
A fine line starting about 100m up the snow slope rightwards from the

Trinity starts and below the obvious and well-defined gully.
1. 60m   (2)   Up snow and over a series of ledges in the gully to below a steep corner.
2. 20m   (3)   Climb the corner, often an interesting ice-pitch.
3. 100m (2)   More easily up snow to reach the ridge.

COULOIR   150m   IV   *

A bold route up the steep V-chimney to the right of Ladies' Gully.
   Start 25m right of that route.
1. 35m   Up easy snow to a small flake belay on the left-hand side of the chimney.
2. 40m   Move right, enter the chimney over thin ice and climb to a small flake. A serious pitch with no protection.
3. 75m   Up the final section of the couloir, then up right to an easy snow finish.

CAVE BUTTRESS   130m   V

A modern route taking the steep buttress just left of Cave Gully.
1. 30m   (1/2)   Follow the ridge left of Cave Gully to a thread belay in a cave.
2. 25m   (4)   Climb the buttress to belay at the prominent block.
3. 25m   (5/6)   Climb the buttress direct to the niche and follow the ridge to twin flake belays.
4. 50m   (2)   The ridge above leads more easily to the top.

CAVE GULLY   125m   III   **

Another fine route, also hard in poor conditions.
   Start some 70m right and higher up than Ladies' Gully, gained from a broad snow ramp running above lower rocks on the right.
1. 45m   (2)   Climb a well-defined and narrowing steep snow gully to below a small overhang.
2. 20m   (3/4)   Turn this barrier by a very steep groove on the left and go up to a cave belay. This can be very trying in poor conditions.
3. 60m   (2)   Exit up left from the cave and climb steep snow to a sometimes corniced exit.

END GULLY   60m   II/I

At the top of the broad snow ramp an obvious short but pleasant gully leads up to the ridge with few, if any, difficulties.

4.4 CLOGWYN DU'R ARDDU

This dark and sombre cliff, the Theatre Royal of Welsh rock climbing, renting the sky with huge sweeps of rock, rarely fulfils its promise as a winter playground. When covered in snow the menace of its steep ramparts is somehow muted, held captive beneath a web of whiteness. Buttresses are well-defined as areas of blankness between the strands of pale possibility, whilst the translucent gleam from the frozen area left of the main crag hints at the pleasures to be found there. Catching the eye, centre stage, a hoary shaft rises from the shadowy depths only to fail at the last gasp. To break through these sunless defences and regain the normality above, will exalt any mind.

Grid Reference: 602555 (OS Sheet 115 Snowdon)
Altitude: 700m - 880m
Aspect: North
Climbing Conditions:
The walls of the main crag do not hold snow well and although ice smears sometimes form, the most reliable conditions are generally to be found on the shattered slopes of Garn Goch, over to the left. The gullies and terraces provide good sport amid the superb scenery, with the Black Cleft providing the most compelling feature of the crag. Some of the buttress routes have been followed to provide very hard mixed climbs, although a good cover of snow is vital to bring these into true winter condition. The crag receives no direct sunlight in the winter months.

Approach:
Take the tourist track towards Snowdon until beyond the Half Way House, where the track turns leftwards and climbs steeply towards the railway. Carry straight on here, first level, then descending slightly to contour below Garn Goch and then the main cliff. The last part of the path can be iced over in places. The track may be gained from the road leaving the A4085 opposite the Royal Victoria Hotel, on the south side of Llanberis. There are obvious parking places at the start of the Snowdon Track, although frost-free roads may allow a start from Hafodty Newydd, but care should be taken to fasten any gate along the road and not to block it in any way. Allow 1 to 1½ hours.

Descent:
From the rim of the cliff, walk back from the edge and then contour east, then ENE to pass above Garn Goch until the railway is reached. This can be followed down with crampons and extreme care (an accident blackspot), until the bridge at Clogwyn Station is reached. The railway or the track can then be followed back to Llanberis.

The Snowdon Ranger Path runs near the crest of the crag and could be followed to Yr Wyddfa if enough daylight remains. In conditions where a rapid loss of height is vital, the ridge can be followed ENE down to Bwlch Cwm Brwynog and Cwm Brwynog follow north (marshy) to Hafodty Newydd, although care should be taken on the ridge as the north edge can be corniced.

The sections of the cliff are fairly easy to recognise. To the left of the main sweep of rock is the broken area of **Garn Goch**, bounded on its right by the small, high rocks of the **Far Far East Buttress**. Right again is the **Far East Buttress**, featured with horizontal breaks which eventually run into the **East Buttress**. The main section of the crag is well-divided by a pair of terraced breaks forming a giant V-shape. The left-hand break is the **Eastern Terrace**, below which is the **Steep Band**. Between and above the two terraces is the **West Buttress**, with the Black Cleft nestling just left of the apex of the 'V'. Parallel to the Western Terrace on the right of the Steep Band is the **Far Western Terrace,** right again being the **Far West Buttress,** before the rocks break up and merge back into the hillside.

GARN GOCH

THE ICE-FALL 100m III ⋆
This starts someway up the broken area, well over to the left, and consists of a steep, stepped ice-fall, with slabby ice above. It is climbed in two long pitches (4,3). Scramble up and left to finish. The small ice-fall just on the left provides some fun.

FARAWAY GULLY 100m II/III
The shallow gully 200m to the left of Boomerang Gully is taken in three pleasant pitches.

Between the last two routes is an area of broken ground with many smaller ice smears and which is worthy of exploration.

MAIN CRAG

BOOMERANG GULLY 230m I/II ⋆
This lies just to the left of the Far Far East Buttress. The base is marked by a set of steep ice-falls (3/4) which may be avoided on the left. Broken ground is followed up leftwards before cutting back up and right over steeper steps, to finish out of a slot which may be corniced.

THE ARÊTE 50m IV
This climbs the snowy arête onto the terrace below Brwynog Chimney, and provides the best start to that route.
1. 50m   Climb directly up the arête to the (Far East) Terrace. It is possible to traverse right to gain the terrace after the first hard section.

BRWYNOG CHIMNEY 50m IV/V
This defines the left-hand side of the Far East Buttress and can be

approached by descending the Far East Terrace, or by the previous route.

1. 50m   Climb the chimney with difficulty past an icicle and continue, sustained and serious, to reach easy snow and the top.

SILVER MACHINE 150m VI **

A fine and varied route, only possible in ideal conditions. Start to the right of the arête where an ice streak forms in a bay, dropping from the foot of the Far East Terrace.

1. 40m   Gain the ice streak from the right, probably using aid and tension, and climb it, exiting right to reach the terrace.
2. 45m   Continue straight up the prominent groove on frozen vegetation to join Naddyn Ddu at 30m. Carry on to snow beneath the overhanging crack.
3. 25m   Climb the ice-chimney just to the right of the crack for 7m, then swing right to gain a parallel line and continue to a stance.
4. 40m   Take the short ice-groove, then easier ground to the top.

JUBILEE CLIMB 210m V ***

Probably the best route on 'Cloggy' when in condition. Mixed climbing gradually becoming more icy. Start below the groove splitting the lower Far East Buttress.

1. 20m   Climb diagonally right to belay below the groove.
2. 45m   The groove is followed with difficulty until easy ground is reached. Flake belay up on the right.
3. 70m   Up left below the overhangs, then left to the snow terrace which is followed to its end.
4. 45m   Carry on diagonally left in a very exposed position, to reach a steep shallow gully which is followed to gain a square-cut chimney on the right.
5. 30m   Continue up the chimney to the top.

EAST GULLY 195m IV/III *

This is the steep rake and gully bounding the left-hand edge of the East Buttress. The top pitch is often mixed but can give good sport. Fine views of the East Wall and Pinnacle areas.

1. 145m (2)   Climb the gully on snow, wide at first but gradually narrowing.
2. 50m (4)   Steep mixed climbing leads to the finishing snow groove.

CAMUS 110m V *

A very exposed route that starts by following East Gully for 100m until a steep snow slope breaks out left into the Far East Buttress. Cross this

148

to below the prominent slanting chimney line that is the substance of the route.

1. 40m   Climb the snowy ramp until a snow basin is gained.
2. 40m   Up left into the chimney line and continue until it closes. Belay on the left.
3. 30m   Move out right and climb steeply on ice to regain the fault. Easy snow leads to a difficult and sometimes corniced exit.

EASTERN TERRACE 220m I *

The left-hand branch of the central 'V'. Gained by steep scrambling diagonally rightwards to reach the terrace proper, before heading back up left onto easy snow. Impressive surroundings.

EASTERN TERRACE DIRECT START 30m III/IV *

The Eastern Terrace has its true start below the Black Cleft, and this often sports an ice-fall. This is taken direct to the terrace, which is followed up and left to reach the ordinary route.

THE BLACK CLEFT 160m V/VI ***

This appears as a striking candle of ice, fed by a spring someway up the dank groove. This ensures that difficult mixed climbing is required above the ice in order to quit the groove. Start where the Eastern Terrace drops away into the ice of the Direct Start.

1. 20m (5)   Gain the ice and climb it direct until a stance on a pillar on the right can be gained.
2. 50m (7)   Move back onto the ice and climb it with runners on the right wall until the ice runs out. Difficult climbing, often aid, leads to a stance 15m up on the left.
3. 15m (6)   Pass the overhang, either directly, or more easily, left then right over a slabby bulge.
4. 75m (3)   Mixed climbing, either direct then right, or on the right, gains an easy snow gully and the top.

WESTERN TERRACE 130m I

This fault line passes through impressive scenery and starts at the apex of the giant 'V'. Gain the terrace, and follow it beneath the overhangs, over one or two interesting steps in a fine position. (At the time of writing (1988), however, the terrace is covered with dangerous debris from a recent rockfall, and so an ascent cannot be recommended.)

WEST END ICE-FALL 35m IV *

In a long cold spell an ice-fall develops, dropping from the Western Terrace at quarter height. This is on the left-hand side of the Steep Band and is climbed direct to the terrace. A serious pitch.

Attempts, with varying degrees of success have been made on Great Slab, which has a difficult entry a little way up the Western Terrace. Under rare true winter conditions, this would provide a mixed route of considerable quality.

RED SLAB   130m   VI   **

This fine and very difficult route, only possible in perfect conditions, may not form in the same line again due to a recent rockfall. The original description is given in the hope that the drainage has not been greatly altered. Follow Western Terrace to the obvious slab after the overhangs where a thin ice smear shows the way.

1.   50m   Gain the ice smear with difficulty and follow it to the source. Exit left and traverse for 15m over the small overhang to a ledge. This is all very serious with no protection.

2.   80m   Follow the chimney line to a ledge, then the gully to the top.

FAR WESTERN TERRACE   130m   II

This is the terrace parallel to and right of Western Terrace. Start below it.

1.   45m   Climb up the slabby ice. A good pitch if the ice has built up.

2.   85m   Easy snow leads up right to the top.

4.5   MOEL EILIO

Grid Reference: 564566 (OS Sheet 115 Snowdon)
Altitude: 510m - 630m
Aspect: North East

Situated below the Moel Eilio Horseshoe on Foel Gron, at the head of Cwm Dwythwch, these short cliffs contain three or four lines that are worthwhile after heavy snowfall. They are gained by contouring into the cwm, past Llyn Dwythwch, after leaving the 'Telegraph Alley' track which starts from above the Llanberis Youth Hostel.

There are three obvious gullies situated high up on the crag. The left-hand pair are II and the right-hand one, which looks steeper, is II/III. All three are 60-70m long and finish on the wide ridge, possibly past cornices. Continuing around the Horseshoe over Moel Eilio provides a pleasant finish.

Three short gullies have been climbed, II/III, 70m, on the SW flank of the mountain. These lie on a broken cliff area called Y Diffws (548572), which is situated above the A4085 SE of Caernarvon near the village of Salem. Access may be gained via a footpath which starts 500m NW along the road towards Betws Garmon.

4.6 YR WYDDFA - THE SOUTH SIDE

CWM LLAN: CLOGWYN DU

Grid Reference: 605533 (OS Sheet 115 Snowdon)
Altitude: 630m - 850m
Aspect: East
Climbing Conditions:
The routes described depend to a large extent on the accumulation of consolidated snow in the large gullies, although Tregalen Groove in particular holds ice quite well.
Approach:
Follow the Watkin Path from Nantgwynant to the footbridge over the Afon Cwm Llan at 620520. Do not cross the stream, but follow a track left up a side stream to the old tramway, and follow this up the valley. From the quarries, strike diagonally up the hillside to the foot of the crag. An old wall which stops at a steep band below the foot of Shadow Gully is a guide. (1½ hours from the road.)

This extensive crag is the most continous area of rock to be found on the massive back wall of **Cwm Tregalen** and it forms the east flank of Snowdon's **South Ridge** some 500m below the junction with the **Beddgelert Path**. **Shadow Gully** divides the crag into two sections: a steep, relatively short, rocky buttress to the left and a massive rambling area of crag extending further down the hillside to the right. The right-hand edge is defined by a huge snow gully, **Tregalen Gully**. This right-hand section of the cliff is steepest at the bottom, above which it degenerates into steep, broken ground with few discernible lines. Right of **Tregalen Gully** is another broken buttress which may be climbed almost anywhere, and to the right again is a less well-defined gully which is not described.

Descent:
Turn left at the top and follow the footpath down the South Ridge of Snowdon to Bwlch Cwm Llan (605521) whence an easy descent to the east leads to the tramway in Cwm Llan.

The modern trend towards perfect rock and car-side crags has served to release the likes of **Clogwyn Du** from the foraging of contemporary climbers. The ridge above may see the passage of hundreds of feet on a good day, but you can be assured of solitude in

151

the confines of the gullies described below. And they are good, honest mountain gullies; deep and long with chockstones, and being Snowdon Gullies, rather special. A gully here, followed by Snowdon and Crib Goch might leave you miles from your car - but what a fine day out.

SHADOW GULLY 250m II/III *

The old ruined wall points up at a prominent cave above and right of the steep band of rock on the hillside below, which bars direct entry to the gully. Go up to the cave, then traverse left across easy ground and go up to the start of the gully proper.

1. 100m (1) Easily up snow through the narrows to the fork where Penumbra veers to the right.
2. 50m (3) Stick hard against the slabs on the left and climb a steep groove to more open ground. A good pitch if taken on the left, although more broken ground to the right offers easier, but less satisfying climbing.
3. 100m (2) Swing round to the left following the slabby edge of the buttress until a vague gully leads out onto the ridge.

PENUMBRA 150m I

The snowy right fork of Shadow Gully may be followed without difficulty to the top.

To the right the crag is quite continuous in its lower third and a number of lines may offer scope for exploration. Towards the left, a slabby groove leads to a prominent V-shaped recess with a large, smooth slab on the left. Above, mixed ground leads upward. Further right, a right-facing chimney beckons and to its right a vague, steep gully heads up towards Tregalen Groove. The edge of the buttress is marked by a deep chasm where the next two routes share a common start.

TREGALEN GROOVE 250m III *

An excellent line which holds a lot of ice.

1. 50m (1/2) A couple of easy steps lead into the chasm where the gully forks.
2. 100m (3) The left-hand fork is a series of stepped grooves cutting into the buttress on the left, giving some enjoyable pitches before the angle relents.
3. 100m (1/2) Easier broken ground above leads to the ridge.

TREGALEN GULLY 280m III

A massive gully giving straightforward climbing after the chockstone has been negotiated.

1. 50m (1/2)   As for Tregalen Groove.
2. 30m (3)   The right-hand fork disappears around a corner where a nasty shock lies in store! Further direct progress may only be possible if the massive capstone is completely banked up. However, the devious will find a way round on the right, only to return to the gully beyond the offending rock.
3. 45m (2)   A couple more steps leads to the easy angled central section of the gully.
4. 100m (1)   Plod on!
5. 55m (2)   Ahead, things steepen somewhat but a groove on the left offers the easiest way out.

CWM DYLI FALLS 150m III

Grid Reference: 650543 (OS Sheet 115 Snowdon)
Altitude: 150m - 300m
Aspect: South East

The gorge of the Afon Glaslyn lies above the power station in the Nant Gwynant and is readily seen across the valley from the road about 2km south of the Pen y Gwryd Hotel. Its height and aspect don't suggest it as a common ice climbing venue, but in rare spells of extreme cold (Ice Ages!), it freezes and has been climbed. It is good fun and gives extended bouldering throughout its length with some pitches up to 4. Turn off the main road at 650522 (only possible if approaching from the SW - or by fancy reversing manoeuvres!) and park beyond the cattle grid by the bridge at 657538. A 15 minute walk leads to the ice.

5. NANTLLE

5.1 **MOEL HEBOG**
5.2 **CWMFFYNNON**
5.3 **CWM SILYN**
5.4 **CWM DULYN**
5.5 **CRAIG CWM DU**

Although considered of little merit in the past, recent years have shown that there is considerable potential amongst these formerly obscure cwms and gullies. There still remains considerable scope for new routes for those with the exploratory urge. Although best in a very cold spell, some of the crags, notably Cwm Silyn, are in condition more often than previously suspected.

5.1 MOEL HEBOG

Y DIFFWYS
Grid Reference: 567476 (OS Sheet 115 Snowdon)
Altitude: 550m - 650m
Aspect: ENE

This lonely peak, although a superb viewpoint, currently only provides one winter line of any note.

Approach:
From the car park at Pont Allen (586483) situated just to the north of Beddgelert, a lane and then a footpath are followed up the hillside towards the summit. Y Diffwys is the long cliff right of the main summit area.

COMPANION WAY 100m II
This is the steep rake that runs up from the left to right in the centre of the cliff, and is a pleasant excursion in good snow. Descent can be made at the left (S) end of the crag, or better, carry on to the Moel Hebog summit.

5.2 CWMFFYNNON

Grid Reference: 537515 (OS Sheet 115 Snowdon)
Altitude: 450m - 650m
Aspect: North
Climbing Conditions:
Requires snow and very cold conditions due to the low altitude and poor drainage.
Approach:
From the lay-by at Simdde'r Dylluan (537533), about 300m west of Drws y Coed on the B4418 road through the Nantlle Valley, follow the track west to Tal y Mignedd and after seeking the farmer's permission return eastwards along the upper track to some higher farm buildings. Carry on through the farmyard and field beyond to a gate leading to the open hillside. Head upwards and rightwards into Cwmffynnon. Alternatively, descend from the Nantlle Ridge down the ridge between Cwmffynnon and Cwm Trum y Ddysgl to the same point.

The climb takes the gully splitting the crag directly behind the small llyn from the base to the summit.

MAIN LEFT-HAND 200m III
Start at a small depression at the lowest point of the buttress, and follow this for about 80m to reach a large cave. Follow the deep gully under the cave and out onto the left side. Carry on to the top, mainly straightforward with two steeper sections, the upper one being the crux.

5.3 CWM SILYN

Grid Reference: 515501 (OS Sheet 115 Snowdon)
Altitude: 550m - 750m
Aspect: North
Climbing Conditions:
Although the climbs are often contained in gullies, the substance of almost all the routes is water-ice. Thus a period of hard frosts is required to bring them into condition.
Approach:
A minor road leaves the A487 at Llanllyfni heading east. Follow this for 1km, then take the narrow lane winding up the hillside SE for 2km to reach a parking spot just through a gateway (495511). This can be reached from the west by finding the same approach lane from the B4418 through the Nantlle Valley. Passing under a slate bridgeway just after leaving the B road is a handy landmark.

Leave the parking spot by the continuation track leading east until after

1.5km the track turns SE into Cwm Silyn. Contouring above the lakes leads to a short but tedious plod up scree/snow to reach the routes.

Upon entering the cwm, the most striking feature is the Ogof, a huge nose of rock with the impressive sweep of the Great Slab on its right. Two huge gullies (Amphitheatre and Great Stone Shoot) mark the transition rightwards to a more broken area at the centre back of the cwm, often seamed with ice-falls. Right again is the eerie precipice of Clogwyn y Cysgod, dripping slime in summer but providing superb hidden gems in winter.

The first two routes are some way around to the left (NE) of the Ogof on the right of the large, prow-shaped crag (Craig Fawr). They are gained by traversing some way across the scree/snow slopes beneath the Ogof until the base of a broad, broken cwm can be gained.

PROW GULLY 250m II
This takes the gully which splits the right-hand side of the upper crag, slabby and indistinct in the lower part but better defined higher up.

BROAD GULLY 250m I
This is the gully right of Prow Gully and just left of the back of the cwm. Again, better defined higher up, it broadens at the top into a fan-shaped snow-field.

The next two routes are found in the steep lower buttresses just round to the left (NE) of the Ogof.

BLACK GULLY 80m III
This is the left-hand of the two steep clefts and can be hard if the lower sections are not eased by snow banks.

ATROCITY RUN 80m V
The right-hand cleft Green Gully, provides a difficult main pitch. Start by the cave at the base of the gully.
1. 35m   Climb the chimney, then the continuation groove to a narrowing of the gully.
2. 40m   The very thin gully provides the main event, sustained until it eases and leads to a large flake belay on the right.
3. 15m   Finish up the gully direct.
An Alpine descent remains over to the left (east), or an Alpine ascent up mixed ground to the top of the cliff.

Around to the right of the Ogof and taking the corner bounding the right-hand side of the Great Slab is:

AQUARIAN WALL   130m   IV/V   ★★★

A popular route giving, when in condition, a climb that ranks with the best in Snowdonia. Start below the corner at the right-hand side of the Great Slab.

1.   25m   Follow the icy corner until a step right and a short hanging icicle gains the groove above. Continue to a poor belay in a niche.

2.   30m   Carry on up iced grooves and slabs, quite steep, to a belay on a small terrace.

3.   25m   Climb diagonally up right for a short way and step around the arête into the continuation groove, which is followed to belay below a steepening.

4.   50m   Follow the groove and shallow chimney on the left until the angle eases. Belay well back on the ridge.

Variation: When the upper groove is not iced, a finish up rightwards can be made.

Right of the Great Slab is a steeper buttress. The next route climbs a hanging ice-fall on the right-hand side of this.

WHITE SNAKE   70m   IV/V   ★★

A difficult and well-positioned climb based on a combination of Upper Slab Climb and West Arête. Start about 15m right of Aquarian Wall.

1.   25m   (4)   Climb the groove into a niche and make a hard exit onto a snow slope on the left. This leads to a large belay on the left.

2.   15m   (4)   Take the corner above to a difficult traverse right to gain the ice-fall. Belay in a groove to the left of the ice.

3.   30m   (4)   Follow the ice-fall to reach the upper snow slopes.

AMPHITHEATRE GULLY   130m   II   ★

This is the first obvious gully right of the Great Slab area and is a good route when heavily iced.

THE GREAT STONE SHOOT   130m   I   ★★

The next big gully to the right is the summer descent route and gives a fine easy snow climb amidst impressive rock scenery.

This marks the start of a less-defined area at the back of the cwm. A number of lines have been climbed here at 2/3 but only one merits individual description.

THE WIDOW OF THE WEB   200m   IV   ★★

This is the most conspicuous ice-fall just left of where the crag steepens again to the right.

1.   30m   Climb the gradually steepening ice corner.

2. 35m   Easily up left to below steep ice.
3. 35m   Climb the ice, similar to Idwal's South Gully but more sustained: a brilliant pitch.
4. 100m   Easy-angled ice to the top.

The right-hand side of the cwm is a strange and sombre cliff line, split by hidden clefts. The upper left-hand end is bounded by **FOUR PITCH GULLY, 100m, II/III,** which is invisible from the floor of the cwm. The deep ravine separated by a big steep buttress from the last route is **LITTLE KITCHEN, 100m, II/III.**

Some 70m down right again lies another bizzare cleft, easily viewed from the approach past the Great Slab and containing two excellent routes.

MASK OF DEATH   120m   IV/V   ★★★
Fine steep ice climbing taking the left-hand branch of the gully. Start as for Bedrock Gully below and belay below the left-hand ice-fall.
1. 40m (5)   Climb up to the left on steep ice and continue directly up the ice-fall, which in some years may be partly detached from the rock.
2. 45m (4)   Straight up the narrow gully until it is possible to pull over into the easier angled upper gully. Boulder belay high up.
3. 35m (2)   More easily up and onto the castellated right-hand ridge to the top.

BEDROCK GULLY   100m   IV   ★★★
A short steep step gains entry to the depths of the cleft and carries on up the right-hand gully line. Start below the short ice-fall after scrambling into the bottom of the gully.
1. 40m (3)   Climb the ice to a steepening, over this to belay above.
2. 20m (3)   Continue in the same line until the angle steepens.
3. 40m (4)   Follow the steepening ice to an exit on the left, a good pitch.

The last route on the cliff before it peters into the hillside is:

COLIN'S GULLY   140m   IV
This is the ice-fall that forms some way to the right of Bedrock Gully.
1. 30m   Climb directly up the ice, moving left to belay at the base of an ice gully.
2. 25m   Follow the gully to a good belay below a steep icy slab.
3. 25m   Straight up the slab to a cave belay on the left.
4. 60m   Move right into the gully line and follow it to easier

climbing and the top.

5.4 CRAIG CWM DULYN

Grid Reference: 497492 (OS Sheet 115 Snowdon)
Altitude: 300m - 450m
Aspect: North
Climbing Conditions:
All the climbs described rely on water-ice, so a period of intense cold is needed
to render them climbable, bearing in mind the low altitude of the crag.
However, every route can be completed in the total absence of snow which
gives the climbing an unusual feel. As a guide to conditions, it is probably fair
to say that if the icy streams on the north side of the Llanberis Pass are well
frozen, then the watercourses of Cwm Dulyn will also be in condition.
Approach: .
This is the ultimate roadside winter crag! Cars may be parked at the end
(488499) of the minor road leading out of the village of Nebo, which is easily
reached from the A487 trunk road south of Caernarfon. An arduous 10 minute
walk along the south side of the lake leads to the crag! However, it is worth
remembering that access to the Nantlle Ridge, of which this is the extreme
western end, has frequently caused problems for climbers and walkers in the
past. It would be sensible to keep a low profile when visiting the crag, particularly with regard to car parking and fence crossing. There have been sheep
worrying incidents here in the past and the farmers are rightly concerned, so
please, NO DOGS.

The crag forms the northern flank of **Mynydd Graig Goch,** which is
the westernmost peak on the **Nantlle Ridge,** and lies above the SE end
of **Llyn Cwm Dulyn**. It divides conveniently into three distinct
sections, each with a number of winter routes. As one approaches
along the south side of the lake, the first section (**The Hanging
Garden**) lies well above (some 70m) the water. It is a massive, broken
crag which is covered in vegetation and the four icy drainage lines may
easily be recognised, assuming that things are 'in nick'. To the left of
the last ice-fall (**Rake End Wall**) an easy rake (**The Rake**) rises up to
the left beneath **The Hanging Garden** as its height diminishes. Below
this rake and just above the lake, is the second section of crag which is
the steepest and least vegetated. This buttress sports a number of rock
climbs, most notably the difficult **Dulyn Groove** which takes the
obvious corner in the centre of the crag. In winter, the two gullies to
the right of **Dulyn Groove** hold a lot of ice. Beyond this crag the
hillside falls back into a shallow cwm. The ground is still steep and the
White Nile and **Runaround Sue** take the obvious frozen water-

courses high on the hillside.

Descent:
From the top of The Hanging Garden, either turn right and follow the blunt
spur easily down to the west end of the lake or turn left and descend The Rake
beneath the left end of the crag. Routes on the central section finish on this
rake which may be descended to return to the foot of the crag. From routes in
the region of the White Nile, it is possible to descend the steep ground to the
right (west) between this section and the central section but it is probably
easier to carry on up to gain the left-hand end of The Rake.

The cwm has a feeling of isolation which belies its proximity to the
road, and whilst it can hardly be described as a classic winter climbing
area, in extended periods of frost it offers by far the best introduction
to pure ice climbing anywhere in Snowdonia. There is just so much
ice! And most of it is set at a reasonable angle, making it suitable for
relative beginners. However, in certain parts there is an absence of
rock for anchors, so a good selection of ice-screws should be taken.
and should the leader be discomfited by the continuous nature of the
ice, he can always take to the vertical heather alongside, where upward
progress may also be possible!

As the lines are strikingly obvious only simple outline descriptions
have been included - if you're in the heather, you're off route! And
watch that you don't get your crampons tangled in it!

The climbs are described from RIGHT to LEFT as one encounters
them when walking in and the first four lines (and variations) lie on
The Hanging Garden.

HEART OF ICE 140m III *
The right-hand line is characterised by a massive icicle fringe high on
the crag. An easy-angled section (2/3) leads to a steep central ice-fall
(4), and the vertical fringe at the top is turned by a deep gully on the
left (3).

Variation Finish
MR. DRAINPIPE OF STOCKPORT 50m 4/5
*The direct finish up the massive icicles at the top of the previous route. First
climbed at a time when frozen drainpipes were all the vogue and the validity
of such ascents was being called into question!*

ICE MAMBA 140m III
Some 50m to the left, a single tenuous line of ice rises steeply through
vegetation. Follow this (3/4) for two pitches until it opens out
somewhat. Now make for an obvious avoidable vertical ice-pillar

160

above. Climb the pillar (5, silly), or avoid it on the left (2, sensible).

CENTRAL ICE-FALLS 140m III
Left again is a wide area of easy-angled ice-falls. Take the most appealing line (3) to broken ground and scrambling after two rope-lengths.

RAKE END WALL 140m III ★
At the start of The Rake, a long concave smear adorns a rocky slab and gives one of the best pitches in the cwm. Climb it, moving left as it steepens (4), to gain the easier angled watercourse above. Move right in a groove (2/3) and continue past one further steepening (3) to the top.

The following two climbs take gullies in the right-hand section of the crag below The Rake.

THE FINAL CUT 50m II/III
The first, straightforward gully beyond the massive boulders on the hillside. It gives an unremarkable but pleasant little climb.

THE CLEAVER 100m III ★
Just right of the main rocky mass of the buttress is a deep gully which rises in two steep icy steps (3,3) to gain an easier angled bay above where it offers two branches. The right-hand one is probably best and it gains a pleasant col on The Rake.

Around in the cwm to the right is a great mass of ice flowing down the hillside. This is:

THE WHITE NILE 100m II/III
Follow the great river to its source. Beware of crocodiles.

RUNAROUND SUE 100m III
Some 30m to the left is another steep stream, easily recognised by two parallel ice-falls, some 5m apart, which separate and rejoin after about 45m. Follow the stream and choose your ice-fall! The left-hand is possibly slightly harder (4) than the right-hand (3/4), but both lead to horizontal ice and *piolet walking-stick*.

5.5 CRAIG CWM DU

This quiet cwm, although clearly visible from the road, has a lonely and mysterious air about it. Never popular, summer or winter, it holds a charm few of it's occasional visitors would dismiss.

Grid Reference: 536551 (OS Sheet 115 Snowdon)
Altitude: 450m - 600m
Aspect: NNE
Climbing Conditions:
Like the other climbing grounds in this area the cwm is relatively low in altitude, although this is somewhat balanced by the northerly outlook. The buttresses are fairly clean but even in summer the gullies are full of water and vegetation, the classic sign of a good winter crag. Thus the crag comes into condition in a prolonged spell of very cold weather but it should be noted that some snow is required to fill out the often drier upper sections of the routes.

There is certainly scope here for future exploration, and intrepid teams are advised to carry the comprehensive rock guide to the crag in order to fully understand the topography of the cliffs.

Aproach:
From the village of Y Fron (Cesarea) (508548), a narrow road can be followed eastwards through the village, taking a left-hand fork, then a right-hand fork down a rough lane through narrow cuttings to a gate. Beyond this, open moor is crossed and the broad shoulder of the mountain rounded to finish up on a small path contouring below the crags. An alternative is to follow the footpath SE across the river and up through the woods into the cwm from Betws Garmon (546563).

Descent:
All routes finish on the rounded summit approaches, and easy descents can be made anywhere on the western slopes.

EDEN GULLY 130m I/II
This is the deep gully over on the left of the crag, bounded on its left by a prominent rib and on its right by a large wall.

SAXIFRAGE GULLY 130m III
The next deep cleft right of the previous route. A worthwhile climb, the middle section providing sustained ice in a deep and narrow cleft which is invisible from below. There are easy snow slopes above and below the hard section.

AVALANCHE GULLY 150m III
This is the dark gully bounding the right side of the central area of rocks. The left-hand ridge overhangs the gully for most of the way. Contains both easy snow and steep ice similar to Saxifrage Gully.

6. LLEYN PENINSULA

Although the **Lleyn** is usually thought of as more of a tropical paradise for holiday-makers from Birmingham than an area for pushing back the frontiers of ice climbing, it does have some fine mountains along its north coast. The northern cwms of **Yr Eifl** are certainly high enough and wet enough to be worth an exploratory visit or two in the right conditions. Of course, the right conditions (several weeks of particularly severe cold) are fairly rare, although each of the recent three winters (85/86/87) has offered spells of this type at some time. To date, only one route has been recorded, and this recently received its first ascent by night! ... But there may be others!

Grid Reference: 357447 (OS Sheet 123 The Lleyn Peninsula)
Altitude: 100m - 300m
Aspect: West
Approach:
Turn off the B4417 coast road to Nefyn in Llithfaen (356432) and follow the road down towards the Lost Valley of Nant Gwrtheryn and the Porth y Nant quarries. The climb is on Craig Ddu which faces out to sea at the head of the valley.

MOONLIGHT FLIT   200m   III/IV   ★★★
The main waterslide on the face gives four excellent, long pitches. The first pitch is the hardest (4), and it eases somewhat above. There are also other minor ice-falls in the same region.

7. MOELWYNION

To the south of Snowdon, beyond Nant Gwynant and the Gorge of Aberglaslyn, lies a range of hills of modest height, stretching from the voluminous flanks of Moel Siabod in the north-east across crag and moor, lake and quarry to shapely Cnicht and the Moelwynion twins, Bach and Mawr, in the south-west. Unfashionable it may be, but go for the views: north to the majestic Horseshoe; west through deep Croesor to the sea where the weak winter sun lights up Tremadog Bay in the afternoon; and south to Arenig, Rhinog, Aran and Cadair in the heartlands of Wales. The West Moelwyns is a place for quiet contemplation in the company of a thousand frozen pools and the rime encrusted remains of an earlier age of modern man.

Away to the south-east, across the Crimea in the Blaenau back-country, lie the East Moelwyns; huge convex molehills, scarred for life by open sores of slate. And deep valleys into which the boglands of the Migneint seep en route for Conwy and Dwy. There is plenty of water in the Moelwyns and when it's cold, the ice appears, to reward the explorer. But don't go expecting climbing - go for the hills and be pleasantly surprised.

Such climbs as are worth describing are listed in an order which may appear rather haphazard - well, it is! The general idea is to start at Moel Siabod, work SW to Blaenau Ffestiniog through the West Moelwyns, then work back to the north through the East Moelwyns.

7.1 MOEL SIABOD

Grid Reference: 705547 (OS Sheet 115 Snowdon)
Altitude: 700m - 800m

Aspect: E or SE

The huge and impressive SE face of Moel Siabod has much potential for winter climbing, although the lack of drainage, and too much south in the aspect usually prevents conditions from building up. Winds from the NW can pile the snow into the major gullies but it rarely consolidates: if it ever does, then there will be some fine sport in the lower grades.

The climbing is in the east-facing cwm above **Llyn y Foel** and is approached in about 1 hour from **Pont Cyfyng** at 734571 on a minor road which crosses the **River Llugwy** from the A5. A good track leads up through old quarry workings and over a shallow, boggy col to the lake.

High above the lake a solitary buttress is split by a gully and also bounded on its right by a large easy gully. The right-hand side of the buttress, between the two gullies, is the line of:

LONE BUTTRESS 80m III

Gain the rib from the left and follow it over mixed ground to the top, avoiding difficulties by excursions from the crest.

EMBRYO GULLY 80m I

The big gully to the right gives a straightforward climb on snow.

Further right are a number of easy gullies which ascend to the rocky spine of Siabod's NE ridge and which in good conditions, may be worthwhile.

7.2 NANTMOR FALLS

NANTMOR FALLS 150m II *

Grid Reference: 651483 (OS Sheet 115 Snowdon)
Altitude: 400m - 550m
Aspect: WNW

This is the prominent steep stream clearly seen from the main road alongside Llyn Dinas, which forms the outflow from Llyn yr Adar and flows into Llyn Llagi. Although its relatively low altitude causes it to freeze only rarely, when in condition it is comparable with Sergeant's Gully in Cwm Glas. Approach in 40 minutes via the obvious footpath from 635490 on the very narrow minor road through Nantmor.

7.3 MOELWYN MAWR

Grid Reference: 658449 (OS Sheet 124 Dolgellau)
Altitude: 600m - 750m
Aspect: SE

Although the aspect is rather unfavourable, some interesting climbs have been recorded on the south-east face of the mountain above **Llyn Stwlan**. Approach from the parking place at 682454 and follow the metalled road beneath the crags up to **Llyn Stwlan**. The climbs start from the traversing Miners' Track some distance above the lake, and are described from RIGHT to LEFT starting with **Central Gully** directly below the summit.

CENTRAL GULLY 150m I
The obvious gully to the summit.

CENTRAL BUTTRESS 130m II
A number of meandering lines are possible on the buttress to the left of the previous route.

SQUARE CUT GULLY 60m II
Some way to the left, a deep square cut gully leads on to Craig Ysgafn on the south ridge of the mountain.

On the col (666453) between **Moelwyn Mawr** and **Moel yr Hydd**, are two huge mine entrances (**Rhosydd Mine**) and a number of practice pitches on iced slabs exist. The west-most hole is the best, and if the weather becomes too inclement, a retreat into the mine adds a new dimension to the day. A straightforward through-trip to 665459 is possible for those with torches.

On the way up the road to **Llyn Stwlan**, a prominent waterfall at 675481 freezes in particularly cold spells. This is reached just before the popular rock climbing crag of **Clogwyn yr Oen** on the way up the road.

FALL OF THE LAMB 60m II/III
The south-facing fall should be tackled on a cold, sun-less day, under which conditions it proves an excellent little training climb, particularly after practice on the waterfalls by the parking place.

Above the back road through **Tan-y-Grisiau** is an area of broken crags called **Craig Nyth-y-Gigfran**, and directly above the Bacon Slicer Factory a prominent two-part ice-fall sometimes forms to the north-east of the main crag. This may have been Britain's first urban ice climb!

THE SLICER 60m IV
Climb the fall with two main pitches. It is possible to descend further over to the right (facing the crag), or more easily (but much longer) by crossing westwards over into Cwmorthin.

7.4 RHAEADR Y CWM

RHAEADR Y CWM 60m IV ★★
Grid Reference: 739417 (OS Sheet 124 Dollgellau)
Altitude: 350m
Aspect: West

This large waterfall is situated in the deep valley below Pont yr Afon-Gam in upper Afon Cynfal and is approached from a lay-by on the B4391. It is rarely completely frozen but is probably climbable at least as often as Aber Falls.

7.5 MAESGWM FALLS

MAESGWM FALLS 150m IV ★★
Grid Reference: 728491 (OS Sheet 115 Snowdon)
Altitude: 300m - 450m
Aspect: NE

A road leads into Cwm Penamnen from Dolwyddelan, passing Carreg Alltrem on the left before petering out at a cluster of farm buildings. The stream is just to the south-west and is followed with increasing interest into the upper cwm below Moel Penamnen. Recent felling in this area has exposed the fall to the outside world.

8. RHINOGS

8.1 CRAIG BODLYN

It is sometimes hard to believe that the Rhinogs are as big as Snowdon, the Glyders and the Carnedds put together. They comprise 25km of rough crag and heather extending from Barmouth in the south to Maentwrog in the north, following a fine, natural ridge line. This only dips as it passes the head of three long and beautifully remote cwms running up from the coast to the west. There is an air of Scottish glens about the range and despite their modest height (up to 750m), the Rhinogs in a biting winter can be a very bleak place indeed.

But what of the climbing? Low and close to the sea, one should not expect too much, perhaps; but the lack of recorded winter climbs may be more of a comment on the lack of exploration rather than the lack of potential. The prospect of long walks, far from the honeypots of the north, explains the lack of interest shown so far and the development of the only crag recorded here owes its existence to the fertile and unconventional mind of Mick Fowler - if the contours are close enough together, there must be climbing! Of course, there may be nothing else, but just to go poking around in the Rhinogs' isolated cwms in the depths of winter will be reward enough for some.

8.1 CRAIG BODLYN

Grid Reference: 650237 (OS Sheet 124 Dolgellau)
Altitude: 400m - 480m
Aspect: North
Approach:
Take the A496 coast road from Harlech to Barmouth as far as Llanddwywe (587224) where a long, straight minor road leads off through impressive portals to a farm complex, Cors-y-Gedol. From here the crag lies 5km to the east along a good dirt road - 2 hours to Llyn Bodlyn and the crag. It is *possible* to drive to the lake, but the gate is likely to be locked, and in any case, may well be when you return! Oh, yes, and there are the drifts across the road! But some may feel that the risk is worth taking...!

The crag extends for about 500m along the south side of the splendidly remote lake, but the major feature is a steep, tall rock buttress at the right-hand end. To its left, beyond a steep ice-chimney line (unclimbed as yet) the crag becomes more broken, passing two more narrow, steep chimney/gully lines to reach the twin ice-falls, starting half-way up the crag. Beyond these is a further easier gully, after which the crag begins to lose interest! The climbs are described from RIGHT to LEFT, as one encounters them.

Descent:

A broad easy gully to the right (west) of the main crag offers the fastest descent to the dam, but it may be slightly easier to return to the shallow valley well to the east of the crag.

The first climb takes the right-hand of two obvious parallel gullies just left of the edge of the major rock buttress on the right of the crag.

CHAIN GANG 150m V *

Difficult and intricate mixed climbing up the steepening gully in four pitches. Each pitch is harder than the previous one and the final crux pitch involves wide bridging on verglas, followed by an exciting pull out left (6).

RISKOPHILIA 150m V *

Similar in quality and difficulty to Chain Gang, this is the parallel line immediately to the left.

High up and some 150m across to the left is a massive fringe of icicles with two free standing pillars, one at either end, which *may* reach the ground. If they don't, it's a long walk out! Approach by scrambling up broken ground to the foot of the ice.

CRYOGENICS 60m V *

The right-hand and more continuous of the two lines. Climb steep ice to the foot of the icicle proper (4). Belay. Climb the icicle, sensitively! (5/6).

THE SCREAMING 70m V *

Start just left of Cryogenics and move diagonally across to the foot of the left-hand icicle (4). Belay. Take the slim, vertical stalactite in an oh-so-tender embrace: 'Fragile - this way up' (6)!

Around to the left is a much easier gully, **DIFFWYS GULLY, 120m, III,** after which the crag peters out into the hillside.

169

9. CADAIR IDRIS

9.1 **CYFRWY**
9.2 **PEN-Y-GADAIR**
9.3 **TWR DU**
9.4 **CWM CAU**

This fine mountain can rival any in Snowdonia with the quality of its winter climbing. Its high, north-facing craggy cwms with their abundant vegetation and drainage provide the potential: unfortunately, its proximity to the warm sea and its relatively modest altitude often combine to frustrate the ambitions of those seeking a winter adventure away from the hurly-burly of central Snowdonia. But venture out when the raw east wind scythes across the mountain, driving snow flurries far out into the Atlantic and sweeping sheets of spindrift across its crags. Only then will Cadair offer up its secret jewels.

THE NORTHERN SLOPES

The northern flank of Cadair Idris presents a long escarpment - one of the longest in Wales - and several cliffs and buttresses are inset to stiffen the rampart. Given good winter snow, this area would provide an endless series of routes: the quality of those few described below suggest that the plums have fallen, but there is still scope for pioneering work in the right conditions.

The starting point for all of the northern escarpment crags is the same, the **car park at GR.698152** on the minor road leaving Dolgellau to the south-west, but the approach to each crag is somewhat different. Although the climbs on each crag are described from left to right as is the convention, the crags themselves are considered from RIGHT to LEFT (west to east) along the escarpment.

9.1 CYFRWY

Grid Reference: 700136 (OS Sheet 124 Dolgellau)
Altitude: 600m - 700m

170

Aspect: North facing

Climbing Conditions:
Climbing on the Western Wing is mainly on steep water-ice but routes on the left end of the crag in the region of Cyfrwy Arête need a good build-up of both snow and ice.

Approach:
For climbs on the Western Wing, approach from the car park (698152), and follow the tourist track towards the saddle (Rhiw Gwredydd) at 691135. Before reaching the saddle, turn off leftwards to reach the foot of the crag which lies to the east of the saddle.

For climbs in the vicinity of Cyfrwy Arête, approach as for Pen-y-Gadair via the Fox's Path to Llyn-y-Gadair, then branch off to the right and ascend snow/scree to the crag.

Two landmarks on the 1,500m long crags may be easily identified; the **Eastern Arête** with its curious truncated tower, and 400m to the right of this, the huge rift of **One Pitch Gully** which cleaves the escarpment. The climbing lies between these two points, with the **Western Wing** some distance away to the right.

Descent:
Either follow the blunt west spur of Cadair Idris easily down to the saddle, Rhiw Gwredydd, and recover the tourist track, or more rapidly if it can be identified, by descending the first wide, easy gully immediately to the right of Barn Door on the Western Wing.

Just left of Cyfrwy Arête is a pleasant easy gully.

EASY GULLY 100m I *

EASTERN ARÊTE OF CYFRWY 130m II **

This is the left-hand ridge which is obvious on the approach, and a prominent square tower at almost half height is a further marker. It is a delight under any conditions, perhaps a miniature Tower Ridge?

Start on its left (east) side.

1. 30m   Climb the easy chimney to the gap behind the square tower.
2. 30m   Climb left across the icy wall above the gap, then back onto the crest.
3. 70m   Another short, steep wall is taken direct and then the ridge is followed easily over broken snow slopes to the top.

Between **Cyfrwy Arête** and **One Pitch Gully** is a steep area of crag furrowed by several gullies. This section is very good under firm snow, and two lines which share a common start are most prominent.

B GULLY 125m III

This slants left from the centre of the area and ends on the upper part of Cyfrwy Arête.

Start in an enclosed, slanting gully just left of the steepest rocks.

1. 45m   Climb ice, mainly on the left of the gully to a wide terrace.
2. 45m   Cross the terrace and climb very steep snow in the same line.
3. 35m   Finish out to the left on the ridge.

C GULLY 140m III

1. 45m   As for B Gully to the terrace.
2. 60m   Slant right up steep snow to an unexpected ridge.
3. 35m   Follow the ridge leftwards to the top.

ONE PITCH GULLY 160m I/II ★

This is the obvious feature already mentioned, and as the name implies, it has a single pitch near the top.

1. 160m   Climb easy snow to the pitch, which although short and safe is rather hard for the grade. Finish up the narrow snow gully above.

CYFRWY WESTERN WING

This area of the Cadair cliffs provides a number of the finest steep ice climbs in Wales. On the right, **The Shining** and **Barn Door** take deep, icy gullies, whilst on the left the deep slabby recess with huge, dripping roofs guarding its left corner, gives the obvious lines of **Colonial Virgin** and the classic **Trojan.**

COLONIAL VIRGIN 130m V/VI ★★★

This fine route takes the icicle which forms in some winters on the right of the huge, curved roof in the left corner of the bay. Start by climbing the easy ice-gully to beneath the roof.

1. 40m   (5)   Climb the groove, then the steep right wall to an ice-ramp under icicles. Chockstone belay.
2. 45m   (6)   Traverse out right and up to the icicle. Up the icicle and slab above to a second icicle. Up this to a stance in the gully.
3. 45m   (2)   Up the gully via easy ice bulges to steep snow and the top.

TROJAN 115m V ★★★

A classic ice climb taking the system of slabby corners and grooves, topped by a triangular overhang on the right at the back of the recess.

It is a natural watercourse giving excellent, sustained climbing at an angle which is never less than 70°. However, it does need a prolonged frost to be in condition, and can become harder as frequent ascents hack away at the tenuous ribbon of ice!

1. 40m (5)   Directly up the corner, negotiating bulges (normally water-ice) to above the narrows. Take a poor stance on a small ledge in the corner.
2. 30m (5)   Continue up the corner, then out diagonally left across the exposed iced slab to a stance just left of the triangular over-hang.
3. 45m (4)   The chimney line above, normally with an awkward bulge at 10m.

THE SHINING 145m IV **

Another fine route taking the deep, narrow gully some 100m right of Trojan.

1. 25m (2)   Up the gully to gain a cave behind the ice-curtain.
2. 45m (5)   Climb the ice-curtain on the right (good Friend protection on right wall) and continue up ice bulges to another cave.
3. 45m (4)   Climb ice in the chimney/groove for 25m to snow. Poor belay below next steepening.
4. 30m (3)   Up steepening to beneath final chockstone and move out right to finish up easy ground.

BARN DOOR 80m III **

This takes the big obvious ice-flow which forms on the left wall of the first wide gully to the right of The Shining.

1. 20m (3)   Make a rising traverse up left beneath the steep ice-wall to a stance below a steep rock wall.
2. 40m (4)   Traverse back right above the ice-wall and up bulging ice to a stance in the vague gully above.
When in condition, the ice-wall may be climbed direct (5), and the route then becomes Grade IV.
3. 20m (2)   Up the gully to the top.

The next wide easy gully to the right (facing the cliff) of **Barn Door**, provides the best descent from all the routes described on the **Western Wing**.

9.3 PEN-Y-GADAIR

Grid Reference: 709130 (OS Sheet 124 Dolgellau)
Altitude: 700m - 890m

Aspect: North West
Climbing Conditions:
As this is the highest of the Cadair crags, conditions will generally be more reliable than elsewhere. Gwth and Rattler depend on water-ice build-up, whilst Central Gully needs a good cover of snow-ice.

This area of terraced cliffs lies directly beneath the summit of **Cadair Idris**, and overlooks **Llyn y Gadair**, to the west of the **Fox's Path**.

Approach:
The crag is easily reached by following the Fox's Path from the car park at 698152 to Llyn y Gadair, from whence a rising traverse rightwards above the lake leads to the foot of the crag (90 minutes from the car park).

The main feature of the crag is an obvious gully on the left-hand side, which crosses two large terraces. This is **Central Gully.** Some distance to the right a number of other, shorter gullies give the lines of the other routes on the crag.

Descent:
Descend eastwards then north-eastwards from the summit of Cadair Idris, following the path until the Fox's Path cuts down steeply to the north-west from a large flat shoulder. This is followed back to Llyn y Gadair.

CENTRAL GULLY 205m III *
The obvious gully on the left-hand side of the crag, crossing two wide terraces which barely interrupt its upward progress.
1. 30m (2)   Up the narrow gully on snow and ice to a bay.
2. 45m (2)   Continue up the gully line, escaping to the arête on the right before moving back left at the first terrace.
3. 20m (3)   Follow the ice-chimney to snow.
4. 20m (4)   An awkward chockstone pitch requiring good snow/ice.
5. 90m (2)   Up easy snow, crossing the second terrace, then follow the continuation gully to the summit plateau.

RATTLER 205m III *
This climb takes a shallow gully line approximately 150m right of Central Gully. Bulges of ice in its upper section are its most obvious feature.
1. 20m (2)   Climb easily up the shallow gully to a good spike and nut belay beneath the first bulge.
2. 45m (4)   Climb two awkward bulges to a snow bay. Nut belay on left under prominent ice bulges.

3. 40m (3)   Climb the wide ice-chimney above to easy ground.
4. 100m (2)   Follow easy mixed ground for about three rope-lengths to the summit plateau.

Right of **Rattler** is a very obvious ice smear about 20m high set at about 60°. By climbing this, and a further two rope-lengths above following an ice runnel, the ice wall of this next route may be seen on the left-hand side of a narrow, steep-walled gully.

GWTH   90m   IV   ★★
As the highest ice route on Cadair, this will probably be the first to come into condition. The ice wall is the natural continuation of the ice runnel on the approach.
1. 45m (5)   Climb the ice wall direct via an icicle at 10m. (Good peg crack below and right of icicle.) Move into a small niche on the left. Follow an ice ramp up rightwards finishing steeply into an easier angled scoop. Stance and belays in a shallow cave on the left.
2. 45m (3)   Continue following the ice flow over a steeper section at 20m, then easy ground to the summit plateau.

9.4   TWR DU

Grid Reference: 719135 (OS Sheet 124 Dolgellau)
Altitude: 600m - 800m
Aspect: North West
Climbing Conditions:
As most of the routes depend on a substantial build-up of both water-ice and snow-ice the crag is rarely in good condition.

The crag is approximately mid-way between the summits of **Pen-y-Gadair** and **Mynedd Moel**, and stands out from the escarpment high above the shallow cwm containing **Llyn y Gafr**. Although, from a distance the cliffs hereabouts appear rather scrappy, closer inspection reveals quite an impressive main buttress.

Approach:
The crag is easily reached by following the Fox's Path from the car park at 698152 to Llyn y Gadair, from whence a long contour eastwards leads to the foot of the crag (90 minutes from the car park).

The main buttress, which towers above a lower area of short rock steps and vegetated terraces is defined on either side by a steep gully line. These are **East Gully** on the left, and **West Gully** on the right.

Descent:
Any direct descent from Twr Du is quite difficult, so the best and safest route is to go westwards above the crags to join the descent from Pen-y-Gadair to Llyn y Gadair via the Fox's Path.

EAST GULLY 200m IV **

The steep ice chimney/gully left of the steep buttress is difficult if taken direct, although easier variations are possible.
1. 75m (3/4)   Grooves and slabs lead via a small bay to the steep chimney section of the gully.
2. 55m (5)   Steep ice leads into the chimney which has a large chockstone near the top.
3. 70m (2/3)   More easily in the line of the gully to the top.

WEST GULLY 200m IV **

This is the vague gully/crack line immediately right of the big, steep buttress and follows the summer route throughout.
1. 40m (3)   Climb just left of the chimney/crack to a scoop. Climb the corner on the right to the base of the ice-smeared slabs.
2. 30m (4)   Climb the ice-smeared slabs to the gully above.
3. 40m (4)   The narrow gully past a chockstone to easier ground.
4. 45m (3)   Climb the gully line over ice bulges.
5. 45m (2)   Take the easiest line to the summit plateau.

WHITE ADDER 170m III/IV

This route takes the distinctive set of grooves on the far right of the crag which are obvious when approaching from Llyn y Gafr below.
1. 40m   Up the initial ice for 10m to snow and continue to second ice-pitch (8m). Belay below the next ice-pitch.
2. 40m   Climb ice, steeply at first, for 20m, then follow snow to belay below ice bulge.
3. 30m   Easy ice and snow leads to foot of steep ice-groove. Peg belays.
4. 60m   Climb the groove to easy ground and the summit ridge.

9.5 CWM CAU

Grid Reference: 712122 (OS Sheet 124 Dolgellau)
Altitude: 520m - 790m
Aspect: North East
Climbing Conditions:
Although the magnificent 300m headwall of the cwm can produce superb

winter climbing, exceptional conditions are required to bring out the best in this area. The main gully lines (Little, East and Great) rely largely on good snow/ice build-up. The routes further right are mainly on water-ice.

Cwm Cau is a vast and impressive amphitheatre scooped by glacial action from the south-east flanks of **Cadair Idris**. The three main peaks of this mountain massif are arrayed around the lip of the cwm: **Mynedd Moel** to the north-east, **Pen-y-Gadair**, the main summit to the north-west, and **Mynedd Pencoed** towering above the dark waters of **Llyn Cau**, to the west. When snow-covered, the huge, complex and vegetated crags which encircle the lake with their tiers and terraces lend a majestic air to this desolate cwm.

Approach:
Approach from the B4405 just south-west of its junction with the A487. Start through the derelict gardens, then follow the stream on a steep, wooded track until the angle eases above the trees and the stream swings westwards to enter the cwm proper. Go around the south side of Llyn Cau to the climbs (90 minutes from the road).

The most obvious feature of the headwall is the imposing sweep of **Pencoed Pillar,** scored on the right by **Great Gully** and on the left by **East Gully.** Left again is **Little Gully** and beyond that several lesser but still interesting lines that rise above the southern shores of the lake. The **Easy Terrace** takes a diagonal line from the foot of **East Gully** across **Great Gully** and then on up with steep walls above and below until it ends at a deep, vertical chimney line. Further right, an area of sloping ramps and terraces lies beneath a steep, wet line of cliffs banded by roofs. **Saturday Night Fever** and **The Ramp** tackle this area of the crag. Further right again, the crags diminish in height and an easy ascent/descent can be made via a broad rake which starts just to the left of a prominent whale-backed rock buttress, just above the lake. This rake leads to the north ridge of **Mynedd Pencoed**, just south of the col at the back of the cwm.

Descent:
For routes in the Pencoed Pillar area, follow the tourist (Minffordd) path down to the south then eastwards above the crags until it descends steeply (beyond Little Gully) northwards to the foot of the cwm, a short distance to the east of Llyn Cau itself.

For routes further right, follow the ridge down to the north towards the col, and descend to the lake via the broad rake mentioned above.

LITTLE GULLY 110m III

This is the conspicuous winding cleft which starts some 100m above the lake. It contains two main pitches, the lower of the two is short on steep snow-ice, whilst the upper involves difficult negotiation of a cave pitch which is frequently verglassed.

THE EAST GULLY 140m III

A more worthwhile proposition than the previous route, it starts some 80m above the south-west corner of the lake on the left of Pencoed Pillar.

1. 30m   Climb iced slabs into the gully and up to a projecting block.
2. 15m   Pass the block by ice on the left.
3. 30m   Steep snow leads to a fork.
4. 65m   Climb either fork up snow with no major difficulties.

THE GREAT GULLY 300m IV ★★★

The great cleft on the right-hand side of Pencoed Pillar should be reserved for near perfect conditons, whence an ascent will fully repay any delay. The scenery en route is particularly grand, bringing to mind its namesake on Craig yr Ysfa. Some of the upper difficulties can be avoided, generally on the right and if this is done Grade III is probably more appropriate.

Start on the right at the foot of the pillar.

1. 100m   Two steep ice-falls lead to a junction with the Easy Terrace.
2. 45m   Climb the narrowing gully until the right wall falls back again.
3. 80m   Surmount short pitches direct, or more easily via snow ledges on the right.
4. 75m   A final steep chimney is climbed over several ice boulders to easy snow.

SATURDAY NIGHT FEVER 200m V ★★

A fine modern line taking the superb ice streak which forms in the vicinity of the summer route The Baron. Start as for The Ramp.

1. 110m   (3)   Follow The Ramp, climbing its first two main ice-pitches, to belay on the large snow terrace below the obvious ice streak.
2. 45m   (6)   Climb the ice streak, crossing a short rock barrier (crux) and moving right below a roof to a large grass ledge.
3. 45m   (4)   Work across leftwards to finish near the deep chimney/gully line.

THE RAMP 200m III *
This climb takes the highest ramp line under the steep wall leading up to the wet, roofed upper crag taken by the previous route. There are three main ice-pitches (of which the middle one is the crux (3)) separated by large snow terraces. Start to the right of the deep chimney line which splits the cliff right of the Easy Terrace.

The following two routes are way round to the right on the south-facing slopes of **Mynedd Moel** and are passed on the approach to **Llyn Cau.**

BIFROST 140m IV
Follows the obvious frozen stream on the south face of Mynedd Moel, and owing to its position, requires an extremely cold spell to bring it into condition. It also melts rapidly in the sunshine!
1. 30m (2) Climb several small ice bulges to a snow bay beneath a 10m ice wall.
2. 40m (3) Climb the ice wall to easy-angled ice beneath a steeper slab with an undercut base.
3. 45m (3) Follow the undercut ice slab to snow, then ice bulges to a good stance beneath a vertical ice-pitch.
4. 25m (5) Climb the vertical ice-pitch to easy ground.

SLAB STICK III
To the right of Bifrost, another ice flow appears in a cold spell and is the substance of this route.

Descent from the above two routes is down a gully to the left (facing cliff) of **Bifrost.**

10. ARAN

10.1 CWM CYWARCH
10.2 ARAN FAWDDWY
10.3 ARAN BENLLYN

Some 20km to the north-east of Cadair Idris and extending south-wards from the shores of Bala Lake to Dinas Mawddwy in the Dovey Valley, lies a range of hills whose true nature is concealed from the distant observer as he scans the far horizon like some feudal Lord from the battlements of his rather superior Welsh '3000'. For those far-away gentle slopes and grassy summits seem trivial to this warlord of the rocky spires and frozen cataracts. But wait a minute, can that be snow, piping the distant hogsback? Surely not, unless some freak, errant shower has mischievously scattered its flakes down there for a joke?

A joke? Hardly, because were it not for the lack of a decent sized cairn, then Aran Fawddwy would be enjoying the last laugh at the fatigued faces of our feudal Lords as they complete their round of the 'Welsh 3's', irresistably drawn across miles of featureless moor and marsh to scale her soft contours: and then to gaze with shock into her rough and craggy eastern cwms.

For the Arans should not be underestimated: Benllyn, Fawddwy, then south to craggy Cywarch; a long, high ridge, drier and colder than the mountains of the coast; hidden cwms and cliffs in a land of waterfalls. And with the winter snows comes the promise of icy adventures far from the madding crowd.

10.1 CWM CYWARCH

Grid Reference: 847190 (OS Sheet 124 Dolgellau)
Altitude: 300m - 600m
Aspect: East or North-East
Climbing Conditions:
Because of its low altitude, these otherwise promising crags are rarely in condition. However, prolonged frosts can produce some good water-ice routes.

The crags of **Craig Cywarch** are plentiful and varied. Many are tucked away on the walls of hidden gullies and streams, but with the exception of **Maen Hir Ice-fall**, the winter lines described are concentrated in the **North Buttress** area, which is towards the head of the cwm, north of the two plantations and west of **Bryn Hafod.**

Approach:
From Dinas Mawddwy on the A470, a minor road leads northwards into the cwm via Aber Cywarch to a car park (853185).

Access to the Arans has always been a thorny issue. Any approach to the east side of Benllyn, including Gist Ddu, from Cwm Croes is likely to meet opposition. Fawddwy is less problematic as it is more remote and may be approached either from Cywarch in the south, or from the east via Llaethnant. Access to the main ridge for walkers has been negotiated from three points only:
1) Cywarch (this does not include an approach to the crags)
2) from the A494 west of the summit of Fawddwy
3) at the far north end of the ridge
Climbers must either use one of these, admittedly rather inconvenient access points, or risk upsetting an already somewhat precarious situation. It is recommended that anyone intending a visit should carefully study the new 1:25,000 Outdoor Leisure Sheet 23 CADAIR IDRIS, with a view to locating rights of way and avoiding walls and fences. No further advice on access to this area is offered in this guidebook.

Descent:
From the top of routes in the North Buttress region, scramble to easy ground, then make a descending traverse north-westwards into the cwm at the head of the Afon Cywarch which is followed back round to Bryn Hafod. Alternatively, and with greater difficulty, locate the steep ramp between the North Buttress and the North Face and descend this.

The descent from Maen Hir Ice-fall is to the right, via the centre of the cwm.

High up on the south side of **Cwm Rhychain** is a gully with a prominent shark's fin pinnacle in it. Just right of this is a steep crag (**Maen Hir Crag**), and right again is an ice flow which forms the substance of the first route.

MAEN HIR ICE-FALL   95m   IV
This gives two steep ice-pitches of 40m and 45m.

When approaching the **North Buttress, North Gully** is the impressive cleft dividing **Central Buttress** to the south, from **North East Buttress** to the north. At the foot of the **North East Buttress**, and close to the start of **North Gully** is the **NNE Tower**, a prominent 20m rock tower.

NORTH GULLY 195m IV

The best of the Cywarch gullies, although all the lower pitches can be avoided. The gully proper starts at a long inescapable runnel leading up to the converging walls pitch (Tombstone Pitch).

1. 45m (2)   Climb the long runnel passing trees to the converging walls.
2. 30m (4)   Climb ice on the left wall to easier bulges above. Follow a groove to a capstone and exit left.
3. 30m (4)   Climb the short undercut wall to snow.
4. 90m (1/2)   Easily to the top.

Beyond **North East Buttress** the crags swing round to become more north-facing. An area of grass terraces is passed followed by the rib and slab structure of the **North Buttress** itself. Further right, the steep descent ramp is passed, and the next crag is the steep and impressive **North Face.**

HOPSIT 75m IV

This route climbs the icy chimney crack in the corner left of the big quartz wall on the left-hand side of the crag. Not often in condition.

1. 35m (5)   Follow ice into the corner and climb it with difficulty to a wide rake on the left.
2. 40m (5)   Take the natural continuation groove on the left.

Right of the **North Face**, a gully containing a striking tower/pinnacle is reached. The tower is **Dinas Llewelyn**, and the gully of the same name runs up to the left of this tower.

DINAS LLEWELYN GULLY 150m II

1. 100m (2)   Climb the gully via many short ice-pitches which are taken direct.
2. 50m (3)   A good steepening ice-pitch leads to the top.

10.2 ARAN FAWDDWY

Summit Grid Reference: 862223 (OS Sheet 124 Dolgellau)
Altitude: 600m - 900m
Aspect: East
Climbing Conditions:
Despite its height, the climbing always lacks continuity and good consolidated snow-ice is a rarity. The Christmas Retreat Gullies rely mainly on water-ice.
Approach:
See the notes in the section on Cwm Cywarch.

Although the area of broken cliff on the east side of the mountain extends for nearly 2km, the main area of climbing is directly above the small lake, Craiglyn Dyfi, and the three routes described all exit close to the summit.

Descent:
Follow the main ridge either northwards or southwards for about 1km until spurs curve around to the east and give straightforward descents back into the large cwm below the crags. But bear in mind the access restriction mentioned under the approach to Cwm Cywarch.

75m above the south end of the lake a fairly continous rocky spur leads directly to the summit of the mountain. The first two routes take gully lines either side of this.

LEFT-HAND CHRISTMAS RETREAT GULLY   150m   II/III
The gully immediately left of the rocky spur.
1. 45m   (2)   Starting at the lowest ice runnel climb several ice bulges and runnels into the confines of the gully.
2. 20m   (1)   Snow leads to bulging ice in a corner.
3. 45m   (3)   Follow the ice in the corner and the steepening slab above to another steep section.
4. 40m   (3)   Take a short steep groove on the right and finish up an ice runnel.

RIGHT-HAND CHRISTMAS RETREAT GULLY   115m   III
The second gully to the right of the rocky spur.
1. 45m   (3)   Climb steep snow to a cave pitch which is passed by an ice ramp on the left.
2. 40m   (2)   Up steepening snow to a final cave pitch.
3. 30m   (4)   Climb the cave pitch direct.

Further right, and just above the lake is an obvious wide gully which exits onto the main ridge just right (north) of the summit. Owing to its NE aspect and height, this is one of the first gullies to come into condition.

AERO GULLY LEFT-HAND   200m   I
Follow the wide main gully with one short easy ice-pitch, to just below the ridge. Now follow the left branch where easy angled ice gains the narrows. Beyond, steep snow leads to a sometimes corniced exit.

10.3 ARAN BENLLYN

Summit Grid Reference: 867242 (OS Sheet 124 Dolgellau)
Altitude: 600m - 880m
Aspect: East and North-East
Climbing Conditions:
Most of the routes described are on water-ice and will come into condition in cold weather, but Tourist Gully needs consolidated snow-ice to be worthwhile.

The cliffs of **Aran Benllyn** standing high above **Cwm Croes** to the east form a natural extension to those of **Aran Fawddwy** to the south. A blunt spur juts out to the east midway between the summits from an intermediate 'bump' in the ridge, forming the only real break in the line of cliffs. To the north of and well below the summit **Llyn Lliwbran** lies in a shallow cwm beneath the imposing fan-shaped dome of **Gist Ddu**, which is the main rock climbing area on the mountain.

Approach:
See the notes under the section of Cwm Cywarch.

Tourist Gully is situated at 867232 on the north side of the spur between **Fawddwy** and **Benllyn**. The line of cliffs continues for some 3km to the north but the climbs described are concentrated in two areas. Just left of the summit **The Great Ramp** crosses the **East Face** diagonally upwards from right to left, starting under a steep section of rock directly below the summit. **Winding Gully** and **East Gully** are based on this feature. The other climbs are on **Gist Ddu** and **Sloose** can be located easily by following the stone wall/fence up from the lake directly to the foot of the impressive corner upon which the climb is based.

Descents:
The notes on access to the Arans under the section on Cwm Cywarch should be considered when planning a descent from anywhere on the main ridge.

The safest descent from Gist Ddu to the foot of the crag is to gain the main ridge above and follow it down to the right (north) descending to the east only when past all difficulties. It is possible to abseil Sloose in two long rope-lengths.

On the north side of the spur between **Fawddwy** and **Benllyn** are a number of shallow gully lines. The first route takes the most pronounced of these.

TOURIST GULLY 265m II/III *
As there are few natural belays a deadman might be useful.

1. 45m   (1)   Climb steep snow in a corner.
2. 45m   (2/3)   Ascend an awkward chimney/groove to snow, then move up to the constricted section of the gully. Poor belay. In lean snow conditions, slabs on the right can be used to avoid the initial chimney/groove.
3. 45m   (3)   An ice ramp leads to a steep exit which can be avoided by the vegetated wall on the left.
4. 45m   (1)   Easy snow leads to the next steepening.
5. 40m   (2)   A short ice bulge leads to more snow. Nut belay on the right.
6. 45m   (2/3)   Steeper snow leads to an exit, sometimes with a cornice.

Below and well left of the summit of **Aran Benllyn** is an obvious ice curtain below the upper end of **The Great Ramp**. The next route makes for the curtain, starting at a narrow gully.

WINDING GULLY   150m   II
1. (1/2)   Short ice-pitches in the gully lead to a 6m ice-pitch.
2. (2)   Climb the ice-pitch to below the curtain.
3. (2/3)   By-pass the huge curtain by climbing on the right via more ice bulges, then move back left above and zig-zag up ice trending right to join The Great Ramp.
          The huge ice curtain has been climbed direct (4).

Starting above **The Great Ramp** and just left of the steep section of rock leading up towards the summit of **Aran Benllyn** is a large shallow gully, **East Gully**. Directly below **The Great Ramp** at this point is a very noticeable 30m ice wall.

EAST GULLY DIRECT   70m   IV   **
A succession of hard frosts are needed to bring the ice wall into condition.
1. 30m   (2)   Enter a gully beneath the ice wall and climb a short ice-pitch to iced slabs. Belay on the right of the ice wall.
2. 40m   (4/5)   Move back left from the belay and climb a slight depression in the centre of the ice wall to a ramp leading off left, or take ice directly above the central depression if in condition.

EAST GULLY   150m   II/III
The natural continuation of the previous route above The Great Ramp.
1. (2)   From the ramp, climb a short ice-pitch to a fork in the gully.

2. (3)   Take the right fork (left fork is (2)) for 15m to a 7m ice wall coming in from the left. Climb this and easier ice bulges above to the summit ridge.

10.4 GIST DDU

Grid Reference: 872255 (OS Sheet 124 Dolgellau)
Altitude: 550m - 650m
Aspect: East
Climbing Conditions:
The routes described rely on water-ice and will come into condition only in prolonged spells of cold weather.

   Gist Ddu is the crag which overlooks **Llyn Lliwbran** and comprises the main cliff (**Central Buttress**) with vegetated areas of rock to either side (the **Right** and **Left Wings**). The first climb takes the gully between the **Left Wing** and **Central Buttress.**

SOUWESTER GULLY 90m III *
The difficulties are concentrated in a 25m pitch near the bottom. Move up to the bottom of the steep groove to start.
1. 25m (4)   Climb the icy groove to a ledge, then continue up the steep chimney/crack, moving right beneath an overhanging block to go up and belay at a large tree.
2. 65m (2/3)   More easily now to the top.

MAGIC MOSS 90m V **
This climb takes the big corner line of the summer route The Trench. It is the first big corner to the left of the stone wall, left of the similar corner of Sloose, near the right-hand side of the crag.
   Climb the corner in two or three pitches (5,5,6) with a crux near the top where the ice runs out. Progress is then made by climbing frozen moss on the left wall - for as long as it lasts!

SLOOSE 90m V ***
The classic of the crag, taking a tremendous line up the steep corner right of Magic Moss.
1. 45m (4)   Follow the summer line straight up ice in the corner to a huge chockstone. Belay above the chockstone on the right.
2. 45m (6)   Traverse back left into the corner at a higher level, then move up just left of the corner to two rock projections. Gain steep ice on the left wall and climb this, passing an overhang on the left at the top to a tree belay on the right.

11. DYFI

Afon Dyfi bites deeply into the heartland of Central Wales, carving a twisting trough from the Arans to the sea at Aberdyfi. Many of its tributaries drain the vast soaking uplands before plunging down into the trough to add their weight to the tumbling waters far below. And often, in their haste to join that babbling brook, they throw themselves lemming-like over the craggy scarps which guard the uplands. Waterfalls abound and when bitter winter stills all motion in the cascading waters, icicles swoop down from on high, their fragile tendrils growing from the dank mossy walls of steep, untouched crags, transforming them into sparkling playgrounds of Ice Age Man.

Dinas Mawddwy on the A470 between Dolgellau and Machynlleth is a natural focus for climbing in the area and the falls are described in a clockwise direction around the village, starting in the north. An OS map, preferably the 1:25,000 Outdoor Leisure Sheet 23 CADAIR IDRIS is an essential tool for any exploration of this area.

11.1 NANT Y CAFN FALLS

Grid Reference: 895207 (OS Sheet 124 Dolgellau)
Altitude: 250m - 450m
Aspect: East
Approach:
The falls are easily seen from the east, from the minor road about 2km past the village of Llanymawddwy towards Bwlch y Groes, and may be approached directly in under half an hour.

NANT Y CAFN FALLS   200m   IV   ★
1. 45m   (1)   Follow easy iced slabs to the headwall.
2. 20m   (4)   Move back down the slabs to a vague ice scoop, the only weakness in the vertical ice wall on the left. Climb it to rock and ice-screw belays at the top.
3. 135m   (2)   Three rope-lengths up the twisting stream bed leads to the top.

11.2   PISTYLL GWYN

Grid Reference: 885196 (OS Sheet 124 Dolgellau)
Altitude: 350m - 480m
Aspect: East
Approach:
A track leads to the falls from the village of Llanymawddwy (¾hr. from the road. The falls occur where a stream flows down 55°-60° slabs and when frozen provide an excellent outing which is sustained but never too difficult.

PISTYLL GWYN   130m   III   ★★★
1. 40m   (2)   Straight up the centre of the ice sheet to a ledge. Ice belays.
2. 40m   (2)   Continue in the same line. Ice belays.
3. 20m   (2)   Up to a tree belay at the top of the ice sheet.
4. 15m   (2/3)   A short steep ice-pitch in the stream bed.
5. 15m   (2/3)   Cross a pool and continue up a further ice pitch to the top.

11.3   NANT EFAIL-FACH FALLS

Grid Reference: 899162 (OS Sheet 124 Dolgellau)
Altitude: 300m
Aspect: South-West
Approach:
From the minor road on the south side of Afon Dyfi some 3½km east of Dinas Mawddwy, a track follows the stream through woodland until the stream swings up left into a narrow gorge behind the hill (y Foel). The falls lie in the gorge and are difficult to see until directly opposite them (½hr. from the road). The SW aspect requires a prolonged period of hard frost to come into condition. Descent is by abseil from a small tree on the right of the pitch.

NANT EFAIL-FACH FALLS   30m   III   ★
1. 30m   (3)   Steep ice at the start and finish, the last move

probably being the crux.

Immediately right of the **Nant Efail-Fach Falls** are some long, iced slabs facing west and giving the following route.

LITTLE EIGER   190m   III/IV
1. 45m   (3)   A long ice-pitch with various bulges to a tree belay.
2. 40m   (2)   Traverse left to a vague gully line which is followed to another tree.
3. 45m   (2)   Continue in the line of the vague gully.
4. 40m   (3)   Ice bulges above to a tree belay on the right.
5. 20m   (3)   A steep awkward snow exit with no natural belays above.

11.4   DINAS MAWDDWY QUARRY

Grid Reference: 852139 (OS Sheet 124 Dolgellau)
Altitude: 350m
Aspect: East
Approach:
A forestry track leads steeply (walk!) up to the quarry from behind the Youth Hostel just south of Dinas Mawddwy (½hr. from the road).

CENTRAL ICE FLOW   50m   V
1. 20m   (5)   Climb the vertical ice curtain to a large ledge.
2. 30m   (4)   The ice wall is taken by its easiest line (on the left). A traverse right under ice overhangs at the top leads to an exit.

The ice-pillar down and to the left of **Central Ice Flow** has been climbed as far as the tree at mid-height, but the continuation groove was insufficiently iced.

11.5   MAESGLASAU FALLS

Grid Reference: 828142 (OS Sheet 124 Dolgellau)
Altitude: 400m - 600m
Aspect: North-East
Approach:
About 1 mile to the north-west of Dinas Mawddwy on the A470 a track leads up a small valley to the south-west. The head of the valley is surrounded by an enormous escarpment through which the falls tumble. They are clearly visible from the main road. Follow the track, then the stream to the start of the difficulties (1hr. walking from the main road).

A magnificent outing, with some spectacular ice scenery.

MAESGLASAU FALLS   200m   IV   ★★★

1. 45m   (2)   From the frozen stream bed climb a steep section then easier ice to boulders at the base of the falls proper.

2. 45m   (3)   Climb an ice-groove on the right then a ramp into the centre of the wall. Belay on screws.

3. 30m   (4)   Climb the steep ice wall on the right to a bay. Belay on screws.

4. 20m   (3)   Move left up steepish ice to a ledge and tree belay.

5. 40m   (2)   Follow the stream line with a short ice wall to the top.

6. 20m   (3)   Steep ice on the left to finish.

11.6   CRAIG-WEN FALLS

Grid Reference: 829174 (OS Sheet 124 Dolgellau)
Altitude: 450m
Aspect: South
Approach:
A forestry track leaves the A470 at Pont Buarth-glas some 4km west of Dinas Mawddwy, and leads in about 1km to the Nant y Graig-Wen, which is followed up to the falls which are situated on the 470m contour. Allow 1hr. from the road.

CRAIG-WEN FALLS   70m   III   ★

1. 25m   (2)   Up ice to a frozen pool at the base of the main pitch.

2. 45m   (3)   Either climb up to the left of the pool or directly above it at about the same standard.

12. BERWYN

12.1 CWM PENNANT
12.2 CRAIG RHIWARTH
12.3 PISTYLL RHAEADR

These rounded grassy hills with their deep, steep-sided valleys form the southern flank of the great valley of **Afon Dyfrdwy**, the River Dee, between **Bala** in the west and **Llangollen** in the east. The cairned twin summits of **Cadair Berwyn** and **Moel Sych**, each reaching 827m, stand atop the main escarpment; glowering eastwards above modest yet craggy ramparts into grassy cwms whose waters are southbound to the Severn and Bristol. For the Berwyns are Wales' true watershed: the great north-south divide.

But, what is this to do with winter climbing? Well, one of these nascent tributaries plunges some 100m into the **Tanat Valley** far below to give **Pistyll Rhaeadr**, one of Wales' highest waterfalls and others take their cue from this. So in a cold spell, the challenge is obvious - but the queue is short!

Approaching from **Bala** take the B4391 across the **Berwyns** (may be impassable under heavy snow) to **Llangynog**. For **Pistyll Rhaeadr**, turn left onto the B4396 and continue on to the village of **Llan-rhaeadr-ym-Mochant**. The other areas are approached from **Llangynog** itself. Or alternatively, if approaching from England, or in the event of heavy snow, leave the A5 at Oswestry with a road map and navigator!

12.1 CWM PENNANT

Grid Reference: Square 0027 (OS Sheet 125 Bala and Lake Vyrnwy)
Altitude: 300m - 400m
Aspect: East
Approach:
From Llangynog, follow a minor road westwards for 3km up Cwm Pennant to a farm complex at the end of the valley. It is best to seek advice from the local farmer as to the best access route and where to park as there are fences and

plantations in the bottom of the valley. The main falls are obvious at the end of the valley and may be reached comfortably in 20-30 minutes.
Descent:
Contour northwards and eastwards around the head of the cwm to gain a track which descends the NE side of the valley back towards the farm.

The main **Tanat Falls** are obvious at the end of the valley with the short, steep **Pennant Fall** just to the left. Some 400m further left and much higher up is a line of crags with **Graig Wen Chimney** slicing through them.

TANAT FALLS   90m   V   **

The main fall gives a fine outing in two long pitches. Similar to, but possibly better than Pistyll Rhaeadr.
1.   45m   (4)   Steep ice slabs are climbed to a ramp which leads to a belay in a cave formed by a large flat rock.
2.   45m   (5)   Climb steep ice directly up the fall.

PENNANT FALL   25m   V   *

The obvious ice-fall in the gully just to the left is 'plonk on' - so don't plop off!

GRAIG WEN CHIMNEY   60m   IV   *

Scramble up to the crag well over to the left where a deep fissure full of ice cleaves the rocks.
1.   40m   (4)   The fine icy chimney is body width (for some!) and leads past some awkward chockstones to a belay on easier ground.
2.   20m   (2)   The snowy arête above is climbed to the top.

The next climb is just above the village of **Llangynog.**

12.2   CRAIG RHIWARTH

Grid Reference: 055267   (OS Sheet 125 Bala and Lake Vyrnwy)
Altitude: 300m
Aspect: South

Just above and to the north of the B4391 at **Llangynog**, there is a steep little crag on the hillside with a prominent 45m ice-fall which only forms in the very coldest of winters.

THE GONAD   45m   V

The steep ice-fall is climbed direct in two pitches (6).

12.3 PISTYLL RHAEADR

Grid Reference: 073296 (OS Sheet 125 Bala and Lake Vyrnwy
Altitude: 300m - 400m
Aspect: East
Approach:
From Llanrhaeadr-ym-Mochnant, follow a minor road NW for 6km up the valley of the Afon Rhaeadr to a parking place below the falls.
Descent:
An obvious rough farm track leads steeply back down on the north side of the falls.

Some 500m left (south) of the main falls, there is an obvious waterslide gully, shown on the map, which offers an excellent route at a more reasonable grade.

CRAIG MWN GULLY 110m II/III **

A fine little route, which after 2 weeks of frost provides four good pitches, gradually increasing in difficulty as it rises. Start by following the stream through trees to the start of the ice.

1. 15m (2)   Up ice on the left of the stream.
2. 25m (2)   More ice on the left.
3. 40m (3)   More steeply now on ice clinging to the left wall, to trees.
4. 30m (3)   Up a short steep wall of ice to a bulge. Pull over into the upper gully and continue to the moor above.

Around to the right now is the main fall. As with similar frozen waterfalls of this size in Wales, it is rare for the whole cascade to become a frozen mass of ice and there is usually some residual liquid in the centre, dividing the fall into two sides.

QUICKSILVER 100m V *

This climbs the left-hand side, and at least three weeks of severe frost is needed to bring it into condition. But when frozen it offer a unique outing.

1. 25m (3)   Start in the frozen pool (about 50m from the car park!) and climb the ice boss on its left to a natural arch. Keep left of this to belay in the second pool, or go up to ledges on the left.
2. 40m (5)   Climb ice on the left of the watercourse (an excellent pitch which forms quickly) to a good ledge and tree.
3. 35m (6)   Climb the fragile groove of ice on the left of the water to easier ground. Then up and out boldly on the ice arch spanning the flowing stream.

CHANDELIER 100m V *

The right-hand side forms somewhat quicker and offers an equally good expedition.

1. 25m (4)   Climb the ice smear rising from the right-hand side of the pool to a tree.

2. 40m (2)   Easily up low-angled ice past trees to belay on rock below the icicles on the upper wall.

3. 35m (6)   Climb the vertical ice pillar just right of the water-fall. Weird ice formations make this technically very hard.

APPENDIX
STARRED CLIMBS
(**NOT** A GRADED LIST)

***	CRIB GOCH TRAVERSE	CRIB GOCH	I
***	PARSLEY FERN GULLY	CWM GLAS MAWR	I
***	BROAD GULLY	CWM FFYNNON LLOER	I/II
***	THE SNOWDON HORSESHOE	SNOWDON	I/II
***	CENTRAL TRINITY	CLOGWYN Y GARNEDD	I/II
***	THE NORTH RIDGE	TRYFAN	II
***	BRISTLY RIDGE	GLYDER FACH	II
***	PISTYLL GWYN	PISTYLL GWYN	III
***	MOONFLIGHT FLIT	YR EIFL	III/IV
***	WELL OF LONELINESS	ABER FALLS	IV
***	THE ANGEL'S TEARS	ABER FALLS	IV
***	Y GULLY, LEFT-HAND BRANCH	CWM CNEIFION	IV
***	SOUTH GULLY	CLOGWYN Y GEIFR	IV
***	THE DEVIL'S KITCHEN	CLOGWYN Y GEIFR	IV
***	BEDROCK GULLY	CWM SILYN	IV
***	THE GREAT GULLY	CWM CAU	IV
***	MAESGLASAU FALLS	MAESGLASAU	IV
***	GREAT GULLY	CRAIG YR YSFA	IV/V
***	AQUARIAN WALL	CWM SILYN	IV/V
***	MASK OF DEATH	CWM SILYN	IV/V
***	WESTERN GULLY	YSGOLION DUON	V
***	THE SOMME	YSGOLION DUON	V
***	MARIA	GALLT YR OGOF	V
***	CASCADE	CRAIG Y RHAEADR	V
***	CENTRAL GULLY	LLIWEDD, EAST FACE	V
***	JUBILEE CLIMB	CLOGWYN DU'R ARDDU	V
***	TROJAN	CYFRWY	V
***	SLOOSE	GIST DDU	V
***	THE BLACK CLEFT	CLOGWYN DU'R ARDDU	V/VI
***	COLONIAL VIRGIN	CYFRWY	V/VI
***	THE DEVIL'S APPENDIX	CLOGWYN Y GEIFR	VI
***	CENTRAL ICE-FALL DIRECT	CRAIG Y RHAEADR	VI
***	CENTRAL GULLY DIRECT	LLIWEDD, EAST FACE	VI
**	SARGEANT'S GULLY	CWM GLAS MAWR	II
**	DOLGARROG GORGE	DOLGARROG GORGE	2/4
**	BANANA GULLY	Y GARN	I
**	THE GREAT STONE SHOOT	CWM SILYN	I

**	CRIB LEM	CWMGLAS BACH	I/II
**	THE NORTH FACE	FOEL GOCH	I/II
**	GRUGOG GULLY	BRAICH TY DU	II
**	THE GRIBIN RIDGE	CWM CNEIFION	II
**	HIDDEN GULLY	CWM CNEIFION	II
**	INTRODUCTORY GULLY	IDWAL SLABS	II
**	DESCENT GULLY	LLANBERIS PASS NORTH S	II
**	CAULDRON GULLY	LLANBERIS PASS NORTH S	II
**	BRYANT'S GULLY	LLANBERIS PASS NORTH S	II
**	PARSLEY FERN LEFT-HAND	CWM GLAS MAWR	II
**	EASTERN ARÊTE	CYFRWY	II
**	YR ESGAIR	FOEL GOCH	II/III
**	CLOGWYN Y PERSON ARÊTE	CWM GLAS MAWR	II/III
**	GREAT GULLY	CLOGWYN Y GARNEDD	II/III
**	RIGHT-HAND TRINITY	CLOGWYN Y GARNEDD	II/III
**	CRAIG MWN GULLY	PISTYLL RHAEADR	II/III
**	NORTH EAST SPUR	Y GARN	III
**	CENTRAL GULLY	YSGOLION DUON	III
**	CNEIFION ARÊTE	CWM CNEIFION	III
**	THE CURVER	FOEL GOCH	III
**	JAMMED BOULDER GULLY	DINAS MOT	III
**	SINISTER GULLY	CWM GLAS MAWR	III
**	LADIES GULLY	CLOGWYN Y GARNEDD	III
**	CAVE GULLY	CLOGWYN Y GARNEDD	III
**	BARN DOOR	CYFRWY	III
**	THE RAMP	CLOGWYN Y GEIFR	III/II
**	THE SCREEN	CLOGWYN Y GEIFR	III/IV
**	SNOWDROP	CLOGWYN Y GARNEDD	III/IV
**	PYRAMID GULLY	YSGOLION DUON	IV
**	PILLAR CHIMNEY	CWM CNEIFION	IV/V
**	THE DEVIL'S CELLAR	CLOGWYN Y GEIFR	IV
**	EAST FACE ROUTE	FOEL GOCH	IV
**	CROWN OF THORNS	LLANBERIS PASS NORTH S	IV
**	WATERFALL CLIMB	CRAIG Y RHAEADR	IV
**	FACE ROUTE	CWM GLAS MAWR	IV
**	WATERSLIDE GULLY	CWM GLAS MAWR	IV
**	INFIDELITY	CWM GLAS MAWR	IV
**	THE WIDOW OF THE WEB	CWM SILYN	IV
**	RHAEADR Y CWM	RHAEADR Y CWM	IV
**	MAESGWM FALLS	MAESGWM	IV
**	THE SHINING	CYFRWY	IV
**	GWTH	PEN Y GADAIR	IV
**	EAST GULLY	TWR DU	IV
**	WEST GULLY	TWR DU	IV
**	EAST GULLY DIRECT	ARAN BENLLYN	IV
**	BLACK CLEFT	DINAS MOT	IV/III

★★	FAIRY FALLS	CRAIG Y DULYN	IV/V
★★	QUICKSILVER	CRAIG Y DULYN	IV/V
★★	WESTERN GULLY (var. finish)	YSGOLION DUON	IV/V
★★	GOLIATH	CWMGLAS BACH	IV/V
★★	PETTICOAT LANE	CWMGLAS BACH	IV/V
★★	DEVIL'S STAIRCASE	CLOGWYN Y GEIFR	IV/V
★★	WHITE SNAKE	CWM SILYN	IV/V
★★	SLANTING GULLY	LLIWEDD, EAST FACE	V
★★	PYRAMID FACE DIRECT	YSGOLION DUON	V
★★	Y-CHIMNEY	LLECH DDU	V
★★	CENTRAL GULLY	LLANBERIS PASS NORTH S	V
★★	SATURDAY NIGHT FEVER	CWM CAU	V
★★	MAGIC MOSS	GIST DDU	V
★★	TANAT FALLS	CWM PENNANT	V
★★	SKID ROW	LLECH DDU	V/VI
★★	THE POLAR BEAR	YSGOLION DUON	VI
★★	SILVER MACHINE	CLOGWYN DU'R ARDDU	VI
★★	RED SLAB	CLOGWYN DU'R ARDDU	VI
★	EASY ROUTE	CWM CNEIFION	I
★	ESGAIR GULLY	FOEL GOCH	I
★	EAST RIDGE	CRIB GOCH	I
★	EAST FACE	CRIB GOCH	I
★	NORTH RIDGE	CRIB GOCH	I
★	GWTER FAWR	CWM GLAS MAWR	I
★	GYRN LAS RIDGE	CWM GLAS BACH	I
★	EASTERN TERRACE	CLOGWYN DU'R ARDDU	I
★	EASY GULLY	CYFRWY	I
★	LEFT-HAND Y GULLY	CWM FFYNNON LLOER	I/II
★	TOWER GULLY	CWM CNEIFION	I/II
★	RED GULLY	FOEL GOCH	I/II
★	Y GRIBIN	CLOGWYN Y GARNEDD	I/II
★	LEFT-HAND TRINITY	CLOGWYN Y GARNEDD	I/II
★	BOOMERANG GULLY	CLOGWYN DU'R ARDDU	I/II
★	ONE PITCH GULLY	CYFRWY	I/II
★	CURVER	CWM CNEIFION	II
★	AMPHITHEATRE 'A' GULLY	CRAIG YR YSFA	II
★	HIGH PASTURE	GLYDER FAWR - UPPER CL	II
★	THE IDWAL STREAM	CLOGWYN Y GEIFR	II
★	C GULLY	Y GARN	II
★	THE RUNNEL	CARNEDD Y FILIAST	II
★	SHORT GULLY	LLANBERIS PASS NORTH S	II
★	THE RAMP	CWM GLAS MAWR	II
★	AMPHITHEATRE GULLY	CWM SILYN	II
★	NANTMOR FALLS	NANTMOR AREA	II
★	AMPHITHEATRE 'C' GULLY	CRAIG YR YSFA	II/III

★	CENTRAL GULLY	GLYDER FACH	II/III
★	TOWER SLABS	CWM CNEIFION	II/III
★	GREY GULLY	GLYDER FAWR - UPPER CL	II/III
★	FORTRESS GULLY	LLANBERIS PASS NORTH S	II/III
★	PTERODACTYL	CRAIG CWM BEUDY MAWR	II/III
★	RAILWAY GULLY	CWM GLAS BACH	II/III
★	LITTLE GULLY	CLOGWYN Y GARNEDD	II/III
★	SHADOW GULLY	CLOGWYN DU	II/III
★	TOURIST GULLY	ARAN BENLLYN	II/III
★	AMPHITHEATRE 'B' GULLY	CRAIG YR YSFA	III
★	EASTERN GULLY	YSGOLION DUON	III
★	WHIPPERSNAPPER'S ROUTE	ABER FALLS	III
★	NANT EFAIL-FACH FALLS	NANT EFAIL-FACH	III
★	Y GULLY, RIGHT-HAND DIRECT	CWM CNEIFION	III
★	WHITE HOPE	IDWAL SLABS	III
★	TWISTING GULLY	GLYDER FAWR -UPPER CL	III
★	CENTRAL ROUTE	CLOGWYN Y GEIFR	III
★	CHICANE GULLY	CLOGWYN Y GEIFR	III
★	COLDHOUSE CRACK	CLOGWYN Y GEIFR	III
★	LADDIES GULLY	CLOGWYN Y GARNEDD	III
★	BUTTRESS CHIMNEY	FOEL GOCH	III
★	DODO GULLY	CRAIG CWM BEUDY MAWR	III
★	THE SQUEEZE	CWM GLAS BACH	III
★	THE ICE-FALL	CLOGWYN DU'R ARDDU	III
★	TREGALEN GROOVE	CLOGWYN DU	III
★	HEART OF ICE	CWM DULYN	III
★	RAKE END WALL	CWM DULYN	III
★	THE CLEAVER	CWM DULYN	III
★	CENTRAL GULLY	PEN Y GADAIR	III
★	RATTLER	PEN Y GADAIR	III
★	THE RAMP	CWM CAU	III
★	SOUWESTER GULLY	GIST DDU	III
★	CRAIG WEN FALLS	CRAIG WEN	III
★	THE GULLY	CWMGLAS BACH	III/II
★	ICE-FALL GULLY LEFT-HAND	YSGOLION DUON	III/IV
★	MOONGROOVES	CWM FFYNNON LLOER	III/IV
★	GREEN GULLY	TRYFAN	III/IV
★	EAST GULLY	GLYDER FACH	III/IV
★	THE NAMELESS STREAM	IDWAL SLABS	III/IV
★	ARCH GULLY	CRAIG YR YSFA	III/IV
★	THE CHUTE	DINAS MOT	III/IV
★	CRAIG Y DWR FALLS	CRAFNANT VALLEY	III/IV
★	EASTERN TERRACE DIRECT START	CLOGWYN DU'R ARDDU	III/IV
★	WEST END ICE-FALL	CLOGWYN DU'R ARDDU	IV

*	EAST GULLY	GLYDER FAWR - UPPER CL	IV
*	PYRAMID BUTTRESS	YSGOLION DUON	IV
*	ICE-FALL GULLY RIGHT-HAND	YSGOLION DUON	IV
*	THE GLASS WALL	CWMGLAS BACH	IV
*	FOUNTAIN OF YOUTH	ABER FALLS	IV
*	DEFFING OUT THE BEN	TRYFAN	IV
*	GRASS ROUTE	GLYDER FAWR - UPPER CL	IV
*	HANGING GARDEN GULLY	CLOGWYN Y GEIFR	IV
*	BANANA SPLIT	Y YARN	IV
*	THE RIBBON	CARNEDD Y FILIAST	IV
*	EAST GULLY	LLIWEDD, EAST FACE	IV
*	CENTRAL GULLY ARÊTE	LLIWEDD, EAST FACE	IV
*	THE WEST PEAK	LLIWEDD, EAST FACE	IV
*	COOL WATER SANDWICH	LLIWEDD, EAST FACE	IV
*	COULOIR	CLOGWYN Y GARNEDD	IV
*	NANT Y CAFN FALLS	NANT Y CAFN	IV
*	GRAIG WEN CHIMNEY	CWM PENNANT	IV
*	JAMMED BOULDER BUTTRESS	DINAS MOT	IV/III
*	EAST GULLY	CLOGWYN DU'R ARDDU	IV/III
*	JACOB'S LADDER	YSGOLION DUON	IV/V
*	PASSCHENDAELE	YSGOLION DUON	IV/V
*	THE STING	CLOGWYN Y GEIFR	IV/V
*	THE FLYING SCOTSMAN	CWM GLAS BACH	IV/V
*	EAST PEAK VIA THE HORNED CRAG	LLIWEDD, EAST FACE	IV/V
*	SHALLOW GULLY	LLIWEDD, EAST FACE	IV/V
*	PROCRASTINATION CRACKS	GLYDER FAWR - UPPER CL	V
*	GALLIPOLI	YSGOLION DUON	V
*	DEVIL'S PIPES	CLOGWYN Y GEIFR	V
*	CASCADE RIGH-HAND	CRAIG Y RHAEADR	V
*	EAST PEAK DIRECT	LLIWEDD, EAST FACE	V
*	WHITE DOVE	LLIWEDD, EAST FACE	V
*	CAMUS	CLOGWYN DU'R ARDDU	V
*	CHAIN GANG	CRAIG BODLYN	V
*	RISKOPHILIA	CRAIG BODLYN	V
*	CRYOGENICS	CRAIG BODLYN	V
*	THE SCREAMING	CRAIG BODLYN	V
*	QUICKSILVER	PISTYLL RHAEADR	V
*	CHANDELIER	PISTYLL RHAEADR	V
*	PENNANT FALLS	CWM PENNANT	V
*	POST WAR	YSGOLION DUON	V/VI
*	CHEQUERED WALL	CRAIG Y RHAEADR	VI

INDEX

DIAGRAMS

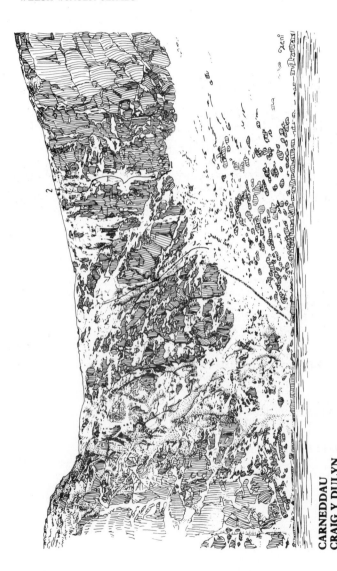

CARNEDDAU
CRAIG Y DULYN

| 1 | ** | FAIRY FALLS | IV/V | 5,5 |
| 2 | ** | QUICKSILVER | IV/V | 5,5, 3/4 |

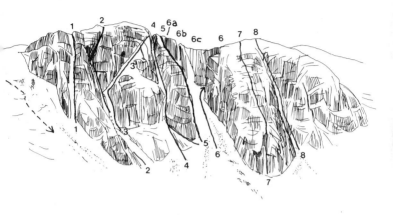

CARNEDDAU
CRAIG YR YSFA

1		PINNACLE GULLY	II
2	★	ARCH GULLY	III
3		BENDING GULLY	II
4		AVALANCHE GULLY	II
6a	★	AMPHITHEATRE 'A' GULLY	II
6b	★	AMPHITHEATRE 'B' GULLY	III
6c	★	AMPHITHEATRE 'C' GULLY	II/III
6		AMPHITHEATRE 'D' GULLY	II
7		VANISHING GULLY	III/IV
8	★★★	GREAT GULLY	IV/V	1, 4/5, 3, 5/6, 4,5,4,1
S	=	AMPHITHEATRE BUTTRESS (NOT DESCRIBED)	

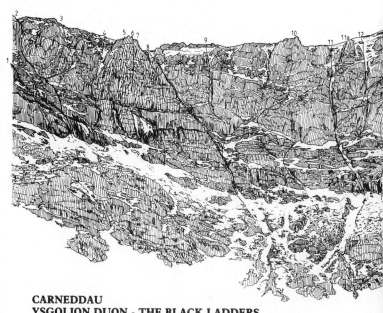

CARNEDDAU
YSGOLION DUON - THE BLACK LADDERS

1		EASTERN ARETE	II/III	
2	★	EASTERN GULLY	III	3,-,-
2a		EASTERN GULLY (ALTERNATIVE START)		
3		PLAYSCHOOL	III	3,3,3
4	★★	PYRAMID GULLY	IV	4/5, 4,1
5	★	JACOB'S LADDER	IV/V	5,5,2
6	★★	PYRAMID FACE DIRECT	V	5,6,4
7	★	PYRAMID BUTTRESS	IV	
8	★★	CENTRAL GULLY	III	3, 2/3, 3,1, 4/5, (3/4), 1/2
8a		CENTRAL GULLY (ALTERNATIVE START)		
9	★	GALLIPOLI	V	
10	★	PASSCHENDAELE	IV/V	

11	***	WESTERN GULLY	V	2,3,4,5, 5/6, 4,1
11a	**	WESTERN GULLY		
		VAR. FINISH	IV/V	4, 4/5, 2
12		YPRES	IV/V	2,2,5,3
13		ARCTIC FOX	V	5, 4/3, 3,5,2
14	**	THE POLAR BEAR	VI	3,6,6,6, 4/5, 4/5, 2
15		TOPCAT	IV/V	
16	***	THE SOMME	V	3,-,5, (4), 3/4, 3,1
16a	*	POST WAR	V/VI	5,5,5
17	*	ICEFALL GULLY	III/IV	2, 2/3, 3/4, 3/4, 2/3, 2
18		NIGHTFALL	III	
19		DAYBREAK	III	
20		FINALE	III	

CARNEDDAU
CRAIG Y CWMGLAS BACH

1	*	THE GULLY	III/II	1,3, 1/2
2	**	PETTICOAT LANE	IV/V	4,4,4,3,4
3	*	THE GLASS WALL	IV	1,4, 1/2, 4
4		STRAIGHT CHIMNEY	III	2,3

CARNEDDAU
CRAIG DAFYDD

1	**	CRIB LEM	I/II
2		DAVID	III	2,3
3	**	GOLIATH	IV/V	5,4, 1/2
4		LEFT FORK	II	2/3, 1
5		CENTRAL TRIDENT ROUTE	II/III	2/3, 2, 1/2, 3,1
6		RIGHT FORK	II/III	2/3, 2/4

Craig Dafydd

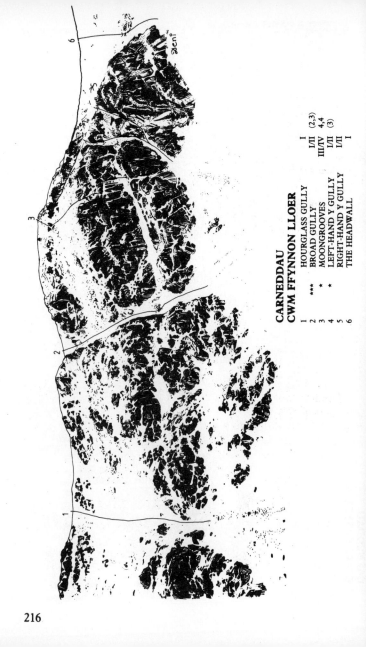

CARNEDDAU
CWM FFYNNON LLOER

1	HOURGLASS GULLY	I	(2,3)
2	BROAD GULLY ***	I/II	
3	MOONGROOVES *	III/IV	4,4
4	LEFT-HAND Y GULLY *	I/II	(3)
5	RIGHT-HAND Y GULLY	I/II	
6	THE HEADWALL	I	

GLYDERAU
TRYFAN

NR	***	THE NORTH RIDGE		
1		SOUTH GULLY	II	
2		NORTH GULLY	II	
2a		LITTLE GULLY	II/III	3,1,4,1,1
3	*	GREEN GULLY	–/II	
4		NOR' NOR' GULLY	III/IV	
5		BASTOW GULLY	II	
6		NO GULLY	I	
HT	=	THE HEATHER TERRACE	I	

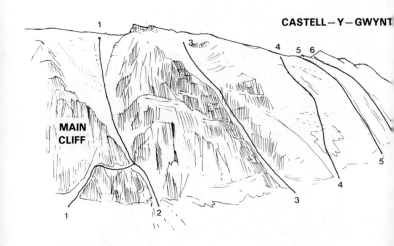

CASTELL—Y—GWYNT

MAIN
CLIFF

GLYDERAU
GLYDER FACH

1		MAIN GULLY	II	
2	★	EAST GULLY	III/IV	4
3	★	CENTRAL GULLY	II/III	
4		PLAQUES ROUTE	II/III	
5		WESTERN GULLY	II	
6		GULLY OF THE WINDS	I	
7		COL GULLY	I	

GLYDERAU
CWM CNEIFION

1	*	TOWER GULLY	I/II	1,2,1
2	*	TOWER SLABS	II/III	2/3, 1/2
3		NAMELESS GULLY	II	1,2
4		NAMELESS FACE	II	2/3, 2/3

GLYDERAU
CWM CNEIFION - CLOGWYN DU

1	*	EASY ROUTE	I	1,2
2	**	HIDDEN GULLY	II	3, (3), 4/5, (4), 3
3	**	PILLAR CHIMNEY	IV	
3a		PILLAR CHIMNEY VARIATION START		
3b		PILLAR CHIMNEY VARIATION FINISH	IV	2,4, 2/3, 3, (3)
4	***	Y GULLY, LEFT HAND BRANCH	III	3,3,3
5	*	Y GULLY, RIGHT HAND DIRECT		

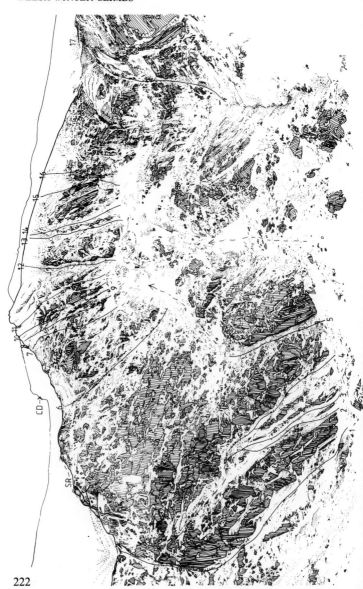

GLYDERAU
IDWAL SLABS

1		EAST WALL GULLY	I/II	2/3, 1/2
2		THE ORDINARY ROUTE	III	2, 3/4, 3,2
3	*	WHITE HOPE	III	3,3,3,2
4		SUBWALL CLIMB	IV	3,4, 3/4, 3
5	**	INTRODUCTORY GULLY	II	

GLYDERAU
GLYDER FAWR - UPPER CLIFF

6		OBLIQUE GULLY	II	2,1, 2/3, (3.)
7		NARROW GULLY	II/III	
8	*	SQUARE FURROW	II/III	3,2, 1/2
9	*	GREY GULLY	II/III	2/3, 5,5
10	*	PROCRASTINATION CRACKS	IV/V	2,4,2
11	*	TWISTING GULLY	III	
12	*	EAST GULLY	III/IV	1/2, 3/4, 2/3
13		CENTRAL GULLY	III/IV	3,3, 3/5, 2/3
14	*	HIGH PASTURE	II	
15		WEST GULLY	III/IV	2,4,3
16	*	GRASS ROUTE	IV	2,4,4
17	**	THE IDWAL STREAM	II	
SR =		SENIORS' RIDGE		
CD =		CLOGWYN DU		

GLYDERAU
CLOGWYN Y GEIFR

B	=	PRACTICE ICEFALLS		
1	***	SOUTH GULLY	IV	3,1, 3/5, (5), 2
2	*	CENTRAL ROUTE	III	3/4, 3
3		GRECIAN 2000	IV	4/5, 1,4
4	*	CHICANE GULLY	III	3, 2/4, 1
5	*	DEVIL'S PIPES	V	5/6
6	**	THE RAMP	III/II	2,3,1
7	**	THE SCREEN	III/IV	3,4
8		THE CURTAIN	-	4
9		DEVIL'S PASTURE	III	2/3, 3
10	*	COLDHOUSE CRACK	III	3,3
11	***	THE DEVIL'S KITCHEN	IV	5/6
A-A		THE GOAT'S PATH	I	
12	**	DEVIL'S STAIRCASE	IV/V	5/6, 5,4,5
13	***	THE DEVIL'S APPENDIX	VI	6,5,5
14	*	HANGING GARDEN GULLY	IV	
15	*	THE STING	IV/V	3,5
16	**	THE DEVIL'S CELLAR	IV	4,5 (4)

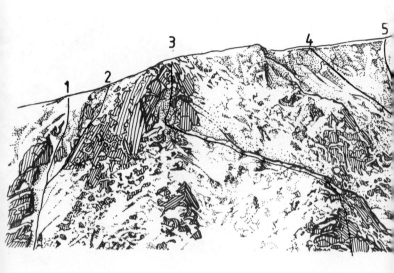

CLOGWYN
Y GEIFR

1		THE TRENCH	I
2		CASTLE GULLY	II/III 1/2, 3,1

GLYDERAU
Y GARN

3	**	NORTH EAST SPUR	II
4		A GULLY	I
5		B GULLY	I/II
6		BC BUTTRESS	II
7	*	C GULLY	II
8		CD BUTTRESS	II
9	**	BANANA GULLY	I

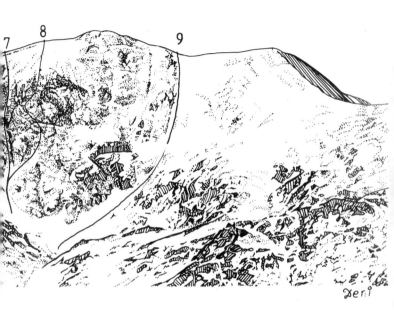

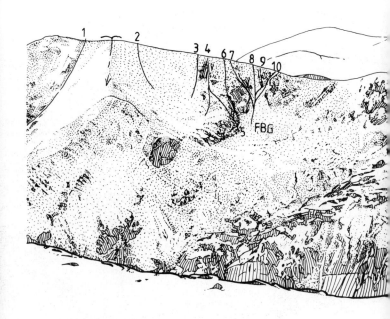

Y GARN

1	**	BANANA GULLY	I
2		SUMMIT GULLY	I
3		SPURIOUS GULLY	I
4		SPUR GULLY	I/II
5		CHICKEN GULLY	II
6	*	BANANA SPLIT	IV
FBG	=	FALSE BANANA GULLY	
7		NO. 1 GULLY	III
8		NO. 2 GULLY	I
9		NO. 3 GULLY	II
10		NO. 4 GULLY	IH

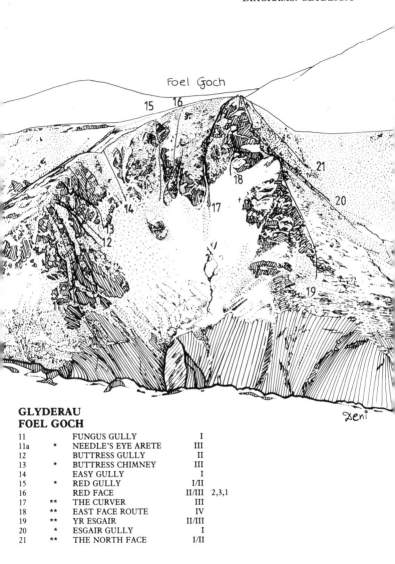

GLYDERAU
FOEL GOCH

11		FUNGUS GULLY	I	
11a	*	NEEDLE'S EYE ARETE	III	
12		BUTTRESS GULLY	II	
13	*	BUTTRESS CHIMNEY	III	
14		EASY GULLY	I	
15	*	RED GULLY	I/II	
16		RED FACE	II/III	2,3,1
17	**	THE CURVER	III	
18	**	EAST FACE ROUTE	IV	
19	**	YR ESGAIR	II/III	
20	*	ESGAIR GULLY	I	
21	**	THE NORTH FACE	I/II	

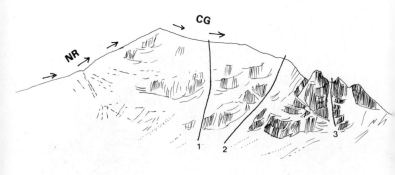

LLANBERIS
CRIB GOCH

NR	*	NORTH RIDGE	I
CG	***	CRIB GOCH TRAVERSE	I
1		ARCHER THOMPSON'S ROUTE	III
2		CARR'S ROUTE	III
3		CRAZY PINNACLE GULLY	II/III

LLANBERIS
DINAS MOT

SG	STAIRCASE GULLY (HIDDEN)		III	3/4, 3,3
1	WESTERN GULLY		III	5
2	WHITE TRASH		-	2/3, 4,2
3	JAMMED BOULDER GULLY	**	III	
4	JAMMED BOULDER BUTTRESS	*	IV/III	
5	BLACK CLEFT	**	IV/III	4,3
6	SAPLING GULLY		III	2/3, 2,3
7	WESTERN STEPPES		II/III	3,3,1, 2/3
8	THE CHUTE	*	III/IV	4

LLANBERIS
CRAIG Y RHAEADR

1	★	CHEQUERED WALL	VI	
2	★★★	CENTRAL ICEFALL DIRECT	VI	5,6,6
3	★★	WATERFALL CLIMB	IV	3,5,3,4,3
4	★★★	CASCADE	V	5,5,5,3
5	★	CASCADE RIGHT HAND	V	
6		GROOVED SLAB	IV	
7		BOTANY BAY	IV	
8		MORTUARY SLAB		5

LLANBERIS
CWM GLAS MAWR

1		FANTAIL GULLY	I	
2	**	CLOGWYN Y PERSON ARETE	II/III	
3	**	WATERSLIDE GULLY	IV	
4	**	INFIDELITY	IV	3,2,3,5,4,4,2
5	**	SINISTER GULLY	III	2,2,4,2
6	*	THE RAMP	II	
7	**	SARGEANT'S GULLY	II	2 TO 4
7a		THE CHASMS	II	
8		THE GREAT GULLY	III/IV	
9		SCHOOLMASTER'S GULLY	III/IV	
10		YELLOWSTONE GULLY	III/IV	
11	*	GWTER FAWR	I	
12	**	FACE ROUTE	IV	3,4,3,2
13		EQUATOR WALLS		6

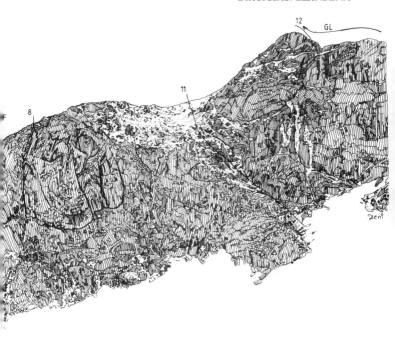

YR WYDDFA
LLIWEDD, EAST FACE

1	*	EAST GULLY	IV
2a	*	EAST PEAK VIA THE HORNED CRAG	IV/V
2	*	EAST PEAK DIRECT	V
3	*	WHITE DOVE	V
4	*	SHALLOW GULLY	IV/V
5	***	CENTRAL GULLY	V

236

5a	***	CENTRAL GULLY DIRECT	VI
5b	*	CENTRAL GULLY ARETE	IV
6	*	THE WEST PEAK	IV
7	**	SLANTING GULLY	IV
8	*	COOL WATER SANDWICH	IV
9		SKIVERS' GULLY	III/IV
10		WESTERN GULLY	I/II

237

YR WYDDFA
CLOGWYN Y GARNEDD

1		THREE PITCH GULLY	III	
2	**	GREAT GULLY	II/III	3,2,1,1
3		INTRODUCTORY GULLY	III	
4		MISTAKEN IDENTITY	V/VI	4,6,2
5	**	SNOWDROP	III/IV	4,2
5a	*	LITTLE GULLY	II/III	
6	*	LEFT HAND TRINITY	I/II	
7	***	CENTRAL TRINITY	I/II	
8		TRINITY BUTTRESS	III	3,2,

9	**	RIGHT HAND TRINITY	II/III	1/2, 3,1
10		SNAKEBITE	III	
10a	*	FALL-OUT	IV/III	
10b	*	LADDIES GULLY	III	3,3
11	**	LADIES GULLY	III	2,3,2
12	*	COULOIR	IV	
13		CAVE BUTTRESS	V	1/2, 4, 5/6, 2
13a	**	CAVE GULLY	III	2, 3/4, 2
14		END GULLY	II/1	
S	=	THE SPIDER		
F	=	THE FLY		

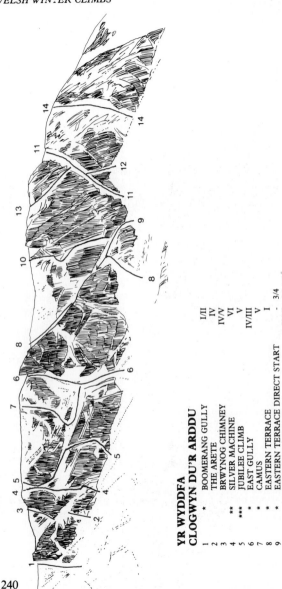

YR WYDDFA
CLOGWYN DU'R ARDDU

1	*	BOOMERANG GULLY	I/II	
2		THE ARETE	IV	
3		BRWYNOG CHIMNEY	IV/V	
4	**	SILVER MACHINE	VI	
5	***	JUBILEE CLIMB	V	
6	*	EAST GULLY	IV/III	
7		CAMUS	V	
8		EASTERN TERRACE	I	
9	*	EASTERN TERRACE DIRECT START	-	3/4
10	***	THE BLACK CLEFT	V/VI	5,7,6,3"
11		WESTERN TERRACE	I	
12	*	WEST END ICEFALL	-	4
13	**	RED SLAB	VI	
14		FAR WESTERN TERRACE	II	

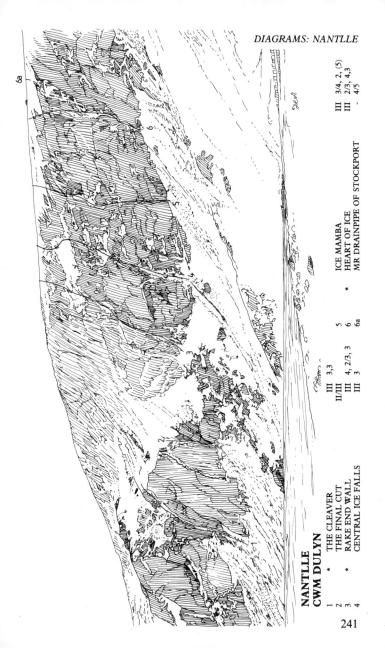

NANTLLE
CWM DULYN

1	*	THE CLEAVER	III	3,3
2		THE FINAL CUT	II/III	4, 2/3, 3
3	*	RAKE END WALL	III	3
4		CENTRAL ICE FALLS		
5		ICE MAMBA	III	3/4, 2, (5)
6	*	HEART OF ICE	III	2/3, 4,3
6a		MR DRAINPIPE OF STOCKPORT	-	4/5

NANTLLE
CWM SILYN

1		PROW GULLY	II	
2		BROAD GULLY	I	
4		BLACK GULLY	III	
5		ATROCITY RUN	V	
6	***	AQUARIAN WALL	IV/V	
7	**	WHITE SNAKE	IV/V	4,4,4
8	*	AMPHITHEATRE GULLY	II	
9	**	THE GREAT STONE SHOOT	I	
10	**	THE WIDOW OF THE WEB	IV	
11		FOUR PITCH GULLY	II/III	
12		LITTLE KITCHEN	II/III	
13	***	MASK OF DEATH	IV/V	5,4,2
14	***	BEDROCK GULLY	IV	3,3,4
15		COLIN'S GULLY	IV	

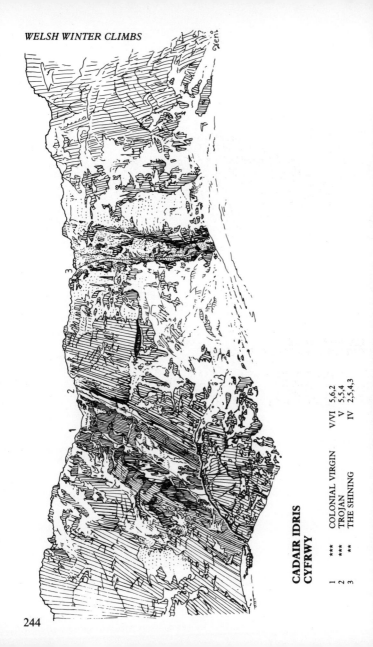

CADAIR IDRIS
CYFRWY

1	***	COLONIAL VIRGIN	V/VI	5,6,2
2	***	TROJAN	V	5,5,4
3	**	THE SHINING	IV	2,5,4,3

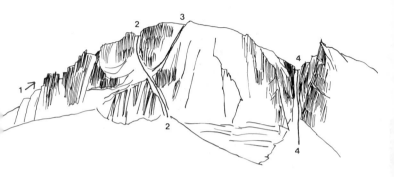

CADAIR IDRIS
CYFRWY: EASTERN SECTION

1	**	EASTERN ARETE OF CYFRWY	II
2	.	B GULLY	III
3	.	C GULLY	III
4	*	ONE PITCH GULLY	I

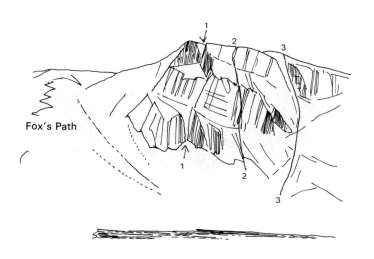

Fox's Path

CADAIR IDRIS
PEN Y GADAIR

1	*	CENTRAL GULLY	III	2,2,3,4,2
2	*	RATTLER	III	2,4,3,2
3	**	GWTH	IV	5,3

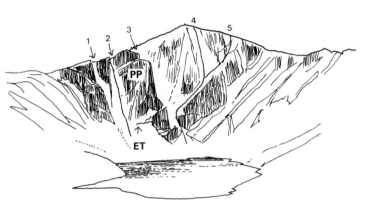

CADAIR IDRIS
CWM CAU

1		LITTLE GULLY	III	
2		THE EAST GULLY	III	
3	***	THE GREAT GULLY	IV	
4	**	SATURDAY NIGHT FEVER	V	3,6,4
5	*	THE RAMP	III	
PP	=	PENCOED PILLAR		
ET	=	START OF EASY TERRACE		

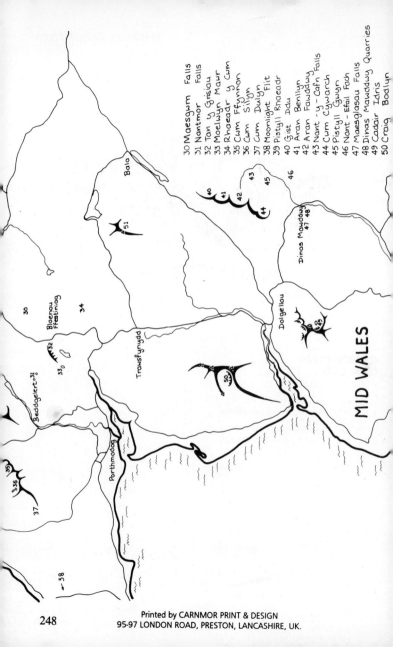

MID WALES

30 Maesgwm Falls
31 Nantmor Falls
32 Tan y Grisiau
33 Moelwyn Mawr
34 Rhaeadr y Cwm
35 Cwm Ffynnon
36 Cwm Silyn
37 Cwm Dulyn
38 Moonlight Flit
39 Pistyll Rhaeadr
40 Gist Ddu
41 Aran Benllyn
42 Aran Fawddwy
43 Nant - y - Cafn Falls
44 Cwm Cywarch
45 Pistyll Gwyn
46 Nant - Efail Fach
47 Maesglasau Falls
48 Dinas Mawddwy Quarries
49 Cadair Idris
50 Craig Bodlyn

Bala
Beddgelert
Blaenau Ffestiniog
Trawsfynydd
Porthmadog
Dolgellau
Dinas Mawddwy

Printed by CARNMOR PRINT & DESIGN
95-97 LONDON ROAD, PRESTON, LANCASHIRE, UK.